ASTROLOGY FORECASTING

The expert guide to astrological prediction

SUE MERLYN FAREBROTHER

RIDER

LONDON • SYDNEY • AUCKLAND • JOHANNESBURG

Rider, an imprint of Ebury Publishing,
20 Vauxhall Bridge Road,
London SW1V 2SA

Rider is part of the Penguin Random House group of companies
whose addresses can be found at global.penguinrandomhouse.com

First published by Rider in 2019
www.penguin.co.uk

A CIP catalogue record for this book is available from the British Library

ISBN 9781846045493

Typeset in 11.25/18 pt Slate Std
by Integra Software Services Pvt. Ltd, Pondicherry

Printed and bound in Great Britain by Clays Ltd, Elcograf S.p.A.

Penguin Random House is committed to a sustainable future
for our business, our readers and our planet. This book is
made from Forest Stewardship Council® certified paper

Illustrations by Alan Sewell

The author and publisher would like to thank Astrolabe Inc (www.alabe.com) for
permission to use Solar Fire 9 software and especially the ET Symbol 3 font.
The author and publisher are grateful to www.Astro-seek.com and
Raphael's Ephemeris for permission to use extracts in Chapter 4.

Huge appreciation and love to my partner, Gert, for endless cups of tea, encouragement and endless forbearance during the writing stage!

And to my talented and dedicated artist friend whose illustrations have enhanced the text. Thank you, Alan.

CONTENTS

Two Natal Charts

The two natal charts for Elaina and Leon on pages x and xi will be used throughout this book to illustrate the fundamental principles of predictive astrology. Once you have read to the end of *Astrology Forecasting* you will be able to interpret them yourself and, by using an *ephemeris* or by consulting my website, to update your own readings of them.

The charts of Leon and Elaina are interpreted in more detail in Chapter 16, which puts their past and future transits into the context of their characters as shown by each of their birth charts.

They are in many ways quite different as people, yet there are some unexpected overlaps.

After reading in these pages about how to make astrological predictions, you'll be able to interpret your own chart and do your own forecasting for years to come. I hope you enjoy the journey!

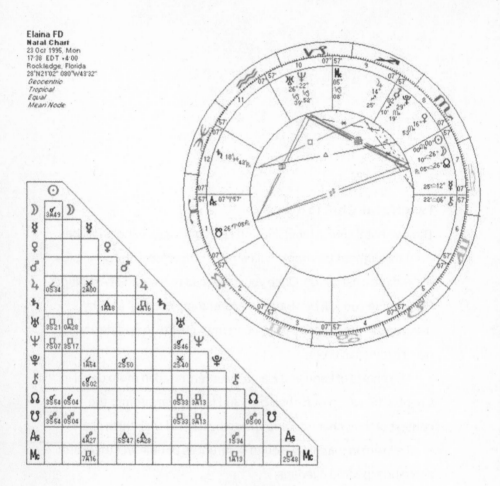

Chart 1: Elaina

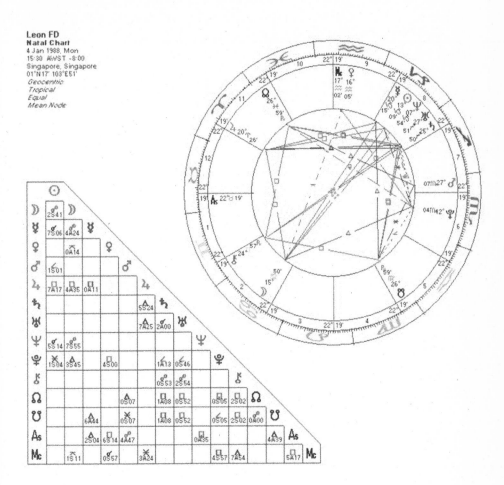

Chart 2: Leon

LIST OF KEY ASTROLOGICAL SYMBOLS

PLANETS

Personal planets	Social or peer planets	Social outer planet	Outer or generational planets
☉ Sun	♃ Jupiter	⚷ Chiron	♅ Uranus
☽ Moon	♄ Saturn		♆ Neptune
☿ Mercury			♇ Pluto
♀ Venus			
♂ Mars			

ZODIAC SIGNS

	Fire	Water	Air	Earth
Cardinal	♈ Aries	♋ Cancer	♎ Libra	♑ Capricorn
Fixed	♌ Leo	♏ Scorpio	♒ Aquarius	♉ Taurus
Mutable	♐ Sagittarius	♓ Pisces	♊ Gemini	♍ Virgo

ASPECTS

Major	Minor
♂ Conjunction	∠ Semi-square
☍ Opposition	⊡ Sesquiquadrate
△ Trine	⚻ Semi-sextile
☐ Square	⚼ Quincunx
✳ Sextile	

NODES

North node ☊
South node ☋

OTHER HEAVENLY BODIES

Ceres ⚳
Pallas ⚴
Juno ⚵
Vesta ⚶

INTRODUCTION

So you want to look into the future?

Let's imagine that you've studied astrology for a while, and you understand the basics of the planets, signs, houses and major aspects. Yet you are aware there is so much more to know. For some of us a further question arises: what's next? What else is there to learn about this fascinating subject? Perhaps that is why you are reading this book: because the art of looking into the future using the symbols of astrology will be described in here. Using astrology to predict what changes may be coming in your life, or anyone's life, is a logical next step for those of us who have become intrigued by what natal astrology can show us. The future beckons – and maybe this is where you want to go too? To learn the methods by which astrologers can reveal potential experiences that have not yet happened? In which case, welcome to *Astrology Forecasting: Learn the expert art of astrological prediction*.

If your interest in astrology has recently been piqued, and you have not yet studied how to interpret a natal chart, I would encourage you to dip into my first book, *Astrology Decoded*, alongside this one. *Astrology Decoded* covers natal astrology in depth, and will help you to build your astrological knowledge step by step.

Learning to understand and interpret an astrology chart is often a revelatory experience. Whatever your approach to astrology before you started learning about its potential, the process of discovering each new factor, and how to combine these factors so that they make sense as a whole, can give rise to astonishment, excitement and even a sense of recognition. How can astrology reveal so much about you? How can this ancient art so clearly describe a characteristic you know you have, or fill in significant gaps in your self-understanding? How is it that the planets of our Solar System in their endless orbit around the Sun provide the snapshot of a birth moment in time and place – which is essentially what a natal chart is – that symbolises the complex personality that each of us is, and will develop through our lives? (As a reminder, astrologers include both the Sun and Moon as Solar System 'planets', for astrology is of course *geocentric*, or Earth-based, so they are included in the natal chart because they appear from Earth to be orbiting around us.)

These, and other related types of questions, are in essence unanswerable. We can describe astrology as a divinatory system that combines a basis of mathematical astronomy with symbolic interpretation. Or we can think of it as a language of symbols that can be learnt. It is not easy to define astrology, except perhaps to say it seems, to those who have studied it, to operate on a system of correlation between that which is above (the planets and stars) and that which is below (that exists on Earth). In any event, astrology is a kind of magical practice of correspondences. Astrology follows the ancient credo that all our earthly experiences have a 'heavenly' equivalent. Nothing happens in isolation: *in other words, we are one with the universe.*

Well-known astrologer Richard Idemon says in his book *The Magic Thread*: 'Astrology to me is the most perfect, all-encompassing, universal model of the human condition.' I am in full agreement with this statement and think it a great shame that many people do not yet understand this. Exactly how astrology 'works' cannot currently be satisfactorily answered in a scientifically provable sense – to the mockery of most of the scientific establishment, many religious systems and numerous hard-headed modern thinkers who do not 'believe' in magic, or in esotericism in general.

Astrology has been ridiculed by certain sections of society for centuries. This is not a new phenomenon. An explanation of how astrology 'works' lies in the realm of the mysterious or magical, and is easily dismissed as delusional in these post-modern times. In centuries gone by, that which could not be rationally or scientifically investigated was often seen as 'magical' by rational thinkers until a method evolved whereby such matters could be measured in scientific ways. Electricity, for example, and magnetism were once seen as 'magical' before they were scientifically or mathematically proven. There are, however, a small number of practising scientists who have investigated the possibility that astrology 'works' and has a scientific explanation that can be measured, as we will see in Chapter 6.

WHAT THIS BOOK IS ABOUT, AND WHAT IT IS NOT ABOUT

This book is about predictive astrology and it will show you what this terminology actually means in practice! It will also describe in some detail each of the various methods commonly used by Western astrologers for predictive purposes, with accompanying examples. However, to begin with, I will be referring to all the methods of forecasting as *transits*. (Incidentally, the meanings of single words or phrases that first appear in italics are explained in the Glossary in the back of the book on page 322.) The word 'transits' is therefore being used initially as a general term, meaning the continuing cycles of the planets as they form connections – or *aspects* – with your natal chart.

In other types of astrological practice, such as Vedic astrology (also known as Jyotish), which originates in India, or in Chinese astrology, other predictive methods are used; but they are not covered in this book. We will follow the most common astrological practices used in countries whose outlook lies broadly within the cultures of the West. This book will take you beyond the meaning of the twelve zodiac signs listed in magazines, newspapers and on websites, which are usually referred to as 'star signs', or more correctly 'Sun signs', and which cover possible events that may happen for those born under each Sun sign for a particular day, week, month or year (e.g. 'Leo is likely to meet up with an old friend this week' or 'Virgo may encounter issues with a work colleague over the next few days', and so on). *Astrology Forecasting* is intended for astrology enthusiasts and students, and will lay out as clearly as possible how to do astrological forecasting yourself, using the whole chart.

You will find a few additions to the steps described in *Astrology Decoded* in relation to interpreting a natal chart. To enhance your understanding of the natal chart, some new techniques will be given, such as studying the Moon's phases, and some different *aspect patterns*. Sections on eclipses and on the four main *asteroids* are also included.

In Chapter 1, I will discuss what can be gained from astrological foreknowledge, and whether this is a 'good thing' or a 'bad thing'. It does, however, remain the case that the natal chart is the basis of individual study, as the interpretation of the forecasting methods described will be based very much on the individual's chart – and what stage that person is at in their life, which obviously makes quite a difference.

What type of information is revealed by studying future transits?

In essence, any type of information can be revealed when studying future transits! But researching a person's transits does not tell you exactly what *will* happen in that person's life. (Thankfully, you may well say!) What it does reveal are the types of encounters, feelings, reactions, events and so on that the person is likely to experience; what their next step could be; or what sort of inner changes may occur. Astrologers sometimes describe this as indicating the next cycle of an individual's life. There could be the potential for a period of good fortune, for instance; or a focus on friendships, partners or romance; work or study concerns; travel; changing interests; changing financial circumstances; spirituality and personal growth – the list of what might be revealed can be as long as the potential variations in human situations!

An astrologer is not – and here I think I am speaking for the vast majority of astrological practitioners – a clairvoyant or a guru who can predict precisely what the future holds for a person, or a fortune-teller who will advise someone exactly what to do next. An astrologer is simply someone who has studied the symbols of astrology, perhaps for quite some time, and who has learnt how to read both the natal chart and the nature of the times we find ourselves in. Your free will, or the freedom to change your own reactions to any given set of circumstances, is always potentially operative. Most skilled astrologers will not advise you what to do, but explain with clarity and care the key characteristics of the upcoming period of time and what types of experiences you might encounter.

If you were hoping for specific forecasts when working with astrology, or advice about the future that will indicate what you should do next, you may be disappointed! Only you can actually decide what to do next. As astrology is primarily a symbolic system, time periods – including the precise time of your birth – are given literally, but need to be understood symbolically. (This will be described more fully in later chapters.) The art of the experienced astrologer is to translate those symbols of time and planetary movement into understandable terminology, and to explain this clearly.

My own prime motivation for interpreting a person's transits is to try to offer useful guidance, based on studying the symbolic and constantly changing Solar System, so that they may find the best way to manage their future experiences or expectations.

SOME PRACTICAL CONSIDERATIONS

If you don't already have your natal chart, this link – www.suemerlyn. com – will take you to a page on my website where you can generate it and then print it out. Or you can generate your own chart at other sites online such as www.astro.com or https://alabe.com/freechart/ You will find that most free birth-chart-generating programs online calculate your chart using the *Placidus house system*, but there is usually an option to change the house system.

House systems

Please note, I use the Equal House method throughout the book. This basically means that the natal chart is divided into twelve houses, which are 30 degrees each, no matter where the birthplace is on Earth. As a reminder, the circular chart is measured in degrees – 360 degrees in total, like any circle – and in astrology, each degree contains 60 minutes of space. As there are 12 zodiac signs, and also 12 equal houses, each of these therefore measures 30 degrees when the chart is divided equally into 12 (30 × 12 = 360 degrees).

However, it's important to remember that houses and zodiac signs are not the same as each other and do not necessarily coincide with each other. On the chart, the houses represent areas of experience and indicate in which area of your life changes are taking place. For example, the 1st house of every chart is about you, your sense of yourself, while the 7th house indicates you and your close relationships with individual others – your close friends, potential romantic partner(s), and also business or study partner(s).

If you prefer to use Placidus, Koch or another house system, you can find ways to convert your chart to your preferred house system online, at www.astro.com for example. For books about the house systems, see Further Reading on page 326. (See also *Astrology Decoded*, page 115, for a short description.) In the Useful Addresses section, on page 328, you will find recommendations for astrology software and mobile/cell phone programs, which will do the necessary calculations for both generating charts and forecasting, as the methods for doing hand calculations are not covered in this book.

A word about your birth time

In every natal chart, the angles and the position of the fast-moving Moon are dependent on an accurate birth time. If the birth time is not accurate, then the angles, the Moon and the house cusps will also not be accurate, which will lead to inaccuracy when looking at forecasting timings. This is because the time and place of birth dictates the rising sign (Ascendant), and therefore all the house cusps. Therefore, I would suggest that you do what you can to ascertain your birth time as accurately as possible. If your mother is not available or cannot remember the exact time, try contacting the hospital records department if you were born in a hospital, or asking other relatives who may know.

If your birth time still cannot be found, you will need either to discount the time-based sections of your chart, or experiment with noting the timing of noticeable life changes and relating this to your forecasting. But first, if you have an approximate birth time, experiment with your Ascendant and Midheaven zodiac signs over a period of time, and see how much you feel you resonate with them, especially the Ascendant. There is a technique for working out birth times in astrology, called rectification, even if you have no idea of your time of birth and do not think you can find out. If you have made every effort to find your actual birth time, if you wish you can find an astrologer who specialises in rectification on the internet.

Additional information

In order to access your individual transits for any time period, you will need to purchase, or consult online, an ephemeris, which is a table of planetary positions (see Chapter 4). Another possibility is to access your current or future transits and other relevant information online at, for example, www.astro.com or www.alabe.com

Two case study charts of real individuals, called Leon and Elaina (not their real names), will also be used throughout this book to illustrate the effects of the various transits at certain times in their lives, based on their charts, as examples of how these may be experienced. The birth charts themselves appear on pages x and xi at the start of this book, while a synopsis of the meanings of these two charts can be found in Chapter 16. A few well-known people's charts and transits will further demonstrate the kinds of events or changes that may be experienced during important transits.

This book will take you through the key forecasting methods and the stages of those methods, as well as how to interpret your findings. While exploring predictive astrology can seem a bit of a complicated business at first, the practice of dealing with the different forecasting techniques step by step means you can take whatever time you need to absorb the information as you go. I hope you enjoy starting out on your new journey of discovery as you embark on the next important stage of learning astrology!

PART I
GETTING STARTED

1.

FOREWARNED IS FOREARMED – OR IS IT?

Is astrological forecasting morally appropriate?

From time immemorial, people have sought methods for looking into the future. The stories about places, time periods and methods used in ancient times for seeking future divinations have grown over the centuries, so that some have become romanticised legends in their own right. Think, for example, of the famous oracle sites that date from at least the time of the ancient Greeks, such as Delphi or Dodona, where seekers would journey to consult with the wise seers, who were reputed to have often been blind or blindfolded so that they perceived with their 'inner eyes'. The desires of individuals in the past who sought foreknowledge were varied, but often it had to do with their domestic lives, such as marriage, family, or prosperity.

Pillars at Delphi

In the ancient kingdom of Babylon (the remains of which are situated in modern-day Iraq), shamans would proffer predictions about the weather, which was important for food production, and about the most propitious times for waging war or the conception of children. Nearly all cultures of the past evolved systems for forecasting the future, from the ancient Egyptians to the aboriginal peoples, from the Asian, South American and African subcultures to the Mayans. Such systems varied like the people themselves and their cultures, but methods often involved translating celestial phenomena and other portents into understandable messages. Rulers and kings of ancient civilisations sought advice gleaned from the sky and other omens through their wise men or women, who were often early astrologers.

The state of the sky and the appearance of the stars were observed for favourable or strange omens; bones were cast, animal entrails were examined; the sighting of certain sacred animals or birds was noted, as well as prophetic dreams: all had meaning for those who were trained to interpret the signs. You may, for example, be familiar with the Bible story of the prophet Daniel, who interpreted the dream of Nebuchadnezzar, the king of ancient Babylon (Daniel, 2).

As it evolved over the centuries, astrological forecasting was frequently used, and astrologers were important figures in many classical and medieval courts. It seems unlikely that most historical monarchs and nobles saw anything immoral in seeking information about the future, as in many cases it was seen as strengthening their position when needing to make important decisions. However, astrology was not just for the nobles. As early as the fourteenth century in Britain, Geoffrey Chaucer described in his *Canterbury Tales* how one of his characters, the Wife of Bath – a lusty soul with five consecutive husbands – blamed her need for sex on her birth chart. (Too much Mars and Venus, prominently placed, she says!) She declared a continuing strong connection with these two planets as she grew older, so her lusty nature did not decline.

Astrological prediction in the West reached its zenith of popularity in the sixteenth and seventeenth centuries, when many members of the population consulted astrologers and sages. Yet there was a factor of dissent against forecasting the future, whether through astrology or through reading other types of omens, amongst certain sections of some societies. Frequently, this took the form of objections from the presiding religious community on the grounds that it was an offence against whatever relevant deity was followed, whose right it was to determine a country's or an individual's future. To seek to know this future or indeed to attempt to change it was, for the ruling religious authorities, anathema and offensive to the deity – including the Christian God – and could be punished by death, or illness or other cursed situations. Much of this attitude from religious bodies was about maintaining power over the beliefs of their congregations, making sure their clerics stayed in control, and that their version of Christianity remained the only acceptable religious practice.

This attitude took on the guise of superstition in some less-educated communities, along with an accompanying fear of incurring the wrath of the deity – who could then deal some nasty cards to you as a sign of disapproval; and it turned many people away from the guidance of wise men and women, and fortune-tellers of all kinds. On an individual level, this negative view of astrology persists for some people in today's world, whether owing to religious belief, or to a form of rationality that only acknowledges that which can be demonstrably 'proved'. The counter to religion, atheism, is a growing philosophy in Western cultures that acknowledges no god and which also dismisses any form of forecasting, except on rationally provable – if somewhat speculative – grounds, such as predicting financial trends.

HOW DID WE GET TO WHERE WE ARE?

As science evolved, mainly from the seventeenth century onwards in Western countries, so attitudes began to change amongst the population as a whole. Objections were raised by the growth of scientific thinking, which required evidence to support any prediction made. The form of astrology mainly practised in the late Renaissance could not provide proofs that satisfied the growing scientific community in the terms they required. This was when astrology and similar practices became underground systems, and ceased generally to be a part of a 'scientific' astronomy, being relegated to 'magical practice' – and therefore ironically became relegated to the realms of ignorant superstition instead. The 'non-scientific' practice of astrology was not revived and brought back into popular awareness until the time of Alan Leo, at the end of the nineteenth and the beginning of the twentieth centuries. Alan Leo was passionate about astrology and revived popular interest in the subject by advertising low-priced astrological horoscope interpretations for the general public, and was inundated with requests, so much so that he had to employ other astrologers to help him keep up with the workload. He went on to found the Astrological Lodge, a branch of the esoteric Theosophical Society, in London in 1915, which is still going strong in the present day.

So where are we now, in this twenty-first century? Predictions based on science, such as weather forecasts, are relied on by many, whether you want to keep a good eye on the coming days for Auntie Margery's garden party, or you are a sea captain whose crew may depend on the accuracy of the shipping forecast for their cargo's safety, and indeed for their lives. In the financial arena, the rise and fall of the stock markets is researched today by suitably qualified astrologers as well as by financial researchers, who have no moral qualms about making future predictions. (Financial astrologers obviously need to be familiar with the world of finance as well as to have extensive astrological knowledge, so it could be argued that the information at their fingertips is wider than those who gain their insights from overtly 'scientific' methods.)

But the wish for a personal insight into their own future remains persistent for many people. With the advent of psychological astrology later in the twentieth century, it may be more appropriate for astrologers to approach forecasting as a means to explore the planetary cycles that are currently specific to you, as an individual, and examining how this period evolves or how you can best use the time to come. This can be seen as being astrologically forearmed. With knowledge of your current or future transits, you can try to make the best of the current or future time periods.

But the question remains: is this a moral activity? As we have seen, some religious communities would object on theological grounds to the use of astrology at all. And many scientific or humanistic thinkers would object to the astrological seeking for meaning in the movement of the planets of the Solar System on the grounds that such interpretations cannot be proved. If any should prove correct, then this can simply be dismissed as coincidental.

So not much has changed since the late seventeenth century, and the dawn of the Age of Enlightenment, you may think. Yet much has. What has changed lies in the attitudes of many people towards non-provable systems such as astrology. Today, not everyone feels driven to perceive the world using only purely scientifically proven methods; we sense there are other useful ways to approach life. The validity of knowing what our transits are and what they indicate for future periods in our lives is now seen by many as psychologically arming us against potentially challenging times, or preparing us to take advantage of propitious planetary periods.

Introducing the Two Study Charts: Elaina and Leon

As mentioned, you will find the birth charts of Leon and Elaina printed in black and white at the beginning of the book, and illustrated in colour on my website: www.suemerlyn.com

These charts have been chosen because they are especially interesting and show that both Leon and Elaina will experience some important transits over the course of a few years. Having absorbed (more or less!) the methods for finding and gaining understanding from the various forecasting systems, one of the most important skills to learn is how to work out what content is most important and should not be overlooked, and what can be discarded – a subject that will be addressed in more detail in later chapters.

The years will pass and the transits to both charts will become history, depending on when you access this book. I will therefore be periodically updating the transits for Leon and Elaina's charts on my website for a little while after this book is published. Hopefully, you will be able to update their charts yourself, should you wish to do so, once you know how to do this by consulting an ephemeris.

You can look at updating your own chart's transits each year too! Being aware of what is going on astrologically for you personally will help to keep you in touch with where the planets are, which is always a good thing for an astrologer to know. (I'd suggest that you focus at first on your transits as they may be the easiest to follow if you have an ephemeris or can access astrological software or the internet.) Incidentally, when you are in the midst of learning astrology, you might also find it very useful to consult a practising astrologer about your own chart at some point, so that you can compare your findings with theirs.

2.
WHAT ARE THE METHODS FOR FORECASTING?

Introducing the four major systems

Although I have been using the generic term 'transits' for ease of description, there are actually four main predictive methods used by astrologers:

- Transits
- Secondary progressions (also known as progressions)
- Solar arc directions (also known as directions, and sometimes as solar arcs)
- Solar return charts

A transit, progression, direction or aspect on a solar return chart occurs when an orbiting planet connects with any natal planet or angle by degree. There are other forecasting methods, but these four are the most important ones. They are used by almost all Western astrologers, often in combination, though not all methods will always be used by each individual astrologer in his or her forecasting work. Below is a brief introduction to each of these methods, which will be fully explained with examples in later chapters. We will also be looking at symbolism versus 'reality', and how this relates to the different forecasting methods.

Measuring space

I have included this short reminder here so that you are clear about how to measure space in a chart before I launch into the explanation of each method. However, if you know this already, feel free to skip forwards!

The way to measure the positions of planets on the chart, or any other astrological feature, is through degrees and minutes. As a recap, the zodiac is a circle of 12 signs. As a circle occupies 360 degrees, each sign occupies 30 degrees. In an astrological chart, every degree of a circle can be further divided into 60 minutes, and further subdivided into 60 seconds. That means that each one of the 30 degrees in a sign contains 60 minutes.

The similarity with the way that time is measured, in minutes and hours etc., of course, neatly correlates with the 60-minute division of 1 degree of space or 1 hour of time – and both of these measurements are in minutes. So the number of degrees of any planet's position can be up to 29 degrees 59 minutes of a sign before its position changes to the next sign. Therefore, 30 degrees of a planet's sign position always becomes 0 degrees of the next sign.

The importance of the birth location

When I am setting my computer program to calculate forecasting for the next year or so, it asks me whether I want to relocate the calculation to the current location (usually where the person lives now) or leave it at the birth place. I always set it for the birth location for any forecasting based on transits, progressions or directions.

The argument for this – for not changing the birth location to the person's current location – is that these three forecasting methods can be seen as astrologically representing the cyclic unfoldment of your inner self, which could be said to be an intrinsic part of who you are, and which links you at some level to your place of birth. Different astrologers have different ideas about this issue, however, and this is one of the areas on which astrologers disagree.

The solar return chart, on the other hand, can be seen as energies of the current location acting on the person you have become, and are becoming at this period of time, so the energy of the resident place can be substituted for the birthplace. (See Chapter 12.)

TRANSITS (T)

In astrology, the term 'transits' applies to the transiting Solar System planets. All planets in our Solar System orbit round the Sun, of course; however, the length of the complete cycle varies greatly from planet to planet – with Pluto and Neptune's orbits, for example, lasting for much longer than a human lifetime. The length of each cycle is known as the transiting planet's orbital period. The movement of all the planets describes a repeating cycle, from the moment of *ingress* into a new sign, or from the formation of an exact aspect with one of your natal planets, through the opposition phase and eventually back to the next conjunction.

The Sun, as the star of our Solar System, sets our Earthly seasonal timing clock based on a year's apparent rotation. In other words, the

Sun has an annual cycle (although it is of course the Earth that orbits the Sun in one year). However, the cycle most of us are most aware of is that of the Moon – from dark New Moon to Full Moon and back to the next New Moon. (See Chapter 9 for more information on this.) Transits are the actual movements of the planets as they follow their prescribed orbits around the Sun, making aspects to the natal chart. A transit occurs when any orbiting planet forms an aspect with a natal planet or angle; for example: transiting (T) Pluto square Moon, or T Saturn conjunct Venus, or T Jupiter trine Ascendant, and so on. In short:

- Transits take place during the actual passage of time, e.g. a normal calendar date, as opposed to some of the other methods of forecasting.
- Transits form the most visible and the most popular forecasting system, and are very often accompanied by tangible changes or events. They are used by nearly all astrologers who practise forecasting.

Transiting planets do not need to aspect a natal planet absolutely exactly to be effective. An ephemeris (see Chapter 4) simply lists the degrees and minutes of a sign that each planet has reached in the last 24 hours. An exact match between the transiting planet and the natal one will have been aligned just before, at, or after the position given in the ephemeris for that day. The period of 'exactness' is usually reckoned to last 1 degree before and 1 degree after the precise match, in terms of the effectiveness of the transit, and is often associated with an event or occurrence at that time; whereas in a listing of planetary positions in an ephemeris, the positions of orbiting planets and the natal positions are precise, as computerised calculations are.

Orbs

Opinions vary as to the approaching or separating *orb* (the distance separated from exactness between transit and natal planet or angle), but it is at a minimum of 1 degree and may be several more degrees. For most astrologers, there is an allowable orb of at least 1 degree away from exactness, whether approaching or separating from the position of the natal planet. However, there are 'wide orb' astrologers who allow up to 6 to 10 degrees as a T outer planet approaches a natal planet. In my opinion, this method suggests that we are all constantly in the grip of some major transit that is still far in advance of the exact aspect – in some cases for many years! I believe that the tighter the orb, the more obvious the transit, generally speaking.

Barack Obama and Jupiter

Here follows an example that shows how a transit can manifest in someone's life (although there are obviously many other ways in which the transit described here could have been experienced). On 10 December 2009, Barack Obama, then President of the United States, was presented with the Nobel Peace Prize in Stockholm. Looking at the astrology of this occasion, he had a couple of meaningful transiting planets aspecting his birth chart at around that time, notably the planet Jupiter as it crossed his Ascendant. Jupiter is usually (though not always) a fairly fast-moving planet, and the Nobel event needed some preparation; hence the degree is not exact to the actual day of the ceremony.

Obama experienced this transit just before the date of the presentation (Jupiter, the planet of celebration and success – amongst other attributes – had just crossed his point of contact with other people at the time – his natal Ascendant.) His diplomacy negotiations with prominent world leaders in the last year had gone a long way towards lessening the threat of nuclear warfare, in the judgement of the Nobel assessors.

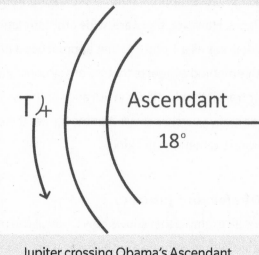

Jupiter crossing Obama's Ascendant

SECONDARY PROGRESSIONS (P)

'Progressing' the chart is a much more symbolic method than transits, in that it is not based on the actual yearly movement of the planets:

- This method holds that each day of a person's life after birth is equivalent to each year of his or her life, i.e. 1 day = 1 year.
- Each secondary progressed planet moves by its natural daily movement over one 24-hour period, which will vary from planet to planet. So for example, the transiting Sun always

moves approximately 1 degree of space in a day, i.e. in one 24-hour period. Therefore the progressed Sun moves that same amount of space in a year. (The Sun does, in fact, vary a little in the amount of space it will move in a day/year.)

- While the same applies to every planet, the inner planets (Mercury, Venus and Mars) and the Moon progress most noticeably in their natural orbits. The planets beyond Mars travel too slowly in 24 hours to be relevant in the technique of secondary progressions, so are rarely used.

- As an example, Mars in its natural orbit travels around 0.5 degrees or a little more per day, so progressed Mars will move on average 20 to 40 minutes of *arc* (space) in 24 hours. (See the Table of Planetary Motion per 24 hours in Chapter 8, page 106.)

- The progressions of planets aspecting the Ascendant and the *MC* (Medium Coeli or Midheaven) are also observed and are meaningful in a progressions reading. Progressions of these angles are themselves taken into account. So p Ascendant or p MC aspecting a natal planet is also significant.

As an example, to find the approximate progressions for a 17-year-old, you would count 17 days from the date of birth, and look up the positions of the planets in an ephemeris on the 17th day. You can always check this for accuracy by putting the question through an astrology software program. The time of birth will make a small difference, most noticeably if you are working this out manually.

So, for people who live a long time, the first 90 days after birth (approximately the first 3 months of babyhood) equals 90 years of life, assuming a lifetime lasting 90 years. (Incidentally, modern Western astrologers very rarely predict the length of a person's life, although I believe there are methods to do this in the Indian system of astrology.)

SOLAR ARC DIRECTIONS (SA)

This method is even more symbolic than that of progressions:

- The Sun's daily movement, as seen from Earth, is the basis for the solar arc-directed method of forecasting.
- Like progressions, the principle that 1 day equals 1 year is the basis of solar arcs.
- The *whole* natal chart is moved forward through the signs and houses by the same 'arc' or movement that the Sun has made in 1 day since birth. This is repeated for the number of years that you want to look at, and the resultant chart is the directed chart – or set of solar arc directions – for that year.
- In this way, you can map out a lifetime using solar arc directions alone if you want to, as it is so simple (although quite a long process). Like the other methods described above, directions make aspects to the natal chart. (See Chapter 11.)

Because only the Sun and Moon, the personal planets and the angles are mainly used in progressions, as opposed to the use of *all* the planets in solar arcs, it follows that solar arcs are often more numerous than progressions. Selectiveness is necessary in order to find the most important ones. The years when one of these planets changes zodiac sign or house in either system often prove key in a person's life.

Bi-wheels and tri-wheels

You can put one chart diagram 'inside' another to show the connections between the forecasting methods more clearly. A *bi-wheel*, for example, is one chart inside a second chart, whereas a *tri-wheel* is three charts, one inside the other, placed together in a 'triple wheel' in order to compare the positions of the planets on the three charts easily.

Overleaf is a *tri-wheel* for one of our main case studies, Leon. All three charts in this tri-wheel feature Mars alone to illustrate the point. The inner wheel, as it says in the top left-hand corner, represents the birth chart for Leon, with his Ascendant at 22° 19′ Taurus in the usual place, on the left of the diagram. The middle wheel shows the position of Leon's secondary progressed Mars on 21 March 2020 at midday, while the outer wheel shows Leon's solar arc directed Mars also for 21 March 2020 at midday, in his 32nd year; both charts being set at his place of birth in Singapore. See how much the planets have moved by progression or direction since he was born, and notice the wide difference between the position of the secondary progressed Mars and the solar arc directed Mars in the same period of time.*

Side note: Incidentally, notice the degrees and minutes of Leon's directed Mars in the spring of 2020, at 29° 53′ Sagittarius. This means, of course, that Mars is about to change sign from Sagittarius to Capricorn, which it does at the end of April 2020. There is a school of thought that considers the 29th degree of a sign as being particularly strong, almost as if the position indicates a 'last gasp' of that sign before moving on. This makes 2020 potentially a particularly significant year for Leon, as a year that stands out in some way when a planet is changing sign or house, especially an inner planet or an angle.

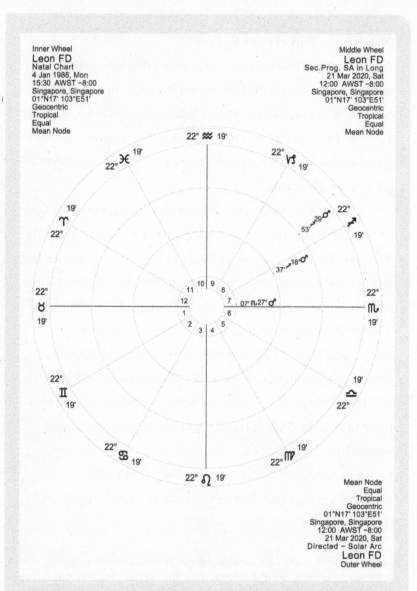

Inner Wheel
Leon FD
Natal Chart
4 Jan 1988, Mon
15:30 AWST −8:00
Singapore, Singapore
01°N17' 103°E51'
Geocentric
Tropical
Equal
Mean Node

Middle Wheel
Leon FD
Sec.Prog. SA in Long
21 Mar 2020, Sat
12:00 AWST −8:00
Singapore, Singapore
01°N17' 103°E51'
Geocentric
Tropical
Equal
Mean Node

Mean Node
Equal
Tropical
Geocentric
01°N17' 103°E51'
Singapore, Singapore
12:00 AWST −8:00
21 Mar 2020, Sat
Directed − Solar Arc
Leon FD
Outer Wheel

Tri-wheel showing the difference between natal, progressed and directed Mars in Leon's chart

SOLAR RETURNS (SR)

The solar return chart is valid for just 1 year:

- The solar return (SR) chart is calculated for your birthday each year.
- When the Sun returns exactly to its natal place every year (a solar return), a new chart is set up for that exact date and time. This is not always the same day as your birthday – this will be discussed in Chapter 12.
- Tighter orbs are used in calculating the solar return than for a natal chart.
- The solar return chart does not replace the natal, but 'overlays' it in meaning.

Sometimes known as a birthday chart, a solar return chart is calculated for the positions of the transiting planets on the day of your individual solar return. The place, however, may change. (This will be discussed in Chapter 12, p 197.) This yearly chart can be read by itself, or in relation to the natal chart.

The benefits of consulting your solar return chart each year as your birthday comes around are that the SR chart highlights the specific areas of experience that you are likely to encounter in the coming year. Continuing transits to the solar return chart, as well as to the natal chart, may trigger some noticeable changes during the relevant year.

Tighter orbs are used for the aspects because of the temporary nature of the SR chart, lasting as it does for just 1 year, and it is usually simpler to interpret than a natal chart. Basically, the most important factors are picked out by the SR chart, which means you can be quite selective when interpreting it. This is actually very helpful as there is quite a lot of other forecasting to consider when making astrological predictions.

A summary of differences between secondary progressions and solar arc directions

To underline the differences between the two 'symbolic' forecasting methods, i.e. progressions and solar arc directions, it is important to remember that when using solar arc directions, every planet and all the angles move forward each year by the amount of space that the Sun has moved, forming aspects to the natal chart. The directed planets can never form new aspects to each other because it is the entire chart that is moving forwards: the relationship between the solar arc planets and angles remains the natal one. The whole pattern of the birth chart simply moves forward at one 'Sun movement' of approximately 1 degree per year. Any directed planets or angles can form aspects with the natal chart.

However, in secondary progressions, each planet moves by the *natural* amount it would normally progress (or retrograde) through in its orbit in a 24-hour day, and forms aspects to the positions of the natal planets. The only progressed planets normally used are Sun, Moon, Mercury, Venus and Mars, plus the natal angles. Aspects with other progressed planets or angles can be formed as well, unlike solar arcs.

WHAT DOES IT ALL MEAN?

Astrology is a symbolic language, which interprets celestial phenomena in terrestrial terms. In this way, it agrees with the ancient hermetic saying 'as above, so below', attributed to a mythical character known as

Hermes Trismegistus. His legendary origins stem from the mythology surrounding the Egyptian god Thoth and the Greek god Hermes, and the discovery of a mysterious set of sacred texts containing the phrase 'as above, so below'.

Each person reading this book has his or her own personal inner life, which is communicable to others to a large (yet not total) extent, but which cannot be objectively proved. The symbolic systems – progressions and directions – tend to reflect those shifts in our moods, emotions, thoughts and inspirations that are just as real to us as the actual events in our lives. That said, directions in particular seem to indicate actual events more frequently than progressions do. Inner and outer experiences are interchangeable in some cases. As an example, moving house represents a very tangible shift of circumstance that is likely to be reflected in a person's transits. But there is usually an inner reaction as well, perhaps visible in the person's progressions or solar arc directions. In other words, directions often coincide with both levels of experience. They certainly represent a departure from the measurable orbiting planets used in transits!

Transits are the most 'real' of all the forecasting methods, based as they are on measurable and observable planetary movements. This being so, transits are considered by the majority of astrologers to be the most important method for looking into the future. They often manifest in a person's life in the form of events that make a significant difference to them, sometimes apparently arising from an external source, sometimes reflecting an internal change that may trigger actions, sometimes both. The most important planets to aspect the chart by transit are the outer planets – Pluto, Neptune and Uranus, plus Saturn and Jupiter, and to a lesser extent, Chiron. (See Chapters 6 and 7 for more details and explanations.)

And the annual solar return chart represents an overall picture of the year to come, but based on your understanding of the natal chart in question. In this chart, differences may occur from the natal chart by shape, elements, modes and polarity, as well as SR inter-aspects with the natal chart.

Forecasting as a key to growth

What is surprising, or hopeful, or revelatory, in assessing your own or anyone else's transits, is that you can see there is always a chance for you to be different, to change your life, and to discover new parts of yourself, or to grow beyond behaviour patterns that may have been holding you back. You are not 'stuck' with the planetary positions or aspects you were born with, or with a lack (or an excess) of an element or mode, or a challenging aspect pattern. Many of your experiences associated with a particular transit, progression, direction or solar return position over the years will 'fill in the gaps' in your natal chart, and bring opportunities to rebalance where this could be useful – although you may well not see it like this at the time! Through learning the techniques briefly described above, you can develop a more mature or philosophical approach to life.

Of course, many people go through their whole lives with no knowledge of how useful or powerful astrology can be, and will discover their own changes, or growth, or progress, just through the process of living. But knowing what is potentially coming (without necessarily seeing all the details in advance!) can give you strength to cope with difficult periods, or the ability to make the most of the time when the universe is moving with you.

3.
TRIGGERING THE NATAL CHART

The natal chart lies at the foundation of any forecasting work, for this chart is the hub of personal astrology, and all forecasting interpretations need to relate back to it.[1] Transits, progressions and directions don't happen in a vacuum, complete in themselves. They manifest in individual ways, depending on the type of person whose chart is being stimulated. And no individual's life circumstances are the same as another's! This chapter concerns itself with the most easily visible of forecasting methods: transits.

Each planet has an essential meaning, but there are many ways of manifesting that meaning. This does not, of course, indicate that a transit can stand for anything you like! The world of symbolic interpretation allows for flexibility, but the orbiting planet retains its essential, and recognisable, significance.

What is important to realise is that the planets are the essence of every astrological chart, and have similar base meanings no matter in

---

[1] To avoid the need for repetition, please understand 'a natal planet' triggered by a forecasting method to mean 'a natal planet or an angle' – i.e. including the Ascendant or the Midheaven (MC).

which context they occur. So whether Pluto is a natal or transiting planet, or appears in other astrological contexts, it still retains a recognisable, though perhaps adapted, interpretation. The same is true of Venus, or any other planet. This is because the planets in astrology represent universal archetypes: all the planets (including the Sun and Moon) are linked to a classical god or goddess who, in turn, are individually associated with certain characteristics.

THE IMPORTANCE OF THE NATAL CHART'S THEMES

When you are preparing to interpret someone's natal chart, before going on to consider their current or future forecasting, what you are seeking to identify are the *themes* of that natal chart: the essential principles that summarise the main characteristics of the person whose chart it is. When considering how a particular transit (or other form of forecasting) may manifest in terms of a person's life experiences, it is worth considering what could be gained or learned from a coming period in relation to that person – and the natal chart can give you clues to that.

To give you an example of how this works, let's imagine you are doing an astrological reading for a woman in her twenties called Mary. When looking at this young woman's chart, you discover that Transiting ('T' for short) Pluto in Capricorn is shortly going to cross her natal Venus in Capricorn in the 8th house, forming an astrological conjunction: T♇♂♀ – T Pluto conjunct natal Venus. This is a transit that will last on and off due to retrogradation for up to 2 years, so it is an important one. It is likely to bring some real-time changes into her life.

To get a handle on its potential meaning, think of a few keywords and phrases for each planet; for example:

Pluto:

Transformational change

Secrecy, hidden qualities

Intensity, compulsion

Death and rebirth

Inheritance

Sexuality

Venus:

Love, romantic relationship

Friendship, companionship

Artistic ability, creativity

Values, attitude towards money

Ways in which Mary may experience her transit could vary from falling in love, to deciding to make a financial investment, adjusting friendships, to becoming involved with a new creative project, or a combination of these. Primarily, Venus represents love and affection, and the ways in which Mary expresses or experiences this. Had this same transit affected the chart of a middle-aged businessman with a similar natal Venus placement, would his experiences have been similar? Possibly not.

So to get an idea how this transit may manifest, you can start by considering what kind of Venus Mary has. You could examine her natal Venus to learn about her natural ways of relating to others, for example her 7th house and Venus's sign, house and aspects. The signs Venus rules can also be taken into account if you want – but my advice is to keep it simple!

Mary's Venus is placed in Capricorn and the 8th house, which indicates that she is cautious when it comes to relationships, and generally does not easily become emotionally involved. This applies for her when it comes to friendships (she may have just a few long-term friendships), or to romance. T Pluto is such a powerful influence that this may change during the period of the transit, and she *could* fall in love. If this does occur, it may be a slow process but would affect her deeply. Or she could perhaps experience changes in her friendships or other types of relationships, such as losing or gaining close people in her life. On another level, she may undergo a shift of personal values or attitudes towards the use of money and possessions.

To give you another example of this variation in response to a major Pluto–Venus transit, a person who has their natal Venus in Pisces aspected to Neptune is likely to have a very romanticised approach to love, and may be a person who falls in love easily – and/or may tend to be intuitively creative. A transit of Pluto to such a natal Venus may well bring a new partner into their life, who may be older (Capricorn) than them, but the romance of such a situation is more likely to embody high idealism, and maybe evoke a feeling of destiny for the person, mainly because of the Neptune influence, which adds a sparkle of mystery to the experience. And because of the intensity brought by Pluto, the relationship with a new partner may be compulsive or obsessive, bringing a certain level of trauma. Returning to Mary, the way you view Mary's natal chart placement is building a sense for you of how she may experience her Pluto transit to Venus. The rest of the chart may help you as well.

So what is the essential learning in this transit? Here, the focus is obviously on Venus and about Mary's way of relating to others, including her sexuality and the ways in which she expresses her sexual needs, as well as her desire to convey and receive love and affection. One experience is very probable, which is getting to know herself better through relating to others, or one significant other. The other ways in which she could experience this transit are given as examples of how broadly an important transit can be experienced, to remind you to keep your thinking wide. But the essence of a powerful transit like this embodies the whole area of you and your relationships. These differing reactions to the same transit will show how important it is to base your individual interpretation on knowing the natal chart.

Mary's natal Venus is not so romantic. Mary has contradictory reactions to Venus issues – she is usually quite down-to-earth and does not easily give way to her feelings (Venus in Capricorn). She will usually take things slowly. T Pluto may shake up her natural cautiousness. Venus in the 8th house is rather different; the suggestion is that she yearns deep down to find an intensely emotional connection with someone else, but would not easily show this. T Pluto conjunct Venus may be an uncomfortable experience for her!

To sum up, to begin to get an idea of how to interpret any transit, pull together a list of key words for the natal planet and the T planet, and try to make phrases from these, as when interpreting natal aspects.

It is important to remember in astrology that the more you work on understanding a planet's meaning, the better you can combine this with the meaning of another planet. This applies whether you are doing a natal chart, or any type of forecasting from transits, progressions, directions or a solar return chart – or any other astrological technique. The planets are, after all, the archetypes that underlie the spirit of astrology. Getting to know them takes practice and experience, and it takes reflection on what that planet is about in principle. Planetary Combinations Keywords are listed in Appendix 1. When I first look at a new natal chart, I try to put myself inside that chart. I try to imagine what it must be like to *be* that person, looking out on the world through the eyes of that chart's Ascendant. The more I keep working on absorbing the core meanings of Pluto or of Venus, as in the example above, the deeper my understanding of them. Gaining an instinctive comprehension of a planet is like trying to describe a dream – not just the strange events that may be present in the dream, but the *feeling* or the *atmosphere* of it.

When trying to understand the meaning of outer planet transits (i.e. of Pluto, Neptune, Uranus), it is useful to consider the position of those planets in the natal chart too. Let's take one of them as an example – Uranus. How prominent is natal Uranus – which natal house is it in, does it have many aspects, is it part of an aspect pattern? If, for instance, Jerry's natal Uranus is conjunct the Moon in the 4th house, it suggests that he needs to feel he has emotional freedom. It may also suggest – using one of the keywords for Uranus (suddenness) and the Moon (feelings) – that Jerry is subject to sudden changes of mood. Compare his natal Uranus with the relative strength of his Neptune or Pluto. It may be that one of the outer planets is natally stronger than the others, so the person is likely to identify with that one the most. So when a transit of the strongest natal planet comes along, it may be particularly important for him, as he has some understanding of it. And sometimes, no one outer planet is dominant on the chart.

Saturn's passage through the chart is often also very noticeable, and transits of this planet are important as well. Jupiter transits are generally shorter (though there are exceptions), and may bring a lightening of mood, depending on the nature of natal Jupiter and the position of T Jupiter. (These transits are considered in Chapter 7.)

Progressions, directions and the solar return chart also need to be observed, but at what level – in other words, how much of each forecasting technique do you need to include? We'll be considering this question in more detail in a later chapter.

Practising for the future

If, so far, forecasting might sound like quite hard work, I won't deny that there is some work to be done, but it becomes easier, and you will get more precise with practice! And it is really revealing and exciting to look into what is potentially coming up for you (or anyone) and how you can make the most of it.

You could try forecasting using someone else's chart; it might be a good idea to start with a close person such as a partner, good friend, or relative. In this way, you can learn more about how astrology relates to them as individuals, before going on to consider what the future might hold for them. Do remember, though, that having a basic understanding of a person's natal chart will help you to interpret their transits, or other techniques, in a more insightful way. This is so important in terms of gaining the most from learning how to interpret forecasting. Perhaps one reason for us to be here on Earth is to understand ourselves (i.e. to live more of our charts), and, to that end, the great internal shift brought by a strong orbiting planet simply opens up a part of us that needed to see daylight.

4.

THE ASTROLOGER'S BIBLE

How to know where the planets are

If there were only one book to buy in order to practise the art of astrology, it would have to be an ephemeris! An ephemeris lists the positions of all the planets on a daily basis for the relevant year and is a truly worthwhile investment. It is quite easy to read, assuming you are familiar with the planets' symbols. (At the beginning of this book, you will find a list of zodiac and planetary symbols to remind you of these.)

You can buy an ephemeris that covers one year, in order to look at the day-to-day positions of the planets during the 12 months in the current year. However, if you'd like to look at your own or anyone else's planets' positions on the day of birth, you'll need a bigger ephemeris that covers a much longer period. When you feel ready, you might therefore consider investing in a 50- or 100-year ephemeris so that you can look at the planets' positions across the years. Most of these give planetary tables for a 50-year period or so, usually from 1900–1950, 1950–2000, or 2000–2050. You can of course access the positions of the planets online, but for ease of moving backwards and forwards in order to see the changing planetary positions, a paper version is better. The best ones are *Raphael's 51-Year Ephemeris,* or *The American Ephemeris* for the twentieth or twenty-first century. You'll find both available on the internet or in a shop that sells astrology books. (A list of websites and shops offering mail-order services is given in the Useful Addresses section, page 328.)

Which ephemeris should you buy?

Raphael's Ephemeris has been published annually since the nineteenth century; it's small and handy to carry, and contains a wealth of astronomical information, as well as the planetary positions for the year in question. It shows the daily phase of the Moon, the aspects between planets for each day, how far every planet has moved in a day, the eclipse dates and times in the year, periods of retrogradation, and much more. It's very useful for checking out the positions of transiting planets as well as for checking the planets' signs for any child born that year. Many astrologers would not be without it, and renew their copy each year!

By the way, *Raphael's* always lists the planets' positions as they appear at noon GMT on each day. This is an important choice if you decide on using a paper ephemeris – know whether an ephemeris gives the positions of the planets at noon or at midnight each day. The paper ephemerides (Latin plural!) I use are all set for the noon positions of the planets, but you can buy one if you wish that gives the positions at midnight. Most ephemerides available online set the daily positions of the planets for midnight at the beginning of each 24-hour period. It is a matter of personal preference, or your choice may be to do with the prevailing convention for astrological calculations in the country in which you live. Owning an ephemeris means you can quickly look up the signs that the planets are in for any given date to get a rough idea of where they are without needing to access astrological software, except for the fast-moving Moon, which can move up to 15 degrees in 24 hours.

If for any reason you are unable to purchase or choose not to buy a paper ephemeris, it is usually quite straightforward to access one online. The simplest way to find this is to input search terms such as 'astrological ephemeris' into an online search engine. There are several online ephemerides available. You may, for example, want to find one that contains the listing for your date of birth, rather than buy an ephemeris that covers 50 years or so, so searching online may be an advantageous way to find this information.

THE IMPORTANCE OF TIME

On pages 44–45, you will find a copy of the page from *Raphael's Ephemeris* that has the entry for Leon's date of birth. Leon was born in the winter months on 4 January 1988 in Singapore, which lies 8 hours ahead of Greenwich Mean Time (GMT, now normally referred to as Universal Time: UT). In spite of the time difference between the two countries, Leon is clearly born on 4 January; he was born at 15.30, Singapore time. My software program has converted his chart to 09.30 UT in order to do the calculations for his chart, but you do not need to be concerned about the methods for converting times as an online astrology calculation program will convert any chart to UT automatically.

Sometimes the conversion of the birth time to UT because of the time zone difference changes the day. After all, the Earth has 24 different time zones, and the greatest distance around our planet is some 25,000 miles or 40,000 kilometres, so it is not surprising that 'days' can change in relation to where we are around the globe. This doesn't change the day that someone celebrates their birthday, though! To give an example, you may recall watching the New Year celebrations on TV, and seeing how Australia celebrates, all bells and whistles, half a day or so before the UK does, and many more hours before America does, depending on in which time zone in the USA you are.

The degree of the rising sign (the Ascendant) changes approximately every 4 minutes. The Earth spins fast! (The question of how the birth time affects the chart is addressed in Chapter 12.)

Taking the other study chart, that of Elaina, the time zone is of course different again because Elaina was born on 23 October 1995 at 17.38 in Florida, USA, which was 4 hours behind Universal Time, still on DST (Daylight Saving Time) on that date. So her UT hour of birth was 21.38.

The positions of the planets are all noted in *longitude* in an ephemeris, and their positions are measured in space along the ecliptic. (Longitude is the type of measurement of space used for positioning the planets.) Therefore, to find the position of every planet on the ephemeris page reproduced below, look in the column marked Longitude, or Long. for short.

There are a number of columns on each table of planets in *Raphael's Ephemeris*; if you find it helps, try placing a ruler across the page by the date, under the planet symbols for 4 January. The first column on the left page lists the date, and the second column is the Sidereal Time, for each day. Sidereal Time can be translated from the Latin as 'star time', 'sidereal' meaning star. It is utilised in astrology for calculating the positions of the planets and the chart's angles – and is irrelevant for our purposes in this book, as we will not be looking at how to do these calculations by hand! The other columns list various ways to consider the Moon's position. The one that concerns us here is the one marked:

☽ Long.

The Longitude Moon has two columns in *Raphael's Ephemeris*: one for its position at noon that day, and one in the column headed '24h', which refers to its position at midnight, twelve hours later. Using the

NEW MOON—January 19, 5h. 26m. a.m. (28° ♏ 21')

2					JANUARY, 1988					[RAPHAEL'S	
D M	D W	Sidereal Time	☉ Long.	☉ Dec.	☽ Long.	☽ Lat.	☽ Dec.	☽ Node	MIDNIGHT ☽ Long.	☽ Dec.	

D M	D W	H. M. S.	° ' "	° '	° ' "	° '	° '	° '	° ' "	° '
1	F	18 41 29	10 ♏ 17 5	23 S 3	11 ♊ 16 51	4 N 50	26 N 55	27 ♓ 8	17 ♊ 30 45	27 N 47
2	S	18 45 25	11 18 14	22 58	23 42 18	5 0	28 17	27 5	29 51 33	28 26
3	Su	18 49 22	12 19 22	22 52	5 ♋ 58 35	4 56	28 14	27 2	12 ♋ 3 30	27 42
4	M	18 53 18	13 20 30	22 46	18 6 21	4 39	26 49	26 59	24 7 16	25 39
5	T	18 57 15	14 21 38	22 40	0 ♌ 6 22	4 9	24 11	26 56	6 ♌ 3 52	22 28
6	W	19 1 11	15 22 47	22 33	11 59 58	3 28	20 32	26 52	17 54 56	18 24
7	TH	19 5 8	16 23 55	22 26	23 49 5	2 39	16 5	26 49	29 42 48	13 38
8	F	19 9 4	17 25 3	22 19	5 ♍ 36 29	1 43	11 3	26 46	11 ♍ 30 39	8 22
9	S	19 13 1	18 26 11	22 10	17 25 48	0 N 42	5 N 37	26 43	23 22 30	2 N 47
10	Su	19 16 58	19 27 19	22 2	29 21 22	0 S 22	0 S 4	26 40	5 ♎ 23 2	2 S 57
11	M	19 20 54	20 28 28	21 53	11 ♎ 28 10	1 25	5 51	26 37	17 37 27	8 42
12	T	19 24 51	21 29 36	21 44	23 51 32	2 26	11 31	26 33	0 ♏ 11 5	14 16
13	W	19 28 47	22 30 44	21 34	6 ♏ 36 41	3 22	16 54	26 30	13 8 54	19 23
14	TH	19 32 44	23 31 52	21 24	19 48 11	4 9	21 41	26 27	26 34 51	23 44
15	F	19 36 40	24 33 0	21 13	3 ♐ 29 6	4 43	25 29	26 24	10 ♐ 30 55	26 53
16	S	19 40 37	25 34 8	21 2	17 40 7	5 2	27 53	26 21	24 56 16	28 25
17	Su	19 44 33	26 35 16	20 50	2 ♑ 18 43	5 2	28 7	26 18	9 ♑ 46 35	27 59
18	M	19 48 30	27 36 23	20 39	17 18 49	4 42	26 59	26 14	24 54 10	25 28
19	T	19 52 27	28 37 30	20 26	2 ≈ 31 19	4 1	23 31	26 11	10 ≈ 8 53	21 8
20	W	19 56 23	29 ♏ 38 36	20 14	17 45 29	3 3	18 25	26 8	25 19 51	15 25
21	TH	20 0 20	0 ≈ 39 42	20 1	2 ♓ 50 49	1 53	12 13	26 5	10 ♓ 17 25	8 52
22	F	20 4 16	1 40 46	19 47	17 38 52	0 S 36	5 S 26	26 2	24 54 34	1 S 59
23	S	20 8 13	2 41 49	19 34	2 ♈ 4 10	0 N 41	1 N 27	25 58	9 ♈ 7 26	4 N 49
24	Su	20 12 9	3 42 52	19 20	16 4 22	1 54	8 5	25 55	22 55 4	11 12
25	M	20 16 6	4 43 53	19 5	29 39 45	2 58	14 8	25 52	6 ♉ 18 43	16 52
26	T	20 20 2	5 44 54	18 50	12 ♉ 52 20	3 51	19 22	25 49	19 20 59	21 37
27	W	20 23 59	6 45 53	18 35	25 45 6	4 31	23 35	25 46	2 ♊ 5 5	25 14
28	TH	20 27 56	7 46 51	18 20	8 ♊ 21 20	4 56	26 35	25 43	14 34 15	27 35
29	F	20 31 52	8 47 49	18 4	20 44 12	5 7	28 14	25 39	26 51 32	28 32
30	S	20 35 49	9 48 44	17 48	2 ♋ 56 31	5 4	28 29	25 36	8 ♋ 59 27	28 5
31	Su	20 39 45	10 ≈ 49 39	17 S 31	15 ♋ 0 36	4 N 48	27 N 22	25 ♓ 33	21 ♋ 0 10	26 N 19

D M	Mercury			Venus			Mars			Jupiter	
	Lat.	Dec.		Lat.		Dec.	Lat.	Dec.		Lat.	Dec.

D M	° '	° '	° '	° '	° '	° '	° '	° '	° '	° '	° '
1	2 S 3	24 S 33	24 S 23	1 S 48	18 S 45	18 S 24	0 N 28	18 S 37	18 S 47	1 S 17	6 N 44
3	2 6	24 11	23 58	1 48	18 2	17 39	0 27	18 57	19 7	1 17	6 47
5	2 8	23 43	23 27	1 47	17 16	16 53	0 26	19 16	19 26	1 16	6 51
7	2 8	23 9	22 49	1 45	16 29	16 5	0 25	19 35	19 44	1 15	6 55
9	2 6	22 28	22 5	1 44	15 40	15 15	0 24	19 53	20 2	1 15	6 59
11	2 2	21 41	21 15	1 42	14 49	14 23	0 23	20 11	20 19	1 14	7 3
13	1 56	20 48	20 19	1 39	13 57	13 30	0 21	20 28	20 36	1 14	7 8
15	1 47	19 49	19 18	1 37	13 3	12 36	0 20	20 44	20 52	1 13	7 13
17	1 36	18 46	18 13	1 34	12 8	11 40	0 19	20 59	21 7	1 12	7 18
19	1 21	17 38	17 3	1 30	11 12	10 43	0 17	21 14	21 21	1 12	7 23
21	1 3	16 27	15 51	1 26	10 15	9 45	0 16	21 28	21 35	1 11	7 29
23	0 41	15 15	14 39	1 22	9 16	8 47	0 15	21 42	21 48	1 11	7 35
25	0 S 16	14 3	13 28	1 18	8 17	7 47	0 13	21 55	22 1	1 10	7 41
27	0 N 13	12 55	12 23	1 13	7 17	6 46	0 12	22 7	22 13	1 10	7 47
29	0 44	11 53	11 S 26	1 8	6 16	5 S 45	0 10	22 18	22 S 24	1 9	7 54
31	1 N 18	11 S 1		1 S 3	5 S 14		0 N 9	22 S 29		1 S 9	8 N 0

FIRST QUARTER—January 25, 9h. 54m. p.m. (5° ♉ 9')

Illustration of ephemeris page for January 1988

FULL MOON—January 4, 1h. 40m. a.m. (12° ♋ 54')

| EPHEMERIS] | | | | JANUARY, 1988 | | | | | | | | | | 3 |

D	☿	♀	♂	♃	♄	♅	♆	♇	Lunar Aspects								
M	Long.	Long.	Long.	Long.	Long.	Long.	Long.	Long.	☉	☿	♀	♂	♃	♄	♅	♆	♇
	° '	° '	° '	° '	° '	° '	° '	° '									
1	15 ♑ 40	12 ♒ 38	25 ♏ 15	20 ♈ 16	25 ♐ 31	27 ♐ 42	7 ♑ 48	12 ♏ 1		△		∠				⚹ ☍ ☍	⊔
2	17 17	13 51	25 55	20 19	25 38	27 45	7 51	12 2		⊔		⊔					
3	18 55	15 5	26 35	20 23	25 45	27 49	7 53	12 4			⊔		☍			☍	△
4	20 34	16 19	27 15	20 27	25 52	27 52	7 55	12 5	☍	☍		□					
5	22 12	17 33	27 55	20 31	25 59	27 56	7 57	12 6			△						
6	23 51	18 46	28 35	20 36	26 6	27 59	8 0	12 8			☍	□	△	⊔ △		⊔	□
7	25 30	20 0	29 14	20 40	26 13	28 3	8 2	12 9				⊔				△	
8	27 9	21 14	29 ♏ 54	20 45	26 19	28 6	8 4	12 10	⊔								⚹
9	28 ♑ 48	22 27	0 ♐ 34	20 50	26 26	28 10	8 6	12 12	△	⊔		⚹			□	□	∠
10	0 ♒ 27	23 41	1 14	20 55	26 33	28 13	8 9	12 13									
11	2 6	24 54	1 54	21 0	26 40	28 17	8 11	12 14		⊔	∠		☍	⚹ ⚹			□ ∠
12	3 45	26 8	2 34	21 6	26 46	28 20	8 13	12 15	□	△			∠			⚹	♂
13	5 24	27 21	3 14	21 11	26 53	28 23	8 15	12 17			∠				∠		
14	7 2	28 34	3 54	21 17	27 0	28 27	8 18	12 18	⚹			♂	⊔	∠	∠		
15	8 39	29 ♒ 48	4 34	21 23	27 6	28 30	8 20	12 19	∠	⚹	□			∠	∠		
16	10 16	1 ♓ 1	5 14	21 29	27 13	28 34	8 22	12 20		△			△		♂	♂	∠
17	11 51	2 14	5 54	21 35	27 19	28 37	8 24	12 21	∠	∠	⚹	∠		♂		⚹
18	13 26	3 27	6 34	21 42	27 26	28 40	8 26	12 22	∠	∠	∠	□				
19	14 58	4 40	7 14	21 49	27 32	28 44	8 28	12 23	♂		⚹	⚹	⚹	∠ ∠	∠	
20	16 28	5 53	7 54	21 55	27 39	28 47	8 31	12 24		♂			⚹	∠ ∠	□	
21	17 56	7 6	8 34	22 2	27 45	28 50	8 33	12 25	∠	⚫	□	∠	⚹ ⚹		△	
22	19 20	8 19	9 14	22 9	27 51	28 53	8 35	12 25	∠	∠		∠		□	□	□ ⊔
23	20 41	9 32	9 55	22 17	27 58	28 56	8 37	12 26	⚹	∠				△ △		
24	21 58	10 45	10 35	22 24	28 4	29 0	8 39	12 27	□		△	♂				
25	23 9	11 57	11 15	22 32	28 10	29 3	8 41	12 28		∠	⊔			△ △	☍	
26	24 15	13 10	11 55	22 40	28 16	29 6	8 43	12 28			⚹			⊔ ⊔	△	☍
27	25 14	14 22	12 35	22 48	28 22	29 9	8 45	12 29	△	□		⚹			⊔	
28	26 5	15 35	13 15	22 56	28 28	29 12	8 47	12 30	⊔		☍	∠			⚹	
29	26 49	16 47	13 55	23 4	28 34	29 15	8 50	12 30	△			⚹				☍ ☍ ☍ ⊔
30	27 23	17 59	14 36	23 12	28 40	29 18	8 52	12 31	⊔	△						
31	27 ♒ 47	19 ♓ 12	15 ♐ 12	23 ♈ 21	28 ♐ 46	29 ♐ 21	8 ♑ 54	12 ♏ 31	⊔	△						△

D	Saturn		Uranus		Neptune		Pluto		Mutual Aspects
M	Lat.	Dec.	Lat.	Dec.	Lat.	Dec.	Lat.	Dec.	
	° '	° '	° '	° '	° '	° '	° '	° '	1. ☉∠♂.♀∠♅.P♂.♂⚹h.
									2. ♀⊥♆.h P♆.
1	1 N 7	22 S 15	0 S 10	23 S 35	0 N 57	22 S 15	15 N 53	0 S 18	3. ☉⚹♇.♂±♃. 4. ☿□♃.
3	1 7	22 16	0 10	23 36	0 57	22 15	15 53	0 18	5. ☿ P♅.♂⚹♅.
5	1 7	22 16	0 10	23 36	0 57	22 15	15 54	0 18	6. ☉ Q♀. 7. ☿⚹h.
7	1 7	22 16	0 10	23 36	0 57	22 15	15 55	0 17	8. ☉P h.☿ ⚹♃.
9	1 7	22 17	0 10	23 36	0 57	22 14	15 56	0 17	9. ☉P♆.☉P h.♀⚹♅.
11	1 7	22 17	0 10	23 36	0 57	22 14	15 57	0 17	10. P♀.☉P♀.♀∠♆.
13	1 7	22 18	0 10	23 36	0 57	22 14	15 58	0 17	11. ☿⚹♂.⊥h.♂∠♆.
15	1 7	22 18	0 10	23 36	0 57	22 14	15 59	0 17	12. ☉□♃.♀⊥♅.
17	1 7	22 18	0 10	23 36	0 57	22 13	16 0	0 16	13. ♀⚹h.
19	1 7	22 19	0 10	23 36	0 57	22 13	16 1	0 16	14. ♀P♂.☉⚹♅.
21	1 7	22 19	0 10	23 37	0 57	22 13	16 2	0 15	15. ☉ Q♇.♀ Q♃.⚹♆.
23	1 7	22 19	0 10	23 37	0 57	22 12	16 3	0 15	17. ☉P♂.☿∠h.□♅.♂□♃.
25	1 7	22 19	0 10	23 37	0 57	22 12	16 4	0 14	18. ☉⚹h.♀∠♅.♂□♃.
27	1 7	22 19	0 10	23 37	0 57	22 12	16 5	0 14	19. ☉⊥♀.⚹♅.♀⊥♅.
29	1 7	22 20	0 10	23 37	0 57	22 12	16 6	0 13	21. ♀∠♃.♂⚹♆.
31	1 N 7	22 S 20	0 S 10	23 S 37	0 N 57	22 S 11	16 N 7	0 S 13	22. ♀⚹♆. 23. ♀ Q h.
									24. ☉⊥h.♂⚹♃.♀☌♂.Q♅.
									25. ☉⊥♅.♀ Q♇.∠♆.△♇.
									26. ♀P♃. 27. ♂⚹♇.
									28. ♂P♆.
									29. ☉⚹♆.♀⊥♃♂P h.

LAST QUARTER—January 12, 7h. 4m. a.m. (21° ♎ 17')

ephemeris, you can see how far each planet – especially the rapid Moon – has moved in 24 hours simply by looking at the positions of each planet for the next day. For our purposes, we can safely ignore all the other columns on these pages: it is only the longitude positions of the planets that we need. (That said, remember that this is an ephemeris for 1988; you will find that the layout of *Raphael's* is more modern-looking now, with even more information in it.)

The rest of the column headings on the page on the right-hand side for January are the symbols for the positions of the planets of our Solar System, in this natural order:

☿　♀　♂　♃　♄　♅　♆　♇

Mercury, Venus, Mars, Jupiter, Saturn, Uranus, Neptune, Pluto

One thing you may find interesting, which you can see in the illustration of the *Raphael's* page, is that this ephemeris gives the Moon's current phase for every 7 days. The example above informs us that the New Moon for the month of January 1988 was on 19 January, and First Quarter was on 25 January. The Quarter Moons are approximately 7 days apart.

Where figures are given for the Sun's longitude and the Moon's longitude in degrees, minutes and seconds, it is common to round them up or down so that the position is given in degrees and minutes only. The seconds are unnecessary. And actually, a person's birth time is often not precisely correct either. Certainly there are many births where the drama of the baby's arrival means no one is precisely recording the time it occurred, so it'll end up being the midwife's best guess!

Another thing you will notice is that the glyph for Pluto is not the same as shown above. What is listed is the alternative way to illustrate

Pluto: it looks like a combination of the first two letters of Pluto's name, PL. The glyph is in fact the combination of the initials of Percival Lowell, the astronomer who predicted the existence of Pluto in 1915, which was eventually proved by Clyde Tombaugh in 1930. This is the alternative symbol: ♇

Not so difficult, really, once you understand how it works! Armed with this basic knowledge of how to read the ephemeris you can not only observe how far any planet (not just the Moon!) has moved in 24 hours, by looking at the positions next day, but, by looking through the ephemeris for any given year, month by month, you can see how much a transiting planet moves in a year, remembering that most planets spend some time every year in retrograde motion (see the Table on page 106). Being able to do this, even though it is only in the form of figures listed in a table of planetary positions, somehow makes planetary motion seem more real.

PART II
THE FOUR KEY METHODS

5.
INDIVIDUAL AND COLLECTIVE

Transiting planetary cycles

As mentioned, each method of forecasting introduced in Chapter 2 will be explored in its own chapter here in Part II. However, it is best to start with the transiting planets to your own chart in your early attempts at forecasting, as transits are the easiest system to find in the ephemeris and it is relatively straightforward to observe their effects. Simple knowledge of where the planets are in a given year – gleaned from an ephemeris – enables you to work out the transits to a natal chart. You can also obtain a list of transits for the required period from an astrological software program or from the websites listed in the Useful Addresses section at the back of this book.

Tip: You may find it handy to make a list of each outer or social planet's moving positions for a year on one A4 sheet, noting the periods when a planet retrogrades, then turns direct, so that you can see at a glance where the planets are in any month without having to constantly consult an ephemeris or online program. For such a list, I suggest you use Pluto, Neptune, Uranus, Chiron, Saturn and Jupiter, and maybe just make a note of the beginning and end dates of the Mean (average) Nodal axis for the year. I always list the eclipse dates and degrees for the year as well.

WHICH FORECASTING METHODS TO USE?

There are those astrologers who *only* use transits when forecasting. But as you progress in learning the various methods, you may find that the finer details of personal discovery, growth and self-understanding are missed when you choose to work with transits alone. By using at least one of the symbolic methods as well, you will deepen your breadth of understanding. This will probably come as your experience grows.

Generally speaking, there is not always agreement amongst astrologers as to which is the best method of these two symbolic methods. There are those who use solar arc directions along with transits, but not secondary progressions, and vice versa. Today, I use both secondary progressions and solar arc directions in my astrological work, although I have been using progressions for longer and have added forecasting using directions to my practice in more recent years. As you can see from the tri-wheel in Chapter 2, page 28, illustrating the movement of Mars in Leon's charts, the SA and p positions of Mars offer two possible options for checking which natal planets are being activated by these forecasting methods. To help you decide whether to use one or both systems, the best way is to try both over a few months to see which seems the most valid, or whether both do.

The solar return chart places emphasis on the current year, but we know it is not usually interpreted in such depth as the natal chart. Rather, it is interpreted as a yearly addition to, and comparison with, the natal chart. Again, there are some astrologers who only look at the solar return chart, but there are equally those who don't use this chart at all. If you choose not to use the solar return chart – as I didn't in my early period of learning forecasting – you won't really miss it, as there is plenty of material available through the other methods. But somewhat illogically, if you do start to use the return chart, you nearly always find something interesting that you perhaps hadn't noticed before – perhaps more of an emphasis to a transit, as you can see it clearly across the chart, a different element/mode balance, or other differences or 'extras' not apparent to you in other ways. One other point to note is that a transit which is passing through in a relatively short period of time, such as only 2–3 weeks or so, can be 'captured' by a solar return chart if it falls near the birthday, and instead of lasting a short time, the influence of that so-called passing transit could last for a year on the SR chart. In Elaina's solar return chart for 2018 (illustrated in Chapter 12, page 201), you will see an example of this in a couple of oppositions to Uranus.

There are a number of possibilities in working with astrology, but your own choices of which methods to use will evolve over time, once you become more familiar with the different techniques. This does not, of course, apply only to forecasting. Other choices will be which house system, what orbs and which planets to use (some traditional astrologers do not use the outer planets). Others will use the fixed stars and the asteroids (see Chapter 15), and so on!

Beyond the individual: the collective influence of transits

The transiting outer planets do not, of course, only affect the experiences of individuals as they aspect natal charts, but can effect great changes in society and attitudes in general. Whether it is that the changing outer planets 'give birth to' new collective ideas, or whether it is that naturally shifting patterns of experience in the world are reflected by the planetary changes, I have no idea. A bit of both probably. Above mirrors below, after all.

An example of a major planetary configuration that happened some 55 to 60 years ago has reverberated down the decades: the mid-1960s brought the example of T Uranus making an aspect to another outer planet; transiting Uranus joined transiting Pluto in the sign of Virgo (T♅☌T♇ . . .) by conjunction in the sky. All babies born in the mid-sixties have this aspect on their charts. The influence of those former flower children is everywhere now – in the prevalence of trendy gym clubs, vegan options on restaurant menus, and greater social equality – and is still in process. This was a short period – in Western countries at least – when the hippie movement, flower power, flowing styles and ideals of free love were in the air. In health-conscious Virgo attitudes were changing – about vegetarianism, meditation, mind-enhancing experiences from marijuana smoking to attending festivals. Martial arts and yoga became fashionable amongst some sections of society. Uranus represents the breaking of the status quo, rebellion, and the bringing in of new attitudes, while Pluto represents major transformations and the death of previous ways.

A new openness and a breaking with older conventions could be said to characterise the period, although, as is often the case with societal changes, years elapsed before the changes became 'normal'. It wasn't until the seventies or later decades that health food shops and yoga venues, for example, began to proliferate across the UK and other Western countries.

These were not the only manifestations of this transit. Protest marches and movements about human rights were also notably part of the period. Demands for equality and the rise of both the women's rights and civil rights movements really got going during the 1960s, as well as the controversial war between the USA and Vietnam. In the world of music, musicians whose influence has been long-lasting, such as the Beatles, Rolling Stones, Bob Dylan, Donovan and many others, first became famous. In a broad sense, their rebelliousness was truly breaking new ground.

In 2012, forming over seven exact aspects (very unusually) until 2015, T Uranus formed a square with T Pluto (T♅□T♇). That is, the two planets both moved from their conjunction at the beginning of this planetary cycle to become 90 degrees apart as seen from Earth – a more testing combination, from awakening and bestirring society with their mid-1960s conjunction to the challenge of the square in the second decade of the twenty-first century.

In the world's collective, this manifested as growing demands for social justice in many countries and over many topics, even though this is certainly not true in countries that are suffering under an oppressive regime, but in some places the citizens have staged protests in Uranian ways, rebelling against such regimes. Uranus brings a more enlightened view of what constitutes true democracy – the will of the people if you like – and Pluto delves beneath the surface of what power is and brings to the surface that which has been hidden or obscured. The square brings disruption and resistance, and extreme reactions from both the authorities and the civilian population.

Even though these two heavy outer planets have moved on in their orbits since 2015 and away from exactness, such is their influence on worldly events that the changes signified by their 3- to 4-year interaction continue to reverberate down the years. Buried anger at political or social injustices erupted in the collective, which had perhaps been germinating over a longer period, and simply needed the 'trigger' of this transit to release it. Hence there are many areas of vicious conflict and protest around the globe, loss of life and property on a grand scale, and displacement of peoples.

There have been other revolutions and revelations that have also made for scandalous headlines in a way that is unprecedented, such as the exposure of corruption at government level in various countries, and the uncovering of sexual and financial abuse in 'high' places perpetrated by certain individuals in positions of power and of trust. This is the kind of manifestation that Pluto especially can bring to the world, and also to the lives of individuals in exposing that which has been hidden.

This is a partial exposé laid only at the door of one transit which is no longer exact. I will leave the subject here, but I hope you can see from this brief explanation the far-reaching effects of an important transit. Your major personal transits can sometimes seem to have a wide-ranging effect in your life, too!

As one of the two outer planets in our Solar System, far away from the gravitational pull of the Sun, Pluto may remain 20 years in one sign, occasionally even a little longer. Neptune's sojourn in one sign could be 15 years or so. This is why both are said to be generational planets, marking the progress of the generations. This is true also of Uranus, Saturn and Jupiter but not for such long periods; see the Table of Planetary Motion on page 106. Uranus spends on average 7 years in each sign, Saturn 2.5 years, Jupiter 1 year. T Neptune is currently in Pisces for 14 years, from 2011 to 2025. Neptune will spend a similar period of time in Aries, from 2025 to 2038.

From the collective to the individual

In an individual chart, it is not only the aspects between T planets and the natal planets that concern us in forecasting, but also the signs on the individual chart, and the changes the outer planets bring as they move from one sign to another. For, at the time of writing, Pluto's current passage through Capricorn (2008–2023) represents a marked contrast to its time in the previous sign, Sagittarius. Whereas Sagittarius tends towards extravagance and not fully considering the consequences of over-spending, exaggerated promises or undertakings, and spontaneous hedonism or simply enjoying life, Capricorn pulls in its boundaries and starts to take life more seriously – which it did (human beings did) too late to ward off the nearly worldwide consequences of the financial crash that began with Pluto's *ingress* into Capricorn. The combined influence of Pluto and Capricorn has resulted in the tightening of restrictions on individuals and on some governments, and has been reflected in the years of austerity in places where that has been the case.

An outer planet's transit through a zodiac sign not only affects the birth chart and therefore the life of an individual, but also describes society's changes on a large scale. Let's look at this in a little more detail, using Pluto as a model for collective change, and looking to the future for both the Earth and for us as individuals . . .

Pluto in Capricorn
♇ in ♑
In the years 2008 to 2023, Pluto traverses the sign of Capricorn. The sign that Pluto is in picks up and exposes collective or individual transformations and potential rebirths that need to be known about; this applies of course to individuals as well, which is why people who know they have major Pluto transits coming can feel anxious (even astrologers!), although it's better to be informed than to be ignorant about them so that we can make the best of these times. Even those people who don't know they have a major Pluto transit on the horizon can feel anxious because they intuitively sense change coming.

To briefly recap, the image of the earthy zodiac sign Capricorn is that of the sure-footed mountain goat, with its extraordinary ability to leap up (and down) to very narrow ledges in mountains, and hold a perfect balance. The astrological sign embodies qualities such as grounded practicality, determination, confidence, ambition and reaching upwards, the capacity to take considered risks and to succeed in business, and in the world; with the purpose of amassing positions of power, prestige, and wealth. The astrological meaning of Pluto in Capricorn tends to bring such qualities to the surface, revealing that which was previously hidden from view. Pluto exposes that which lies below the surface whose time has come to be revealed to the world in some way.

During Pluto's years in Capricorn, when it has brought secret deals to light from the underworld of corporate agreements and shady affairs, the world has undergone some extraordinary shifts. Take a moment to reflect on other major changes and exposés that have occurred during Pluto's time in Capricorn, affecting many countries in the world, for example: the revealing of fraudulent government and multi-nationals' practices in many countries, including tax evasion or punitive pricing; the manipulation of the media; corrupt leaderships and presidential stances – resulting in some countries engaging in violent conflicts, and the displacement of peoples; the forceful persecution of whistle-blowers; the exposure of the stark inequalities in many countries and societies; scandals, abuses and misuses of power, to name just a few.

Much can be achieved through the persistence and determination of Capricorn, together with Pluto's natural inclination to enhance our general awareness of what has been hidden in the world. Much of that which was hidden, or information about those individuals or organisations who were responsible for keeping it below ground, has surfaced. Many people's perceptions or understanding of that which was previously secret knowledge is continuing to go through a process of revelation, in many countries.

From death or transformation comes a rebirth, and a new awareness of individual personal power to effect real change is continuing to
emerge from Pluto's underworld. The process continues today, when-
ever you are reading this, for Pluto's force for change does not stop as
the years roll on.

Retrograde phase

An outer planet will always enter a *retrograde* period once a year while
transiting the position of a natal planet. As a reminder, retrograde
motion is an optical illusion as viewed from Earth – the planets don't
actually travel backwards! (Remember that astrology is *geocentric*. It's
what a planet looks like it is doing when viewed from here on Earth.) If
this is the case, it will cross a degree in its retrograde period, before
crossing back again, passing the natal degree of the relevant natal
planet by the same aspect three, four or even five times. So usually
there will be at least three periods of intense experience, and calmer
periods when the T planet is not exact. Uranus transits always last for
approximately a year at least; those of Pluto or Neptune usually last
longer.

This equally applies whether the T planet is making a conjunction,
opposition, square, trine or sextile or a minor aspect, to the natal planet
or angle concerned.

Transits of Neptune, Uranus, Saturn, Jupiter

To see the connections with planetary movements and social or
large-scale change, it is helpful to view these planets in a collective
way, as well as on a more personal level. Areas ruled by each of
these planets may feature in the news, or be more localised.

Neptune collective issues can be to do with oil, for example, so possibly incorporating transport systems, oil rigs, spillages; gas – escapes or explosions; water problems e.g. floods or scarcity, and so on.

Study the meanings associated with these planets, consult your ephemeris and then take a look at the news headlines for that day: can you see any connections between events and the transiting planets?

It is important to realise that the meanings associated with each planet remain essentially the same whether you are interpreting the planet in the natal chart, or by any relevant method of forecasting. Therefore, the more you can expand your perception of the astrological meaning of the planets, above all other factors in a birth chart, the more your understanding of interpretation will grow. In the Further Reading list on page 326, you will find recommended astrology books that will also enhance your knowledge.

Know – and love – your planets!

6

TRANSITS 1: THE OUTER PLANETS

Distant Pluto, Neptune and Uranus

You may think that the three 'generational' planets – Pluto, Neptune and Uranus – are so far away from our planet Earth that they could not possibly exert any influence on us. However, the energy of these transiting outer planets usually brings changes to both the collective level and our personal experience, as illustrated in the example of Pluto in Capricorn given in Chapter 5.

These planets are held in their orbits by the immense gravity of the Sun, and they shine with a certain amount of reflected sunlight from our powerful star, depending on which planet it is and how far away from the Sun it is. These planets have only very minor, if any, actual physical influence on planet Earth, but this is not how this influence appears to operate astrologically. This is one of those frequent misunderstandings in assessing astrological meaning by non-astrologers. Logically, it would seem that if any planets of the Solar System were having any effect on human affairs, there would be some kind of physical component (such as a magnetic force or other property).

This is, for example, the thinking of an unusual scientist, who became fascinated with the sky from an early age, and qualified in adulthood as an astronomer, now retired. Dr Percy Seymour wrote a number of scientific papers and books explaining his theory that astrology 'works' because of the magnetic influence on the Earth from the Sun and the orbiting planets in space. One of his books is titled *Astrology: The Evidence of Science*, and he is to be admired for having the courage to persist in his approach, which is highly unpopular amongst his fellow scientists, who almost universally condemn his theories as 'pseudo-science'.

Unfortunately Dr Seymour's books and papers have done little to debunk the prevailing worldview that astrology is unprovable, scientifically speaking. And, while many astrologers admire and appreciate his theories about magnetic fields and astrology, and find it encouraging to have support from a member of the scientific community, they would be inclined to focus instead on how powerful the symbolism used in astrology is, allowing human qualities to emerge from myth which were gradually correlated with the Solar System planets.

I often liken a transit or progression as acting like a mystical 'spotlight' that picks out a part of ourselves that lies hidden in our chart, and which holds it up for examination; each part of our inner character is revealed in turn as the planets move. Over an average lifetime, you will experience an opportunity to grow and expand each part of your soul, or your inner self, or whatever expression describes this best for you. Whether or not you can take this opportunity on board will be your own choice. (Though it certainly doesn't always feel like an opportunity!) But you do have autonomy. Resistance to change is nearly always possible, and you can choose to reject your challenges, although sometimes it takes a great deal of effort to resist the learning process the universe is apparently offering you.

Practicalities and recapping

Astrological opinions vary on the orb used for T planets from 3 degrees to 5 degrees ahead and after the natal point is exactly aspected. Personally, I tend to look about 1 degree before and after the exact period, but it varies. Some individuals are more sensitive to an approaching transit than others.

In terms of when during a major transit a definite event may be experienced, it often seems to be the case that it is the last exact hit that manifests the event, with more inner changes experienced in the beginning of the transit. This is of course not always the case. My statement is based on my experience of working with transits over the years. Later on in this chapter, there is an example or two of the 'last hit' phenomenon.

The *average length* that a transit lasts overall on the chart is different for each planet. This depends on the length of the orbit of that planet and its distance from the Sun, which of course changes its consequent speed through your chart. Its orbit, and therefore its total transit length, is recapped under the description of each planet.

The *essential meaning* of an outer or social planet transiting a chart is listed below by each planet. Further reading can expand this information, so do check Further Reading on page 326 and explore astrology sites!

♇ PLUTO

Average transit length: varies between 1.5 to 3 years long. Occasionally, important Pluto transits can last as long as 5 years, but this is rare. As we have seen, the passage of Pluto near the edge of the Solar System, orbiting the central Sun, lasts approximately 248 years, which means it averages 16–20 years in each sign or equal house. This means that transiting Pluto traversing the natal degree of a planet or angle on the birth chart, with its inevitable retrograde motion back and forth over that point, is usually a slow process.

Myth: Pluto (known as Hades in Greek myth) was the Lord of the dark Underworld, god of the Earth, and of death and rebirth. His father was Saturn, also known as Kronos. Pluto had a fearsome reputation in ancient Greek or Roman thought, for he annually stole away the warmth at the end of the summer, bringing the cold death of winter and the dark months. No one emerges unchanged from an experience of the Underworld.

Essential meanings of Pluto:

- Major shifts, and far-reaching changes or endings in your life.
- The process of death, rebirth or renewal – journeying through unconscious patterns or complexes to an expanded understanding of an aspect of life.
- Experience of the use or abuse of power or manipulation – yours or someone else's.
- Issues that are buried or hidden being exposed, or secrets that are revealed.

Discovered: in 1930

Pluto rules: Pluto is the modern ruling planet of the zodiac sign of Scorpio. Scorpio is also traditionally co-ruled by Mars. Pluto is often thought to be the 'higher energy of Mars', which represents Pure Will.

A modern myth: is Pluto a dwarf planet? (And therefore meaningless?)

Before I go on to write about transiting Pluto, I need to dispel the rumours about astrologers' continuing use of Pluto as a meaningful planetary symbol . . .

In 2006 the astronomical scientists determined that because of its small size and distance from the Sun (amongst other definitions), Pluto should be downgraded in its definition as a planet of the Solar System, and henceforth be referred to as a *dwarf planet*. Astronomers of course base their definitions of a planet on the physical characteristics that people have discovered, as far as they can be determined from here; and they are continuing to discover more information through probes and fly-pasts of this distant body. No symbolic meaning is ever attached to bodies in space by astronomers, because they are basing their definitions on empirical science.

Like their erstwhile counterparts back in the seventeenth century and before, astrologers have naturally always perceived a wider and a meaningful view, which is the basis of our art – that all bodies in space symbolise varying qualities. (Although, none of the outer planets were known in the seventeenth century.) Of these many bodies, the Solar System planets assume the most powerful of symbolic meanings. There are now a myriad of other bodies known to us on Earth, including many stars and smaller bodies such as Ceres or Eris or Sedna – some of which are known to astrologers as asteroids (though former 'asteroid' Ceres is now designated astronomically a dwarf planet) – comets, the moons of the planets, and so on. Many of these have a symbolic meaning and purpose in their own right to astrologers, although a discussion of these is beyond the scope of this book, except for the asteroids.

In the case of Pluto, it is true that this distant body is indeed small in size – though materially immensely dense and heavy – and is influenced by the gravitational pull of Neptune, but whatever title scientists assign to it, astrologers know that its symbolic meaning remains unchanged. Indeed, the planet Pluto symbolises one of the most important forces for inner and outer transformation in the astrologer's 'toolkit'. Its very material characteristics form part of its meaning. Its influence can indeed be experienced as a profound one (which may be experienced as heavy or dense).

Pluto transits

Transiting Pluto has one of the most noticeable influences of all the outer planets. Its impact does of course depend on the nature of the transit. If Pluto is transiting one of the *luminaries* in a major aspect, for example – the two planets that form our basic sense of ourselves, the effects can be life-changing, for Pluto can take people to the depths of themselves. Every Pluto transit is important, whether it is major, such as T Pluto conjuncting, squaring, or opposing a personal planet or angle – e.g. T Pluto opposition natal Sun; or a seemingly 'lesser transit' such as T Pluto sextile Saturn. Each Pluto transit will not return again in precisely the same combination in a lifetime.

Transits of this outer planet to a natal planet or angle very often mark 'crossroads' years, or periods when major events or inner transformations occur. A death, a shift of perspective, a change of career or residence, or other potentially life-changing experiences may occur. Sometimes, a Pluto transit that affects an individual's life may have an echo in an event that affects many people.

To get to the essence of transiting Pluto and natal Mercury as experienced by Leon in 2018, see what you can gather from keywords for the transit itself (see below).

On Leon's chart, Neptune, Sun and Mercury in Capricorn and the 8th house are noticeably prominent, as is his natal Moon in Cancer in the 2nd house opposing all his Capricorn planets. Pluto has been crossing all his Capricorn planets, one after the other since 2011, but as the natal conjunction is not tight, he will probably have experienced each as a separate transit. T Pluto conjunct natal Neptune is of course not personal, and will be experienced by everyone born in a similar time period. But we are looking for what stands out amongst the transiting planets, from Jupiter to Pluto; and Leon was nearing the end of this series of Pluto conjunctions on his chart plus T Pluto opposing his Moon in Cancer in 2018 to 2019.

During approximately the same period, Leon will have experienced his Saturn return in the sign of Sagittarius and the 8th house. (See page 93 on the Saturn return.) This occurs when T Saturn returns to its natal place after about 29 years orbiting the Sun, so when Leon turned 29 years old. His Saturn is of course in Sagittarius and the 8th house. I will come back to this period later on when we look more specifically at his forecasting and what was happening for Leon during these years.

So can you see why Leon's 29th to 30th years are particularly significant ones over the course of his life? So many planets are being triggered in approximately the same time period that transformational changes are very likely, both outwardly in his circumstances and internally in terms of the ways in which his attitudes and feelings undergo a shift. (I will give you an update on Leon's experiences during this period after describing T Pluto conjunct his Mercury.)

T♇ơ☿ Pluto conjunct Mercury

First, try to come up with your own keywords for Pluto and Mercury. Then put the keywords together in phrases before looking down the page at the keywords and suggested phrases provided here.

Keywords for Pluto and Mercury

Pluto
- Change/transformation
- Buried, hidden, secretive
- Ending – death and rebirth
- Control, power, manipulation
- Obsessions, intensity, depth

Mercury

Thinking, type of mind, communication style

Speech, ideas, beliefs, arguments

Connections with others

Inspirations, learning

Perception, insight

Suggested phrases

Here are some suggested ways to interpret the experience of T Pluto conjunct Mercury:

- Changing your own or someone else's thinking process, and a deepening of thought.
- Using powerful persuasion to transform another person's attitude. (A good example in literature is Richard's manipulation of Anne's perception of him in Shakespeare's *Richard III*, Act I, Scene II.)

- Withholding secrets, manipulating a situation by arguing.
- Making powerful speeches or writing in an inspirational way.
- Using words in a sharp or cutting way to analyse or destroy.
- Learning new skills that potentially transform your life in some way.

This transit will last over a period of time, in and out of exactness (because of retrogradation) for a couple of years or so, varying from being a background influence at times to being a constant stimulus at other times during its passage. The particular aspect which connects the two planets will have an influence as well, of course. Generally speaking the conjunction is the most powerful, followed by the hard aspects (square, opposition) and the flowing ones (trine, sextile), but aspects can sometimes not conform to type. Even a trine can still bring disturbing experiences, or a square can sometimes bring surprisingly beneficial changes. Much may depend on the strength or otherwise of the planetary combination on the chart.

Leon's experience during his Pluto–Mercury transit
First, have a look at the position of Leon's Mercury, just to get some ideas about it. It is in Capricorn and the 8th house, like his Sun and Neptune. He became a little bit familiar with this repeating Pluto transit after it crossed his Sun in 2014 to 2015. Leon's Mercury has an exact aspect: square natal Jupiter. It is also opposition Moon, though less strongly. In essence, this describes Leon's need for frequent travel and for deepening and expanding his spiritual journey through encountering many cultures. Reading voraciously since childhood has widened his thinking. T Pluto triggers his mental world, and deepens his natural ability to organise and structure his future plans.

Months of transit exactness: February; July; December 2018, and almost exact from August to December 2019

In January 2018, Leon returned to Singapore after graduating from his English university. He then found a job as a library assistant – very appropriately for his transit – searching for and sorting books(!). He took time out to travel to diverse countries, meeting others, communicating with non-English speakers, and all the while continuing to diversify his absorption of new knowledge. He also took more training courses in India, one of which coincides with the last exact transit in December 2018, so this was particularly inspirational as he felt his mind was absorbing instruction at a heady rate. He does actually say that during 2018 (acknowledging also the echoes of his Saturn return, which brought a personal overall evaluation of where he is going) he experienced a deepening of his spiritual practice and plans for the future.

Contrasting experiences of the same combinations of planets
Elaina: Elaina's natal Mercury is at 12° Libra. Pluto, as an orbiting planet at 12° Capricorn, formed a challenging square aspect to her Mercury in Libra during 2014 to 2015 (T♇□☿). Mercury in Libra is fair-minded and prefers to avoid arguments if possible. The planet is positioned on the 7th house side of Elaina's Descendant, so there is a further emphasis on a peaceable approach to expressing her ideas and thoughts, especially with close others. When Pluto comes to square this Mercury, she may have found herself being more forceful than formerly. Remembering that important transits are often marked by events as well as psychological changes, this was a period when Elaina was very much focused on deciding her future course of study at university and she

went through a period of learning what really interested her. Pluto inclined her to in-depth research before she settled on her direction. T Pluto was deepening and shaking up her thinking and her interests. This transit is a square, so she may have had some challenging issues to deal with, and may have had to stand up for herself and defend her position.

So – a very similar transit but different experiences of it. This comparison between two people affected by the same transit is an indication of how important it is to take the individual's particular chart into consideration when assessing how forecasting can affect their lives.

In the months of the exact square for Elaina, due to the retrograde motion of T Pluto at 12° Capricorn, the transit was around as a background influence for almost the whole of 2014 to 2015. These transits 'fade in and out' over a period of time.

We become aware of the inner changes that are taking place quite clearly, or there is a gradual transformation of ourselves without our particularly noticing because the change is drawn-out.

Pluto and the Sun

T♇ ☍ ☉ *T Pluto opposition Sun*

Here is an example of how a different aspect between Pluto and the Sun can manifest itself, with a brief breakdown of how I arrived at the following interpretation. Also, this is an example of a 'last hit' transit event.

In this instance, Pluto's influence will reflect on the whole bundle of the individual's Sun sign, house and aspects. This transit will indeed bring one of the more major change periods that a person is likely to experience in their lifetime. Why is this so? Because the Sun in your chart symbolises your sense of who you essentially are, and what direction you are following. But this is an opposition – and there is a strong likelihood that what changes will affect someone else in your life, and may have a dynamic/shocking/transformational effect on you. This can be quite literal, as transits often manifest as a tangible event.

Paul has Sun in Gemini conjunct Uranus in his 4th house close to his *IC* (Immum Coeli, the point directly at the base of the chart), in his birth chart. In 2007, he received the upsetting news, out of the blue, that his brother (4th house and IC = family; brother = Gemini) had died suddenly of a heart attack = Sun conjunct Uranus. This was at the last 'hit' of T Pluto to his Sun, which is when an outer planet transit often seems to manifest as an event (this is not always so, but does frequently occur). This affected his life for the following 3 years or so, as not only did he have to deal with his loss, but he also had to deal with his brother's complicated estate, as his brother had died unmarried and intestate. Even though Paul felt himself to be quite a confident man in a stable situation in his own life, the experience knocked him sideways.

♆ NEPTUNE

Average transit length: Neptune takes approximately 165 years to orbit the Sun, and transits of Neptune to the natal chart usually last for 1 to 2 years, although they can sometimes last as long as an average Pluto transit.

Myth: whereas Neptune's brother Pluto was the god of the lower realms, Neptune himself (called Poseidon in Greek myth) was the Lord of the Sea, the god of Water, and of merging, oneness and dissolution. In the sea, all the separate drops of water have merged together to form the oceans – as any other body of water forms a pond, a lake, a river, etc. In time, all things are eroded and ultimately dissolved by water, a most mysterious substance. When Neptune became enraged, he called forth the destructive power of water, traditionally by striking the ocean floor with his trident, causing storms, floods and shipwrecked mariners. Floods that ruin property and bring chaos can be a frightening consequence of uncontrolled water, like overwhelming emotion. Yet Neptune can equally lift your soul to the heights of mystical experience, bringing healing.

Essential meanings of Neptune:

- Our connection to God, or the universe, however we conceive this.
- Oneness, merging, divine yearning, fusing.
- Love and compassion, empathy and sympathy, sensitivity and spirituality.
- Inspired creativity, imagination, psychic or intuitive insight.
- Fantasy, dreams, idealism.
- Delusions, deceptiveness, the dissolution of structures and the chaos of dissociation.
- Neptune asks: what is reality?

Discovered: in 1846.

Neptune rules: Pisces. However, Neptune is Pisces' 'modern' ruling planet, and Pisces is traditionally co-ruled by Jupiter. Neptune is thought to be the 'higher energy of Venus', representing Divine Love. Neptune is in Pisces until 2025, when it will enter the sign of Aries.

Neptune transits

As you can see from the list of essential meanings above, the meaning of a Neptune transit is often rather difficult to pin down. The experience of someone in the middle of a Neptune transit to their chart can be bewildering, or equally it can be uplifting and inspirational. Transits of this planet to the personal or social planets on your chart tend to dissolve your reality, engender illusions, incline you to contemplation, stimulate your creativity or increase your intuitive faculty . . .

If you are generally a grounded kind of person, with a down-to-earth and practical approach to life, a major transit by Neptune to one of your personal planets or an angle can be very disorienting, and make you feel out of sync with yourself. You may find yourself being, for example, much more easily moved than normal, uncharacteristically sentimental or overwhelmed with compassion, inspired to take up a creative or spiritual activity, or feel more inclined to escapism, whatever form that takes – from watching fantasy movies, or joining an art or dance class, to taking consciousness-altering substances, or any one of many different ways to escape mundane reality.

Or you could simply feel lost.

A different kind of person experiencing the influence of T Neptune but who is more of a reflective thinker or dreamer, or not perhaps particularly practical, could become highly motivated and inspired, or seek to escape to a more beautiful place, whatever that means to them. Neptune transits seem to take you out of yourself, and need containing if they are to be meaningful. Some of these can put you in danger of losing touch with reality, whatever your usual experience of reality is.

Let's look at how T Neptune featured in Leon's chart from 2017 to 2018.

T♆⚹☉ Leon – April, August 2017, February 2018

T Neptune sextile Sun
(This list for Neptune, below, is simply an abbreviated version to put it into context next to the list for the Sun.)

Keywords for Neptune and Sun

Neptune	Sun
• Merging, search for perfection	Core self
• Idealism	Sense of purpose
• Compassion, empathy	Centre of being
• Formlessness, 'God' connection	Life force
• Spiritual love and romance	Joyful energy

Suggested phrases for T Neptune sextile Sun
- Sense of merging with the universe, spiritual uplifting
- Aiming high to an ideal of perfection
- Feeling inspired with a sense of purpose
- Compassion and empathy for others
- Joy in loving others, or another person

Leon had T Neptune in Pisces sextile his natal Sun during 2017–2018. As this was a 'soft' aspect, he did not experience a blurring of his sense of identity in a challenging way, but his encounter with this transit was nevertheless interesting. At the time the transit started to approach, Leon was in the later stages of completing his Master's degree at university, reading Religious Studies, and was in the process of preparing and writing his final dissertation. He finished this and submitted it, and gained his MA qualification. We need to look at Leon's natal Sun position to place this transit into its context in Leon's chart. Leon has both Sun and Mercury in Capricorn natally, which suggests a natural ability to write in the structured manner that a final dissertation essay usually requires. The Sun is in Leon's 8th house, a watery house of emotional expression, and the Sun is sandwiched between Mercury and Neptune natally.

In this case: Neptune = inspiration; sextile = enjoyable effort; Sun = sense of oneself.

This transit helped him by triggering an opening-up of his inspiration and imagination, perhaps lending a well-thought-out (Capricorn) yet poetic style (8th house) to his ability to express himself in writing.

Apart from how the transit enhanced his Religious Studies course and helped him to gain his Master's degree, Leon met up with close friends from the past, which was an ongoing pleasure, and selflessly gave yoga workshops for no charge. He returned to Singapore in January 2018 and continued giving yoga classes for free. He is also a musician and is in two bands, each playing different types of music – a metal band and a progressive rock band. This occupied some of his time in 2017–2018. One of the bands released a third album in 2018. He is now increasingly involved in his spiritual practice and feels he may be moving away from playing music as much as he once did. This transit reflects this changing phase of his life well. His focus and purpose (Sun) has changed during this time. Neptune of course rules the arts in general, especially music, so his interest in creative occupations may change but probably will return.

TΨ□♃ Elaina – March, October 2018, January 2019
T Neptune square Jupiter

To give you a different example of T Neptune so that you can begin to see how you go about interpreting these transits, here's an instance of Neptune aspecting one of the 'social planets' – that is, Jupiter or Saturn. The other case-study person, Elaina, had T Neptune square natal Jupiter (TΨ□♃), which was exact in March 2018 and continued in and out of retrograde exactness until February 2019. The two planets came close enough to register with Elaina before that date, in 2017 as well. Looking at Jupiter's natal position, as we did for Leon's natal Sun, we see that Elaina's natal Jupiter is in Sagittarius and the 9th house, sextile to her Mercury, semi-square her Sun and square her Saturn.

How complicated that list of aspects sounds! But break it down into simple parts and give each keywords, and it becomes more manageable:

Let's consider her natal aspects: Jupiter–Mercury enhances her ability to express herself, and maybe inclines her to exaggerate; Jupiter–Sun suggests an optimistic life philosophy, but the semi-square inclines her to exaggerate a bit too; and Jupiter square Saturn shows that a need to find her purpose in life, while balancing self-doubts (Saturn) against belief in herself (Jupiter), is likely to be challenging. The sign and house position of her Jupiter echo each other (her Jupiter is in Sagittarius and the 9th house), indicating that her outlook, philosophy and approach to life are areas that she constantly strives to expand. Her education is very important to her and she is looking for her purpose and meaning in life. She puts in a lot of effort with Aries rising as well as her fiery Jupiter. Mars conjunct Pluto in the 8th house gives her the energy, if not the obsession, with forging ahead and finding answers. This combination is intense because of her depth of feeling (Pluto in the 8th house) and Mars conjunct Pluto focuses this energy – both planets seem to push (at times) for what she wants. This applies to most areas of her life, including romance. Her intensity is a part of herself that she finds hard to hold back even though she is aware that she could come across as too intense for some people! (We will be looking at this in more detail in later chapters.)

So how might T♎□♃ manifest in her life?

Her natural wish to be generous and give of herself and her time (Moon and Mercury in Libra 7th) is stimulated by this transit. She will feel idealistic (Neptune) and want to give to others, but it is important for her to try to remain grounded so her big heart does not get too damaged; she is more inclined than normal to reach out to needy people. This transit suggests that she could be taken advantage of, so she needs to try to maintain her boundaries. There is, however, an aspect on her solar return chart for 2018 that may help here (see Chapter 12).

♅ URANUS

Average length of transit: the orbit of Uranus around the Sun is approximately 84 years. The average length of its transits is approximately 1 year. Uranus stays in one sign for approximately 7 years.

Myth: Uranus is the Lord of the Sky, the god of the air. Together with Gaia, creator goddess of the Earth, these two deities caused the formation of the Earth and sky and then separated the two. *Ouranos,* to give him his Greek name – which still means 'sky' in modern Greek – was the son of Gaia, for his mother was also his mate, in the strange way of ancient myths. He was the father of a race of giants, called the Titans. Uranus rejected his offspring, finding them not at all up to his expectations, so at the request of his mother Gaia, Kronos, the youngest Titan (also known as Saturn), castrated his father in order to stop any more children being born. Anything can happen in a myth!

Essential meanings:
- Revolution, rebellion, radical shift
- Independence, freedom
- Breaking rules, doing it your way
- Awakening, breakthrough, insight
- Suddenness, unexpected, extreme, fanatical
- honesty (sometimes brutal)
- truth, clarification and cutting through confusion

Discovered: in 1781.

Uranus rules: Aquarius, as the modern planetary ruler. Aquarius is also traditionally co-ruled by Saturn. Uranus is said to be the higher energy of Mercury (representing the Higher Mind). Uranus entered the sign of Taurus in May 2018.

Uranus transits

Transiting Uranus (depending on the particular combination with the natal planet) does not 'pull any punches'; it can break things wide open, which can be a painful process. When Uranus transits someone's birth chart by a challenging aspect (e.g. by square or opposition), it usually brings disruption in its wake. The effect of this planet in transit is perhaps primarily experienced as a wake-up call. It could often be likened to a flash of lightning that seems to come out of nowhere. It can be felt as a shift in thinking, in beliefs, in attitude. On the other hand, and often when a Uranus transit is a trine or a sextile, a person may have unexpectedly inspirational ideas, or gain freedom and assert their independence from some situation.

Those periods when our basic ideas about life (perhaps formed in earlier, quieter times or childhood) are shaken up by disturbing events are often accompanied by a challenging Uranus transit and can be uncomfortable to say the least. We may suddenly leave a situation, or another person may leave us, or a cherished philosophy of life may be shattered. There are many ways in which T Uranus may manifest, but it does not make for a stable and steady set of circumstances. Some individuals may embrace such times, and find excitement in everything changing around them, but most people will be bewildered by the speed of change or of the instability of their world while the transit lasts. Things may not go back to 'normal' even when the transit ends, for something has changed and things are unlikely to revert back to where they were. There is no denying that changes are happening.

T Uranus may affect the greater environment around someone as well. As one example, your place of work may be going through a time of 'adjustment' in which some employees are made redundant, or you may encounter a new belief system that gives you a different per-spective on life. (Please remember these are only suggestions, and absolutely not certainties!)

It is worth noting that Neptune and Pluto, with their long orbits around the Sun, and therefore apparently around us, do not return exactly to their natal positions in the course of a normal human lifetime. The only possibility of the experience of a return of an outer planet is of transiting Uranus, with its 84-year orbiting cycle, which therefore will return to its natal degree and sign position at the age of 84.

Uranus square Uranus

When we are around the age of 21, the first significant and challenging aspect of outer planet T Uranus to itself on the birth chart is T Uranus square natal Uranus, when transiting Uranus forms a 90-degree aspect to its natal position (T♅□♅). This will occur twice in an average life span, the second time being when T Uranus is three-quarters of the way through its solar orbit, and it squares natal Uranus from the other side when we are in our early to mid-sixties.

The meanings of both of the T Uranus square Uranus transits are in essence similar, yet because there is a big difference in the age at which we experience them, they will naturally not be experienced in the same way. This is a period marked by the wish to do things differently from what has been our experience in life before this time. So in our early twenties, many of us are establishing our own path in life, perhaps being a student, leaving the parental home or building towards our own direc-tion, or career. For some, this could be the time for starting a family. However, in our sixties, this square may coincide with becoming part-time at work, or with retirement, or it may show as taking up something new, or approaching an area of life differently.

To experience this square for a third time, a person would need to be about 105 years old! And I am not sure what the transit would mean to a person of such an advanced age . . .

Elaina's Uranus transits

Elaina's chart has the Uranus–Neptune conjunction in Capricorn of the mid-1990s, so it is generational for that period of time. In the 10th house and square Sun and Moon, her experience of this is likely to be noticeable. The conjunction of Uranus and Neptune is about having a strong sense of social injustice as a generational approach to life, and awareness of political abuses of power. In her 10th house and Capricorn, this affects her choice of direction. Because Elaina has the double square to both her Sun and Moon, her thinking and feelings are affected. Take a moment before reading further to try to work out what this may mean on her chart. Think of keywords for Sun and for Moon. And add to those if you can. What does the conjunction between the two luminaries mean? See what you can make of it.

Sun: sense of identity, creative centre, purpose in life
Moon: inner emotional life, needs, instinctive reactions

Here are some ways to understand the aspect, that is: Uranus conjunct Neptune square Sun conjunct Moon (♅ ☌ ♆ □ ☉ ☌ ☽), which sounds very complicated. As ever, the advice is always to break a complicated-sounding configuration into its component parts. Take one of the interpretation examples for the Uranus–Neptune conjunction – a strong sense of social injustice – and put it together with the challenging aspect of the square, with her central sense of who she is and what she needs from her life (Sun–Moon.) Given its placement in her chart this suggests that, going forward, she may incorporate this into her working life in some way. So – she could become an advocate for those who have suffered corporate injustice; or this could become a tenet of whatever she does. She is qualifying in not-for-profit management when she graduates. There may well be opportunities for this natal aspect to come into force in her life in some way.

The following 'double' transit of the Moon and the Nodes that was Elaina's experience in 2017–2018 illustrates how both planet and Nodal axis can work together:

T♅☍☽☌☊– *T Uranus in Aries opposition her Moon conjunct North Node in Libra*

In autumn 2017, Elaina had T♅ in Aries crossing her 1st house, with T♅ (T Uranus in Aries) conjuncting her South Node (T♅☌☋) – therefore Uranus was also in opposition to her Moon conjunct North Node, both of which are in her 7th house. T Uranus moved on to oppose her Sun in 2018 when it entered Taurus, which was in turn featured on her Solar Return of October 2018, which lasted until autumn 2019. (See Chapter 12.)

T Uranus triggering the Nodal axis and any closely aspected planets at the same time, especially across the 1st to 7th houses, the houses of the self and of relationship with close others, suggests there was a likelihood that Elaina would have a challenging experience in the area of personal relationships during this period. She is likely to be really sensitive when she has transits from Uranus, especially to personal planets, because of the importance of Uranus with Neptune on her chart. Any new relationship could possibly be seen as a 'karmic' meeting by some astrologers (i.e. accompanied by a feeling of destiny, that the two people have known each other before somewhere) because of the

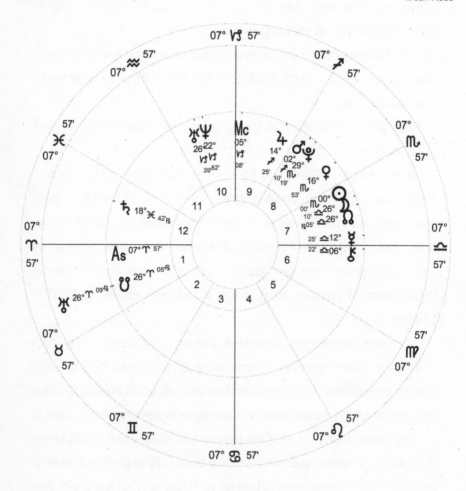

Inner Wheel
Elaina FD
Natal Chart
23 Oct 1995, Mon
17:38 EDT +4:00
Rockledge, Florida
28°N21'02" 080°W43'32"
Geocentric
Tropical
Equal
Mean Node

Outer Wheel
Elaina FD
Transits Chart
28 Oct 2017, Sat
10:00 EDT +4:00
Rockledge, Florida
28°N21'02" 080°W43'32"
Geocentric
Tropical
Equal
Mean Node

Bi-wheel for Elaina's chart and her Uranus transit

involvement of the Nodal axis. The Nodes are often involved on a person's chart in relationship situations, which may or may not mean that everything will work out well! (There will be more on the Nodes in Chapter 14.) The nature of such an experience may have been a sudden meeting (Uranus) or a surge of feelings towards someone (Moon) that was perhaps not entirely smooth from the beginning, but which held a spark of excitement.

What happened: Elaina did indeed meet another possible boyfriend in early October 2017, when she had the Uranus–Moon transit going on. It was not exact, but heading towards exactitude in November. The transit remains valid during the whole period that it is operational, until it definitively moves on. She fairly quickly found out that communication was not particularly regular from his side (they lived in different towns, but in itself that is not much of a barrier in these days of easy communication). She says she has already learnt more patience, and although when they meet in person she really likes his company, this relationship has caused her a lot of emotional confusion owing to his lack of consistency.

Uranus often does not offer stability, but electric fascination with another person who somehow also causes emotional frustration. By the time T Uranus opposition Moon finished, Elaina had agreed with her 'boyfriend' to just be friends, although she had been left with turbulent emotions, such as anger, frustration and bewilderment. But because the Moon and Sun are so close on her chart, T Uranus shortly afterwards also opposed her Sun and North Node (T ♅ ☍ ☉ ☌ ☊). This potentially hurtful disruptive opposition, especially to a person's essential Sun and Moon or other personal planets, can be hard, manifesting as it very often does through our relationships with others. Uranus often does not offer easy experiences, yet can bring excitement, new understanding and awakening. (In autumn 2018, Elaina met a new partner, which will be astrologically addressed in Chapter 16.)

The midlife crisis

Most of us are familiar with the idea of the 'midlife crisis', which runs roughly from the age of 37 to 42. Whether that is your midlife is debatable as people are on the whole living longer (at least in Western countries), but there is no denying that for many this period does coincide with a shift of focus. To turn 40 doesn't exactly make you into an elder, but the first flush of your youth is gone, and turning points may be experienced; for example, at this age, a person might change their job or their marriage, move house or country, or otherwise make a fairly noticeable change.

This period is marked astrologically by T Pluto squaring natal Pluto at about the age of 37 to 38, followed by T Neptune square natal Neptune and T Uranus opposite natal Uranus, both in your late thirties to very early forties (♇ □ ♇, ♆ □ ♆, ♅ ☍ ♅). If any of these outer planets on your chart fairly closely aspects a natal personal planet (especially Sun, Moon or an inner planet), the more likely it is that you will go through your personal version of the midlife crisis as the other planet is also triggered.

A client of mine went through a big shift when her T Uranus opposition to Uranus happened as part of her midlife crisis at the age of 39. Her natal Uranus is closely conjunct her natal Sun. At this time her partner of 9 years left her for another woman, apparently suddenly, and she went to live abroad for a couple of years to recover from the upset.

A word here – this period is not always a difficult time. For some it could mark a deepening of a belief, a relief at no longer being so young, a 'fated' meeting, and so on. If you do go through a major change then maybe this period is about clearing out some of your previous circumstances and starting anew. Astrology can put even important changes into perspective, and in time may bring better understanding!

The next most important transits that you are likely to experience are those of the 'social planets', Saturn and Jupiter, which we will be looking at in more detail in the following chapter.

7

TRANSITS 2: JUPITER AND SATURN

The great red spot and the icy rings

In this chapter, I will look at the planetary returns of Jupiter and Saturn. I will also look at other transits of these two 'social' planets to natal planets or angles, in order to set the context. As there isn't the scope in this book to cover every transit in depth, the Planetary Combinations list in Appendix 1 will start you off with interpretations. You can of course also look up meanings of various forecasting combinations in other books listed in the Further Reading section.

I do, however, encourage you to work out your own interpretations of various transits, progressions or solar arc directions as well, based on your personal understanding of the meanings of the planets, the angles, and the type of aspect between them.

'SOCIAL' PLANETARY RETURNS

Because of the planet's relatively short orbit of 12 years, the return of T Jupiter will be experienced every 12 years when the planet returns to its place at birth. This is the case for everyone at the ages of 12, 24, 36 and so on – as Jupiter orbits every 12 years. The return of T Jupiter will be experienced at least seven times if you have a long life, and the seventh

Jupiter return will coincide with the Uranus return at the age of 84. Not surprisingly, many people experience a meaningful event of some kind around this age.

In the case of orbiting Saturn, its return to its natal place will happen every 28 to 29 or so years, so our first Saturn return occurs when we are that age; our second Saturn return occurs at about the age of 56 to 58, and the third (for some) will happen at about the age of 85 to 87.

All the planets in the Solar System will eventually return to their natal place in an individual's chart as they orbit the Sun – remember that from an astrological perspective these planets appear to be orbiting the Earth – and the slower-moving ones often bring key experiences in life. The returns of Mercury and Venus are not much noted in astrology, mostly because they usually are so fleeting, while Mars returns every 2 years or so (see pages 100–1, towards the end of this chapter for more on this, if an individual is particularly attuned to Mars).

Every planetary transit to anyone's natal chart carries echoes of that planet as it is placed natally. A returning planet is a revisit to its natal placement, and therefore places an emphasis on a person's life in that area.

JUPITER RETURN

Recapping the meaning of Jupiter, natally or by any kind of transit:
Where your Jupiter falls – the sign, house and aspects – you search for meaning or purpose; you seek to expand your life experience and to grow and learn.

- Seeking meaning and purpose in life, and inner fulfilment, whatever form that takes for the individual.
- Exploring life through travel, mentally or physically.

- Finding out in which ways and circumstances fortune smiles on you. (For instance, would you describe yourself as a lucky person, generally speaking?)
- Your sense of humour and your personal philosophy of life.
- How broad-minded or adventurous you may be; how easy or otherwise you find it to seize opportunities that arise in life.

Obviously, your Jupiter return at the age of 12 will not be experienced in the way you will experience it when you are 24, 36 or 60. Yet a similar quality prevails. At 12, or around that age, many children in different countries change schools, and progress from young childhood learning to higher-level studies. Jupiter likes to learn, so for many this may be an exciting time (even if a little scary). It's also a time when many young people are continuing to develop their ability to think and form their own opinions and ideas.

For some, the returns of Jupiter to its natal place, followed sequentially by a reiteration of the natal Jupiter aspects by transit, may not be as powerful, or even as noticeable, as the experience of the Saturn return. It depends on how much the individual is attuned to the meaning of natal Jupiter. It also depends on how deeply your Jupiter transits have been experienced over the years.

Take as an example the chart of Elaina: in 2019, she experiences her 2nd Jupiter return, at the age of 24. Her natal Jupiter is in Sagittarius and the 9th house – a classic example of a 'strong' Jupiter, as it falls in both its own sign and its own house, with Sagittarius the sign on the cusp of the 9th house. (This will be explored in more detail in Chapter 16.) Jupiter's aspects are mixed – sextile Mercury and trine the Aries Ascendant, plus square Saturn and semi-square the Sun. Her chart suggests that she is generally well attuned to the energy of Jupiter. She places a high value on the university course she is currently pursuing in the USA, with graduation in June 2019. She also has strong ideals about helping people to stand on their own two feet and find their own power (especially women).

As a clear example in our times of ways in which Jupiter can manifest in big events, American President Donald Trump was exactly at his half Jupiter return in Libra when he was elected in November/December 2016. T Jupiter opposite natal Jupiter can bring high honours, but also can indicate over-confidence, and feelings of omnipotence.

Other transits of Jupiter

Given the generally expansive nature of the planet Jupiter, it is natural to interpret Jupiter transits to the chart as bringing a positive influence. I have mentioned one of Jupiter's noteworthy physical attributes in the subtitle to this chapter: its 'great red spot'. We don't know everything about this feature, but we do know that it consists of a massive storm which is bigger than our whole planet, and that it has been raging at super-speeds for some centuries. In terms of astrological symbolism, the suggestion is that the planet's enormous size, together with this mysterious stormy area, can make it overwhelming in its influence. Jupiter's massive size in comparison with the rest of the Solar System's planets has underpinned its astrological symbolism as the planet of expansion and growth. But the long-term presence of the great red spot also suggests that the nature of the king of the gods, Jupiter or Zeus, is not to be trifled with; he has immense power which he can use for good or ill.

As a general rule, when forming a flowing, easy aspect to a natal planet, such as a trine (120 degrees) or a sextile (60 degrees), transiting Jupiter is likely to bring feelings of enjoyment or good will, depending on the planet transited. As it's Jupiter, the challenging aspects such as the square and the opposition to the chart often bring some kind of over-enthusiasm, exaggeration or self-indulgent circumstances. Jupiter embodies 'doing it big' and its more negative qualities often err on the side of excess! However, this is not always a major issue.

T Jupiter conjunct a natal planet is 'neutral' and can be experienced as an enhancement of new learning; or feelings of being overwhelmed by too much to do or learn all at once.

In 2017 to 2019, case study Elaina had some very active transits to her chart. Some years are relatively quiet in terms of transits, and some are busy! She had T Jupiter traversing the end of Libra and moving through into the next sign, Scorpio, in 2017. Given that her North Node, Moon, and Sun are close together in her 7th house of relationship, and although they are in adjacent signs (Libra and Scorpio) they are still conjunct, in dissociate conjunction, being less than 8 degrees apart, and Jupiter crossed that conjunction in late 2017. At the end of 2017, T Jupiter moved on to conjunct natal Venus, at 16–17 degrees Scorpio, in Elaina's 8th house.

These Jupiter transits possibly suggest a new relationship, perhaps with a new romantic partner. They could also indicate changes in her life in terms of friendships. Jupiter conjunct Venus was exact in December 2017, turned retrograde in March 2017, moving back across her Venus again at 16 degrees Scorpio in May 2018 and then finally moved on past Venus again in August and September 2018. The presence of the North Node exactly conjunct the North Node during her Sun–Moon transit (which is part of the triple conjunction on Elaina's chart for any transiting or progressed planet that aspects it) suggests that any new friendship or relationship in her life can bring not only pleasure (potentially) but that there is a value in the whole experience that can enhance her life in some way. This could take a relatively tough form, though it could equally bring much joy. (There is an important addition to this in the next chapter on progressions, and on benefics, see page 119.)

What happened: Elaina did indeed form a new relationship with a guy, and also changed her living situation, moving into a house with friends, having been living alone, just after this transit ended (remember what I said earlier about how often it seems to be the case that actual events happen as the transit ends or shortly thereafter).

Do remember that transits of Jupiter sometimes only last a few days, and that it moves through a whole zodiac sign in about a year (30 degrees of space). When this planet is not in a retrograde period, it is reasonably fast-moving. So when T Jupiter takes up to 9 months to move backwards and forwards across a planet or angle on the chart, as it does in the above example of transiting natal Venus, it is likely that there will be a noticeable effect in the person's life. On the other hand, some short Jupiter transits can pass over the chart without always being that apparent in terms of the individual experiencing 'big' changes.

SATURN RETURN

Recapping the meaning of Saturn, in the chart or by transit:
The combination of Saturn's natal sign, house and aspects will describe the individual expression of Saturn in a person's natal chart in more detail, but the meaning of this planet is essentially about the following qualities:

- Attitude to responsibility, discipline and organisation.
- Serious approach to life, recognition.

- Sense of reality and structure.
- Striving to achieve goals.
- Acknowledging limitations, 'hard edges'.
- Sometimes referred to as the Lord of Karma or the Great Teacher.
- Consolidating your position – promotion, qualification.

For example, if Joe's natal Saturn is in Leo and his 5th house (let's say with only trines or sextiles to other planets), some of the ways in which he experiences that placement may be as a burning desire to be seen by others as talented, or creative, or simply worthy of recognition. Yet, for all kinds of reasons, he may find it hard to accept these qualities in himself and may be inclined to play down his naturally creative self, feeling unworthy even of the praise of others, especially during his youth. The compulsion to achieve an ideal or a mission to attain perfection in his goals may block him from trying to achieve his goals, as Saturn is a demanding energy, associated with the 'if I can't do it as well as (so-and-so), then I'm not going to do it at all' syndrome. 'So-and-so' could be a famous and established person that he admires and envies, or simply a friend or colleague.

When Joe reaches the age of 29, opportunities arise for him to confront his view of himself, and maybe to acknowledge his own ability at last. He might be offered a chance to show what he can really do at work or in a more personal area of his life, and the practical nature of the planet Saturn may inspire him to rise to the occasion in spite of his anxiety. Joe knows by now that the praise or appreciation of others, important and pleasurable as that is, is not enough. Joe has to take this on board and build his own self-belief.

So the Saturn return brings back challenges that Joe has perhaps struggled with in his earlier life, but also may bring the 'golden opportunity' that he needs. There is no guarantee that Joe will be able to take a chance that is offered – which may last anything from 2 weeks to the best part of a year, depending whether transiting Saturn has a retrograde period during the time of its return. It can sometimes be the case that a Saturn return only lasts a couple of weeks if T Saturn does not go through a retrograde period at that time. The point is that a person experiencing a Saturn return often goes through anxious feelings, and for some this can be crippling until the fear is faced – and that might not occur until some time in the future. This is of course just one example of a million ways in which a person may experience his or her Saturn return. But as a general rule this period of time around the 28th to 30th birthdays marks a period of reflection, of reaching a crossroads or making an important decision, which will be as varied as each individual person's life patterns are.

I have another illustration of a Saturn return to share with you: Leon, the subject of our male case study chart, experienced his Saturn return throughout 2017 at the age of 29. It recurred three times: exact in February; in May to June, when it was orbiting retrograde – the time of his final exams at university; and exact again in November after orbiting direct again. This was significant for Leon, making 2017 a landmark year for him. His natal Saturn is in Sagittarius, conjunct Uranus in the 8th house, with mixed aspects – trine Jupiter in Aries, semi-square Pluto, opposition Chiron and square the Nodal axis. Have a look at his chart. For him, this was an important year, during which he graduated with his Master's degree in Religious Studies in November 2017 – on T Saturn's last 'hit'. Shortly after this, his student visa ran out and he returned from London to his place of birth in Singapore. His Saturn had then just entered the sign of Capricorn. For some people, the return year is when qualifications are awarded, or a worldly opportunity arises; some get married, some get divorced, have a child … the possibilities are many in terms of concrete occurrences. (Remember the earthy nature of the planet, so external recognition is important.)

I have referred to the 'icy rings' of Saturn in the subtitle for this chapter. You may find it useful to use the symbolism here for recalling the meaning of the astrological Saturn. The position of this planet in the Solar System as the last planet visible with the naked eye, and its rings composed of hard substances like permanent space ice and rock, suggests limitations and hard-edged boundaries, or consolidation.

Most people – even when a lovely positive and tangible event occurs around the time of the Saturn return, which it certainly can– also perceive this period as marking a kind of turning point in one's life, maybe a kind of ending, perhaps of youth or childhood. Astrologers hold that a person does not really become grown up, or reach maturity, until the Saturn return, following straight after the progressed Moon Return (see Chapter 8).

Tangible events often occur at this time, and the implication is that the way someone's life has developed during their earlier years has led to this experience. In this sense, all transits simply build on previous experience, especially significant transits of the same planet. What is behind this statement is the idea that the person has already experienced something of the nature of the T planet earlier in their life so may be better prepared. It is true that if you have *consciously* experienced a transit such as T Neptune or T Saturn to a personal planet, then your memory of what happened at that time may forearm you to some extent.

Sometimes, this is difficult to trace ... unfortunately it is of course not so simple as 'reward or punishment' for fulfilling your potential – yet the nature of any transit, including returns, does retain its parameters of meaning. A return usually seems to offer a chance to revisit the meaning of the planet concerned and maybe to renew your connection with what it represents for you.

Other Saturn transits

Elaina had a significant Saturn transit to an angle throughout 2018 – T Saturn conjunct her MC in (T♄ ♂ Mᴄ) or ♑. It was exact in February, again in July (because of retrogradation), and a final time in November, so it was a whole-year transit. If you recall, the Midheaven (MC) governs the direction in life, career, ambition, reputation and how others see us. So events that focus on these areas of Elaina's life are likely, including potential career developments and concerning the opinions of others – perhaps such as university tutors? Her MC is Capricorn, so comments or recognition may come from people in authority, and it is in the 9th house, so her university is probably featured, and is likely to be key in her life.

What happened: Saturn conjunct her Capricorn MC mainly seems to have taken the form of a year of what Elaina describes as incredibly hard work. I asked why she had three part-time jobs as well as her studies, and had been setting up an exhibition during this period. The reason for this is another one of Saturn's favourite set-ups – money. The jobs have been paying Elaina's tuition fees. It also looks good on her CV (resumé as it is called in the States) – her Saturnian reputation. She is trying to obtain a job before she graduates, and feels she needs a good record.

*

On a larger scale, and looking more collectively, since approximately the end of 2014 Saturn was transiting through Sagittarius, outlining a period of excess, both financially on a larger scale in terms of national and personal debt, and also in bringing out tales of abusive conduct in individuals prominent in authoritative bodies such as governments, the Western movie world, and show business in general.

Saturn stays on average two and a half years in each sign, as you can see from the dates given. Saturn entered the sign of Capricorn in December 2017.

When considering a returning planet transit, be aware that after this transit has passed, all the natal aspects to that planet will be repeated, for now the transiting planet is going to pass them all again. (Just to remind you, your birth chart is itself a transit of the date, time and place that is frozen by each baby's birth.)

So when Leon has his Saturn return in 2017, T Saturn will then go on to echo the natal position – to conjunct Uranus, square the Nodal axis (remember that if a planet squares one of the Nodes, it will always automatically also square the other one, because they form an axis), and conjunct Neptune, and so on. In spring 2018, Leon had Saturn conjunct Neptune transiting. It was exact in March, May and December. Possibly the most noticeable effect of this repeating natal aspect was that he felt able to make a dream or a visionary idea become a reality. (The planet of groundedness meets the planet of merging and no boundaries!)

Jupiter and Saturn combined
Following on the heels of his Saturn return in 2017, case study Leon had a number of Jupiter transits starting at the end of 2017 and continuing into 2018.

The most important of these included T Jupiter:

- trine Moon – T♃△☽
- opposition Ascendant (conjunct Descendant)
- square MC/IC
- sextile Mercury T♃⚹☿

I have briefly summarised this list, looking at these transits from a past year, to give you an idea of how to go about interpreting them. Hopefully this will help you when considering important Jupiter transits, at least in principle.

- Look at natal Jupiter: in *Aries, 11th house, ruled by Mars.* Make keyword notes and put it together.
- Make brief notes, even just the keywords, to get an idea how this little series of Jupiter transits lead one into another, as Leon experienced them.

Interpretation:

- Natal Jupiter – the desire to grow through doing things his own way. Uncompromising in his principles and philosophy, he was influential for others.
- *Jupiter trine Moon* – nurtured by travelling, loves learning, natural teacher.
- *Jupiter aspecting all his angles and sextile Mercury* – the desire and need to communicate, to listen to those he considered knowledgeable, on training courses, and to store these learnings in his mind so they became part of the direction he was building in order to guide others as well as himself.

Coming out the 'other side' of his Saturn return, Leon found that his world had somehow shifted and become more open. He felt that he achieved something that was very important to him during 2017, and that he could enjoy the feel-good experience of having had the planet of opportunity and enjoyment (Jupiter) making a flowing aspect (trine) to his emotional centre (his Moon in Cancer) as he entered 2018. The years 2019–2020 will bring other transits of Jupiter but I hope this has given you an idea how to approach these. The Jupiter transits, along with T Neptune trine Moon, happening over part of the same period, suggested the changes he experienced during this time were no less than life-changing, affecting both his reputation and his relationships with important people in his life, and enhancing his spiritual path.

And T Neptune was trining his Moon from Neptune's position in mid-Pisces as well as T Jupiter in Scorpio. We will return to this combination towards the end of the book, when the topic is on the blending of material. It is important to remember that transits or progressions rarely happen in isolation, and the challenge is to assess the relative balance of various factors and put the whole picture together.

Mars return

A brief word about the Mars return, which occurs approximately every 2 years, when Mars orbits back to its exact same position as at birth. A person's response to this period will depend on the nature of that individual's connection with his or her Mars energy. The duration of this return may vary from 2 to several days, depending on whether Mars is in a retrograde period or not at the time of the return, and given that its speed of orbit varies somewhat.

I have known individuals who are particularly sensitive to their assertive or war-like qualities and who usually experience some kind of forceful energy at the point of their Mars return – perhaps until they become less sensitive with the passage of time.

On the other hand, there are those who apparently do not notice T Mars passing over the Mars on their charts. Some people are more affected by Mars crossing its natal place than others – though many people will experience themselves being more aggressive, or more inclined to stand up for themselves than they normally would be.

I once had an astrology client who had a super-sensitive connection to her Scorpio Mars, and she contacted me for an appointment. She explained that every time T Mars returned she seemed to hit some difficulty: she needed to confront someone, or she had some issue with a physical discipline she was practising – running, gym, etc., or some other event occurred that was evidently Mars-related. After a few times, she recognised it and found ways to counteract it and calm the forceful energy she experienced every time.

8

SECONDARY PROGRESSIONS: THE INNER PLANETS

A day for a year

Astrologers often quote from Ezekiel 4:6 to 'explain' the basis of progressions: *'Thou shalt bear the iniquity of the house of Judah forty days: I have appointed thee each day for a year.'* The argument is that, in this way, the Bible offers a precedent for the idea that one day of life symbolically equals a year. Well, maybe. But wherever the idea originated, the fact is that progressions – especially concerning significant changes of sign or house, or direction – are effective in describing current experiences.

As explained in Chapter 7, your transits often result in noticeable events in your life. In Chapter 3, I looked briefly at the meaning of secondary progressions, and explained that the mainly inner planetary movements of the Sun, the Moon, Mercury, Venus and Mars – plus your Ascendant and MC – are usually less tangible and more about your changing inner landscape. Your feelings and moods are primarily what are affected by your progressions, and even your overall outlook on life, which will change with the passing years.

It is not that there is a clear division into external and internal changes along the lines of 'transits = outer experiences that affect me; progressions = affecting my emotional orientation to life', yet that is how many people studying astrology tend to see it – in order to distinguish between these different methods of exploring the cycles of our lives. And it is not a bad way to differentiate between them, except that the fact is that the majority of people are more affected by that which happens *to* them, or is brought about by their own actions, than by the often more subtle changes in their personal lives. In other words, you usually *do* experience your transits, in a way that affects your life appreciably, especially if you are experiencing a major transit, or a series of major transits involving one or more outer planets – or a lingering Saturn (and to a lesser extent a lingering Jupiter) transit. It is useful to remember, however, that many transits that recur because of retrogradation often have a more tangible impact on the second or third exact 'hit'. (The examples in the last chapter may give you a clue!)

But it is possible for busy people to push aside states of mind, or emotional responses, more easily than a major event such as a change of job or location, or any other life-affecting occurrence. This is not true for everyone, of course, but it is so for many, depending on what feelings you are experiencing!

Because transits, as we have seen, are usually interpreted with an emphasis on tangible occurrences, and because they can be accessed with relative ease, they are the most important form of forecasting that astrologers use. Having said that, secondary progressions certainly do have an effect on our inner lives, and there are certain key progressions that we are very unlikely to miss, such as the changing of a planet into a new sign or house, or crossing an angle.

But then, if a person is not aware of astrology, as most people are not, these periods are not going to be recognised for what they are, and will of course not be named, although change will be experienced. The forecasting methods explained in this book can all be experienced at a number of different levels: astrology simply reflects life, from clearly concrete events to subtle personal reassessments.

One other thing to remind you about, as this can cause confusion: your birth chart will remain your personal birth chart throughout your life. But transits, progressions, solar arc directions and the annual solar return chart will 'overlay' the natal chart for the time period that these are in effect, adding their energy to your birth chart. One of the many beautiful things about learning astrology is that it shows us how we all have the capacity to be different, as the moving planets cast light or darkness on the person we experience ourselves to be. And the effects of a number of these changes remain after a particular transit or progression has passed. Our shifts of mood or attitudes, usually triggered by our transits, progressions and so on, do bring differences in a long-term way: we potentially grow and learn – or not, as the case may be.

Some hints and tips about progressions

Below is a table (page 106) that shows you how much each planet moves in its orbit in 24 hours. This table will help to clarify why astrologers consulting progressions use mainly the luminaries, the inner planets, and the progressed angles in assessing progressions, because the daily movement is small but visible. This is opposed to using the social or outer planets. Indeed, by contrast, the planets from Jupiter out to Pluto move very little and even more slowly due to their distance from the Sun and the length of their orbits.

The table also provides information about how long each planet is retrograde p.a. (per annum, i.e. per year) and, in the case of the planets from Jupiter outwards, how far each planet moves in days by progression (90 days), which equals 90 years in its orbit over a long human lifetime.

As a reminder, neither the Sun nor the Moon can have retrograde periods (because the retrograde illusion only occurs when viewing – from Earth of course – a planet transiting the Sun, when either Earth appears to overtake that planet or vice versa) but all the other planets do. As soon as you count up the movement in space of any planet in 24 hours, you are actually assessing each planet by progression and interpreting it as representing a year of the person's life.

How long is a progression's meaning in effect?

Conventionally, a progression is usually most effective when it is exact, but due to slow movement, it can last as a background influence for a few months. In the case of the progressed Moon, the orb either side of exactness is usually between 0.5 degree and 1 degree, so most straightforward p Moon progressions last about 2 months, unless the aspect repeats, as illustrated below. The progressed Moon will fairly frequently aspect a planet, and often a month or two later will aspect the same planet again, but in its progressed stage. (Or vice versa. Sometimes a progressed planet is aspected first if it is retrograde at the time.)

It can be the case that two progressed planets form a major aspect with each other. A progressed planet aspecting another progressed planet occurs from time to time. So for example, in February and March 2021 Leon experiences p Moon square natal Saturn (p☽□♄), but in June 2021, the progressed Moon has caught up with the slow movement of progressed Saturn, and reconnects by square with that planet, so Leon will have p Moon square p Saturn (p☽□p♄). In my experience, the inter-

Table of Planetary Motion

Periods of inner/personal planetary motion + retrogradation for progressions

Planet	MOTION p.d.	Max ℞ period p.a.
Sun	57m–1deg 1m	
Moon	11.47–15.12 deg	
Mercury	1.5 deg (average)	3 x 25d every year
Venus	1 deg 12m max	40d (not every year)
Mars	30–40m max	81d (not every year)

Periods of Outer Planetary Motion + Retrogradation

Planet	Max motion p.d.	p.motion over 90y.	℞ period p.a.
Jupiter	14m	15 deg	4 months
Saturn	7m	10 deg	5 months
Uranus	5m	6 deg	5 months
Neptune	2m	2/3deg	5 months
Pluto	2m	2/3deg	5 months
Chiron	2/3m	3 deg	variable

Abbreviations:

d = day   p.a. = per annum

deg = degree   p.d. = per day

m = minute   ℞ = retrograde

p = progressed   y =year

pretation is hardly changed. This lengthens the period that the progression's meaning is effective – about 5 to 6 months. It may not be absolutely exact in the intervening few months, but for Leon it is like experiencing this progression for the whole period. Incidentally, the Moon squaring Saturn by progression suggests a period of needing to give attention to his emotional life (family or women), which seem to require his energy. The square also suggests that he tends towards feeling defensive, possibly encountering disapproval or criticism, and wanting to protect himself – a rather vulnerable period. (More information on the progressed Moon can be found in Chapter 10.)

Progressed planets other than the Moon last a variable length of time. In practice people do of course vary in their sensitivity to progressions, and if a p planet is changing signs or houses, it is likely that the individual will experience the shift over a period of time, especially if it is the Sun changing sign or house.

So, you can see from the table that the movement of Sun, Mercury, Venus and Mars in 24 hours is very small, and therefore the movement of the planet during the year that is represented by that 24-hour period is likewise small and subtle. Even the Moon, as our relatively speedy satellite, does not move more than half a sign maximum in 24 hours. But because of the very slow and minimal movement, the effects are usually lasting. Small orbs are used, see above.

Do not forget too that if Mercury, Venus or Mars are retrograde during any section of the period being studied, these planets will progress 'backwards' until they turn direct. Check this out by looking at an ephemeris if you can. Any year will do. Choose one of the inner planets when it is in its retrograde period, and note its backward progress so you can see how it is moving and maybe aspecting other planets when it is being seen as a progression.

And no matter where in the world the person has moved to since birth, the place of birth is always used when looking at a progressed chart or list of planetary movements for any date. This is because progressions (and solar arc directions) are an unfoldment of who the person is, which of course is an internal process, and is not dependent on the person's location.

Use only major aspects to all natal, or progressed, planets or angles in assessing which progressions to consider. Generally, the conjunction, square or opposition are the most powerful, but also the trine and the sextile if they look meaningful. A trine or a sextile can bring positive energy and emotions! Minor aspects, such as semi-squares, sesqui-quadrates, semi-sextiles or quincunxes between planets or planets and angles, can be ignored as they are very likely to be unnoticed in the course of life – though there are always exceptions.

What stands out as important

- Progressed Sun: A change of house or sign, which shows a re-orientation of your sense of personal identity. (See below.)
- The p Moon changes sign or house approximately every 2.5 days (= 2.5 years), and these changes of orientation, interests, and feeling responses to life are usually quite noticeable. Major p Moon aspects vary largely per year, as these depend on the distribution of the natal planets. Some years there are relatively few, other years there are very many, so discrimination must be exercised.
- A progressed angle changing sign or house. Remember that if the p Ascendant changes sign or house, the Descendant will change as well. Equally, if the MC changes, then so will the IC, as both of these angles are an axis.

- The changing of the progressed lunation cycle (approximately every 3.5 to 5 years). See page 166.

Using the Equal House system of 30 degrees per house, the Sun will only change house on average once every 30 years. The same is true for a change of sign. That year will therefore stand out.

A progressed planet making an exact major aspect to a natal planet on the birth chart, or to another progressed planet, happens quite frequently, so note the natal strength of the planet being aspected – its position, what it rules, how it is integrated, etc.

Progressed Sun

p Sun = a shift in your sense of yourself, or a new area of your life assumes greater significance, with new interests or a new attitude.

Progressions involving the p Sun are likely to be particularly significant and will bring inner and possibly outer changes at a profound level. There can be several years when there are no p Sun progressions, depending on the distribution of planets around the natal chart. Check this out for yourself using an ephemeris.

As all zodiac signs measure 30 degrees in length, and if your Sun at birth is at 5 degrees of a sign, then you will be 25 years old before you experience the change to the next sign. Or if your Sun is at 23 degrees of a sign, you will be 7 years old when the Sun enters the next sign, and so on. So this changing sign will take place much earlier for some people than for others, depending on the degree of the Sun at birth in the individual's chart. This means that by the age of 30 at the latest, everyone will have experienced a change of progressed Sun.

Have a look at Elaina's chart – her Sun is exactly at the beginning of Scorpio, at 0° 0'. So Scorpio is a sign that will have a strong role in her sense of identity until she is 30 years old, when her Scorpio nature will be overlaid by some Sagittarian characteristics. So 2025 is a significant year for Elaina.

So depending on what happens in your individual life, you may have a hazy or a strong memory of the difference, or there may have been an event that happened at that time. Progressions can also mark an event of some kind. The effects are not all inner experiences. (See the example of Peggy on page 111.)

MEANINGS OF PROGRESSED PLANETS BY SIGN OR HOUSE CHANGE

To understand how a change of sign or house for the p Sun is so noticeable for the vast majority of people, remember that the p Sun moves on average 1 degree through a sign in 24 hours. This of course equals one year of life as a progression.

If your p Sun changed either sign or house when you were very small, you might not have had much, or any, conscious awareness of this shift. On the other hand, you might, if a change in your young life had significance at that time period, e.g. you were aware of a parental difficulty, a house move, or the birth of a sibling. You are far more likely to recall an event or family change, of course, if you were, say, 15 or 25 when the change of sign or house took place.

To find when your own Sun changed signs, as a rough estimate, count forward through the years using 1 degree as an average movement of the Sun, starting at the number of the degree of your natal Sun until you reach the end of the sign at 30 degrees. (See the examples

above, but be aware that the minutes of the degree can make a difference – sometimes you need to round the minutes up or down to the
nearest whole degree; see the example of Peggy below). It is easier to
do this by counting through an ephemeris, but you can work it out on
your fingers! That year of your life is likely to have had some particular
significance for you.

If p Sun made a major aspect to another planet or angle one year,
that year too assumes importance in your life. Because there are often
years when there is no major p Sun activity, so the years of change stand
out. When the p Sun is changing house, the affairs of the new house are
likely to be key, and a contrast with your involvement with those matters
indicated by the previous house occupied by the Sun – but after the
change year has taken place, this is more likely to become a background
influence. In a 90-year lifetime, your p Sun will only change sign or
house three or at most four times (so if you are born with the Sun in the
late degrees of a sign you could experience four changes in a long life).

Example: p Sun changing from Gemini to Cancer at age 5
When Peggy was 5 years old, her progressed Sun moved into Cancer
from Gemini, where it had been since birth. (Thus her Sun at birth was
at about 25° Gemini. Her Sun was actually at 24° 46′ Gemini, and I have
rounded it up to the nearest whole degree, so using 25°.) As she was a
child, she had little control over what happened in her life. Her parents
moved to a completely different area of Britain. The primary school that
Peggy attended in the new location determined her educational experience for the rest of her schooling, and the move affected other
aspects of her life, for the family was now isolated in terms of their proximity to the extended family, which had been geographically close in
the previous location. So a whole set of new experiences was set in

motion when Peggy's Sun changed signs. A year before that her brother had been born, presaging the move to come (when her Sun had reached 29° Gemini before moving to 0° Cancer in the next year).

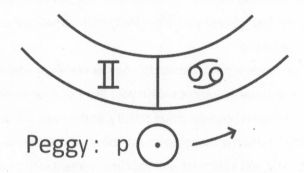

p Gemini Sun moves into Cancer in Peggy's chart

PROGRESSED MOON

The progressed Moon is a special case, due to the speed at which it moves in its orbit in 24 hours. Look up the Moon column in an ephemeris for any month and year, in order simply to follow the Moon's daily movement. Or you can look back to Chapter 4 and the page from *Raphael's Ephemeris*, where you can see the changing signs very easily – run your finger down the column of the Moon in longitude (the way in which all the planets', including the Moon's, orbital movements are measured). You will see that the Moon changes sign every 2.5 days on average, which means in progression terms that it changes sign every 2.5 years.

A whole chapter is dedicated to the progressed Moon (Chapter 10), so I will simply say here that its essential meaning is about the shifting patterns of our inner emotional lives, and how our feelings, moods, needs and orientation change as the Moon passes through different houses or signs, or aspects natal or other progressed planets. The

Moon represents the feminine, subconscious self. It's an important planet that merits in-depth treatment.

RETROGRADE PERSONAL PLANETS

If Mercury, Venus or Mars is retrograde at birth (therefore on your chart), then you are likely to experience these planets (or some of them) turning direct at some point in your life. This should be noted when assessing a chart, as it will in all probability be a year when you experience some kind of inner shift. (See the individual planets below.)

There are various ways to interpret retrograde natal personal planets. Generally, there seems to be a consensus of opinion about the meaning of such planets:

- Hidden qualities, energy turned inside, holding back.
- Shyness, difficulty in 'standing up and being counted'.
- May be thought of as a 'late developer'.
- May be a deep thinker, but hard to express thoughts.
- Sometimes there may be a reluctance to put self forward.

These ways to view natal retrograde planets underlie the interpretation of progressed inner planets.

Check on your chart whether Mercury, Venus or Mars is retrograde on your birth chart, and if so, note how many days (years) after birth that planet remains retrograde. Then check forwards in an ephemeris to which year any of them turned direct: was this year notable for you in terms of the meanings you understand for these planets?

Usually the changing planet 'stations' – slows down its movement as seen from Earth as it shifts to the other direction – which prolongs the process (marked 'S' for 'stationary' on the chart by many computerised astrological software programs). You can find this in an ephemeris by checking the daily listing of any planet's degrees when it is approaching turning retrograde or turning direct (marked as 'R' or 'D'). If you look at virtually any planet as it approaches changing direction, you'll see that its degree is repeated several times as it 'slows down'. Not surprisingly, this places an emphasis on the meaning of that planet at that time, which is especially personal to you if it connects to something on your chart.

Personal planets that are direct at birth: it is possible you will not experience them changing direction in your lifetime. Check back to the table above, but here's a reminder as to why:

Natal retrograde Mercury
By the age of 25 at the latest, Mercury will turn direct. This is because it stays retrograde for a maximum of 25 days. Mercury will turn retrograde on average three times every year, but then stays direct for up to 3 months (about 90 days, which equals 90 progressed years).

This changing direction from natal retrograde Mercury to direct seems to bring out a more outgoing way of expressing yourself and your ideas. Retrograde Mercury is more preoccupied with inner reflection and thoughts and may not be very forthcoming in youth. But retrograde Mercury people often experience a distinct shift in the way they communicate after the planet turns direct.

Natal retrograde Venus
By the age of 40 at the latest, Venus will turn direct. Venus stays retrograde for 40 days maximum, then can stay direct for up to 1.5 years = 150 years by progression.

Venus turned direct mainly reflects your changing attitudes towards relationships, and what you are looking for in this area of life. You may find that the types of people who become close to you are changing, or your own way of relating to others may undergo an adjustment. Turning direct may also bring an increased interest in financial matters, shifting personal values, or the developing of new creative abilities.

Natal retrograde Mars

Mars can stay retrograde for up to 81 days, and then turn direct and stay direct for up to 2 years. A shift of direction is usually very noticeable in an individual's preoccupation with 'Mars matters', not surprisingly, such as developing a new interest in physical activities, greater assertiveness, changed energy levels, or changed awareness of one's sexuality and so on. Or you could decide to join the army, for example, and undertake a dangerous job! It could also manifest as bursts of energy in the year it changes direction.

The years when one of these planets changes direction is usually significant, representing a shift which will only happen once in our lifetime, if it happens at all.

Other natal retrograde planets and points

It is of course possible, and for many people, likely, that some of the social planets (Jupiter and Saturn) or the outer planets (Uranus, Neptune, Pluto and Chiron) are retrograde at birth. However, I do not consider this of any great personal importance, especially as far as the outer planets are concerned. Check back to the Table of Planetary Motion on page 106 to remind yourself how long each of the outer planets remains retrograde: the outer planets are all retrograde each year for about 5 months, and Jupiter, Saturn and Chiron are retrograde for shorter periods every year. When the outer planets are retrograde for so many months, large numbers of people across the world also have retrograde outer or social planets at birth. This is therefore generational rather than personal, and has little individual significance. Only the meaning of retrograde personal planets are noted as important (i.e. Mercury, Venus, Mars). You will find interpretations for Jupiter and Saturn retrograde in other books or websites if you have either of these retrograde on your chart and are curious to see what other writers make of this.

The Mean (average) Nodal axis is of course not a planet, so its retrograde motion is not relevant here.

THE PROGRESSED ANGLES AND YOUR BIRTH TIME

All the angles are subject to progression, as well as the planets. It's important to remember that as the Ascendant changes, so too does its opposite point – the Descendant. The same applies to the Midheaven (MC) and its opposite point, the Imum Coeli (IC).

Progressed Ascendant–Descendant

This is about your changing view of life in your personal world and the way you relate to others, as well as any changes you may want to make in terms of what you need for yourself or from other people. If the p Ascendant aspects, or is aspected by, a planet – natal or progressed – especially by conjunction, then the energy of that planet will be absorbed, and experiences are likely to occur that embody that planet in some way. The person may come to new realisations, take up a new interest or make different types of decisions, for instance. For example, the p Ascendant aspecting natal Jupiter will bring out a philosophical attitude to life circumstances, or may urge you to take on a bit more than you can comfortably handle, depending on your natal Jupiter position and the nature of the aspect!

Progressed MC–IC

The Midheaven–Imum Coeli axis concerns our unfolding sense of direction, longer-term goals, reputation, and inner purpose, as well as our sense of place, safety, family and home life. When a planet connects with the MC–IC, our ideas, choices and needs concerning our future will become the focus of our attention. Because this axis also indicates our relationship with our parents, this may be affected also.

Turning to Elaina's study chart, Elaina's MC changes signs in 2020 from Capricorn to Aquarius, which will probably presage an interesting development with regard to her career. It's not a progression that occurs very often in a person's lifetime. In fact, it will not occur again for 30 years, as the MC only moves a degree or so in a day, like the Sun.

Elaina – a progressed aspect in practice

Elaina had a meaningful progression that was experienced for a month or two as it approached, which was exact in December 2017, and which then remained viable for the next few months, even when it passed exactitude, because that is the nature of progressions – the effects can last up to about 6 months. Progressed Venus conjuncted her natal Jupiter, in the sign of Sagittarius and the 9th house (p♀♂♃♐9).

A combination of the two 'benefics' (see next page), ♁ Venus conjunct Jupiter (especially when they are not aspected on the natal chart, so are relatively unfamiliar with each other) suggests new feelings of joyfulness and wanting to celebrate something, an enjoyable social life and being drawn to activities that bring pleasure. Jupiter (making things bigger) serves to enhance these feelings, to exaggerate them, even to exceed boundaries. It could have had a more external meaning too, in that Venus also represents that which we value.

Venus is important in Elaina's chart. Can you see why?

It is important because the planet is rather isolated, with only one aspect, a trine to Saturn, which suggests a strong loyalty to people close to her, and the potential for making commitments, albeit often quite cautiously. It is also not in a comfortable placement on her chart. Venus, ruler of Libra and Taurus, is said in traditional astrology to be in her detriment (uncomfortable) in Scorpio, and Venus is also in the 8th house: Scorpio's natural house. Venus's energy is romantic, loving, sensitive, compassionate, whereas Scorpio inclines her to be passionate, secretive, with powerful feelings – not feeling very happy with the intensity that Scorpio brings to most things! To complicate this, Venus rules Elaina's Moon in Libra, which indicates her sensitive emotional nature, and that one-to-one relationships are particularly important for her. So she longs for intimate relationships with others, seeking sweet romance but also passionate intensity – sometimes hard to reconcile.

Planets with only one or no aspects in the chart are disconnected from the wholeness of the chart, as are planets in their *detriment* or *fall* – out of their natural affinity with a sign. Planets so placed are either awkwardly expressed, or they are over-expressed. It is not easy for Elaina to manifest her Venus position in the best way, and she may make some choices of partner that don't always bring the happiness she seeks, as she learns from experience!

Benefics and malefics

In the 'traditional' astrology of previous centuries, there were two planets known as *benefics*: the planets Venus and Jupiter, which were said to bring positive experiences, such as love, growth and good fortune to the life. Naturally there were also two planets known as *malefics*: these were identified as the planets Mars and Saturn, bringing suffering, hardship or misfortune. These views are seen as somewhat simplistic in today's modern approach to astrology, and they have largely fallen into disuse by the modern astrologer. But there are an increasing number of astrologers who have incorporated older terminology into a modern or a psychological approach, and these terms have their value.

Generally speaking, the combination of Venus and Jupiter suggests easy growth, a philosophical attitude, and a capacity to enjoy life.

The malefics, Mars and Saturn, *do* represent harder qualities than do Venus and Jupiter, however. In natal charts or in forecasting, whether through a transit or a progression or solar arc, Mars in any combination aspect with Saturn represents qualities such as control, structure or discipline. There can also be a quality of endurance and holding on through periods of self-doubt or fearful anxiety.

In addition to progressed Venus in Sagittarius conjunct Elaina's natal Jupiter in December 2017, transiting Jupiter in Scorpio was crossing her natal Venus – creating an interesting example of a progression and a transit occurring together (T♃ ♂ ♀♏ 8).

The transiting energy is experienced for a period of time before and after an exact aspect at the same degree (although it is often shorter afterwards). In Elaina's case, from December 2017 transiting Jupiter was conjunct natal Venus, then exact again in its retrograde phase in May, and passing back across exactitude in August and September, for the third time, thereby emphasising its importance.

Remember that astrological forecasting is not a neat system with definite beginnings and endings, but rather a process of flowing into existence and then fading as an influence as the last period of exactitude wanes. (When a back-and-forth transit is not in exact aspect, its influence is less but not entirely faded during the period under consideration.)

Bearing in mind that 'lucky' Jupiter can mean a financial windfall (maybe from another person in Elaina's case, as the conjunction falls in the 8th house of 'other people's money'), or some other luck with money, this could have been the case for Elaina under this transit. However, in view of the repeating combination of the 'benefic' planets, it seemed that a new relationship was the most likely interpretation.

Indeed, keeping the ebb and flow of energy in mind, from the autumn of 2017 Elaina had an on-off relationship with a man, that was not very satisfactory. In December 2017, the conjunction of progressed Venus and Jupiter was picked up and extended by the Jupiter–Venus transit. This transit repeated for the second time in May 2018 (because Jupiter turned retrograde), and she met someone new who she really liked during the second phase of the transit following the progression. So what could have been a passing progression had they met during the progression of her Venus to Jupiter in December 2017 turned into something potentially more serious.

This relationship was progressing slowly at the initial time of writing. But a few months later, looking back, this relationship has not lasted very long either. Elaina has experienced some ups and downs on the relationship front, as she met yet another guy in October 2018. The new boyfriend and Elaina were working together on organising an exhibition at the museum where Elaina is part-time employed to help pay for her tuition costs while she is still at university. This seemed to be going well, but in April 2019, her boyfriend brought the relationship abruptly to an end, and she was not entirely sure why. It seems she is not currently very lucky with the men she meets, and the emotional traumas are not easy to handle.

The significance of progressed Sun and Moon

Although the example above is a telling illustration of the impact of a progression of Venus (enhanced by the accompanying transit), the fact is that in the world of progressions, the ones most people actually experience are the changing of sign or house. Refer back to the Introduction page 7, to the note about birth time. If this is not accurate, then the house cusps will also not be accurate, resulting in inaccurate timings for forecasting techniques.

Such movements are most readily observed when it is the p Sun or p Moon that is crossing a house or sign cusp, or making a major aspect to another planet or angle. This is because of the importance of the symbolic meanings of both luminaries in human experience.

Before I go on to explore the meanings of the other major forecasting techniques – solar arcs and solar returns – I am diverting to a very important part of understanding the astrological meaning of one of our luminaries – the Moon. The phase of the Moon that an individual is born under is a significant part of forming an overview of the chart, along with the elements, modes, polarity and quadrant emphasis. This is also relevant to the progressed Moon phase, as the next two chapters will reveal.

9.
A NATAL MOON INTERLUDE

The Phases of the Moon

If you are wondering why this chapter dedicated to the natal Moon is included in a book about forecasting, here are some of my reasons:

- Near the beginning of this book, I stated I was intending to cover not only forecasting methods, but also to build upon the foundations established in my first book, *Astrology Decoded,* by including some new natal subjects. The Moon's phase is one of these.
- Because the natal chart is the basis of all forecasting, so the experience of a transit, progression etc. varies to some extent according to the patterns of the individual birth chart. While not every part of the meaning of the chart can be fully covered here, knowing your natal Moon's phase forms a part of astrological self-understanding for the owner of the chart. This is why my two case studies' forecasting examples also cover a short interpretation of their charts.
- Comparing the Moon's phase that you are born under with your current progressed Moon phase (in Chapter 10) shows you in which ways you have grown over the years.

We are all aware of the changing Moon in the sky, never the same from night to night. And indeed sometimes, slightly mysteriously, it is even visible during the day. (This is because the earlier the Moon is in its waxing (growing) cycle, the earlier it rises, rising later as it moves through its monthly progress.) Over the centuries, people have made all sorts of associations with the Moon. The Sun and the Moon were of course the most easily visible to our ancestors of all the heavenly bodies, and still are to us. But whereas the Sun's daily rise and set is more or less predictable, the Moon's is less easy to follow. Together, the interaction of the luminaries formed the basis of some of the earliest types of primitive astrology, as earthly events were observed to be apparently linked to certain heavenly phenomena. Notches found carved on ancient animal bones have been identified by modern scientists as marking the passage of time, the Moon's phases and the progress of the female reproductive cycles.

But depending on the geographical location, the time period, and the eye of the beholder, very different impressions of the Moon are formed. For a couple in a warm climate, out at night, the Full Moon shining its bright beams across water is often associated with romance. For a person who has perhaps been influenced by Bram Stoker's stories of Dracula, or by mythological werewolf stories, the silvery light of the Moon can speak of unearthly terrors. There are those who are aware of and troubled by the tarot's Moon card, number XVIII, meaning uncertainty or lack of clarity. Some individuals have a sensitive response to the Full Moon, and can be disturbed a bit more easily than others. The bright Moon is such a 'normal' phenomenon in the night sky, and yet because of its connections with strange events or individuals in folk tales, horror stories and our dreams, perhaps it is not surprising that it has a reputation for causing a rise in mental health issues.

Many cultures, past and present, have personified the Moon as a female deity, such as the Greek goddesses Artemis and Hecate, the Roman goddess Diana, Egyptian Isis or the Chinese lunar goddess Changxi. However, the ancient Babylonians worshipped a male Moon god, Sin, as did the Aztecs: the male god Tecciztecatl, amongst others, so neither gender predominates, but there are very few cultures who have not assigned a deity or two to the Moon.

And for the student of astrology, the symbolic meanings of the Moon are many, ranging from femininity, family, home, childhood and mothering/nurturing, to the subconscious, instincts, the past, memory, emotional security, sense of belonging . . .

Do you know the Moon?

If I were to ask you the current phase of the Moon in the sky tonight, would you know? Is it waxing or waning, Full or New?

As an interesting exercise, I would like you to keep a Moon Diary. In a notebook or diary, record the changing phases of the Moon in the sky every night. Begin with the next New Moon, sometimes also known as the Dark Moon (temporarily invisible), which lasts 2 to 3 days (at the start of the waxing phase), and continue noting down the phases until the following New Moon – about 27 to 28 days. At Full Moon, the Moon will enter its waning phase. If you are unsure of the phase, the sky is too cloudy(!), and you don't have access to an ephemeris, you can find this information easily on the internet.

One more thing: as well as making a note of the daily phase of the Moon, try to notice how life is for you on each day and how you feel. During the waxing phase, for example, do you feel as though you are growing or opening up to new possibilities, and building structures of some kind? During the waning phase that follows the Full Moon, do you feel that you are consolidating your situation, expressing your creative side and letting go, and that you are more inclined to 'go within yourself' than at the waxing phase? You may or may not have any particular awareness of this.

Whatever your experiences, and regardless of how they fit with the traditional qualities associated with the Moon's phases, it can be a fascinating experience to follow the Moon through its cycle. Apart from anything else, this exercise puts you more in touch with what is happening in the sky, and sharpens your awareness of the patterns of relationship between the Earth, Sun and Moon.

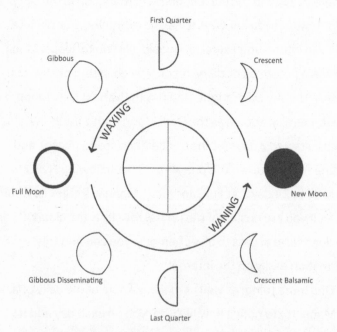

The Moon's phases: the illuminating Sun's rays light up the Moon from the right-hand side of the diagram

YOUR NATAL MOON PHASE

The rest of this chapter is devoted to exploring your natal Moon phase, the phase you 'came in with', which shows clearly on your birth chart. This is often an overlooked area when making initial observations about a person's chart, and many astrology schools and tutors do not devote much space to it; however, an understanding of it can enhance your natal interpretation work.

You may well find that identifying your own natal Moon phase will be interesting to you when recording your Moon Diary, especially when comparing your current p Moon phase with your natal one (see next chapter). There are eight phases of the Moon in the course of one complete natal lunar cycle, which will vary slightly in length – lasting 27 to 28 days in total.

Each Moon phase covers 45 degrees of space, and there are eight sections of 45 degrees each in the Moon's orbit of the Earth, which, like any circle, consists of a total of 360 degrees. (While the Moon's orbit is at a 5-degree angle to the Earth and is not a perfect circle, it still covers 360 degrees of space.) Looking back at the table in Chapter 8, you'll be reminded that the transiting Moon's movement is between just under 12 degrees and just over 15 degrees per 24-hour period, so on average, the Moon moves a little more than 13 degrees a day, and stays in one sign for approximately 2.5 days. If you can access an ephemeris, you can easily check this movement out for yourself, looking of course in any Moon's Longitude column (if there is a choice). If you have a *Raphael*'s, don't forget to check the Moon column marked '24h.' to see where the Moon has moved to by midnight on the day you are looking at. (By the way, in the examples below, the shapes given are for the northern hemisphere. In the southern hemisphere the shapes are reversed except for the Full Moon.)

The natal Moon phase is the relationship between the natal Moon and the natal Sun. To clarify the two opposite lunations:

- The New Moon phase happens when the Sun and Moon are close together in the same part of the sky (maximum 45 degrees apart) at birth.
- The Full Moon phase happens when the Sun and Moon are opposite each other on either side of the Solar System as seen from Earth, with the Earth in the middle, at birth.

In the 'waxing stage' the Moon is *ahead* of the Sun by sign and degree. A New Moon phase can of course begin in any sign, but taking the natural order of the zodiac as an example, the Moon's waxing phase would be from 0° Aries to the end of Virgo. This applies until we reach the Full Moon position, where the Moon starts to be referred to as being **behind** the Sun, continuing from 0° Libra to the end of Pisces. An example of an almost exact Full Moon phase chart is that of Marc Bolan, lead singer of T. Rex in the 1970s, who has his Sun at 6° 27′ Libra, almost exactly opposition his Moon at 8° 51′ Aries. Although the chart clearly has a Full Moon aspect, the position of the Moon is now counted as being **behind** the Sun by 177° 36′ rather than ahead, and is into the waning phase.

There is an easy way to work with what might seem to be an awkward way of dividing the 360-degree circle's degrees into eight sections: 45 degrees is a sign and a half, so just go to the next sign round from the Sun following the natural zodiac order, and add half as much again to reach the limit of one phase. So, starting theoretically at 0° Aries as the beginning of the New Moon phase, the next (Crescent) phase would begin at 15° Taurus. The following phase (First Quarter)

Marc Bolan
Natal Chart
30 Sep 1947, Tue
12:30 BST −1:00
Hackney, England
51°N33' 000°W03'
Geocentric
Tropical
Equal
Mean Node
Rating: A

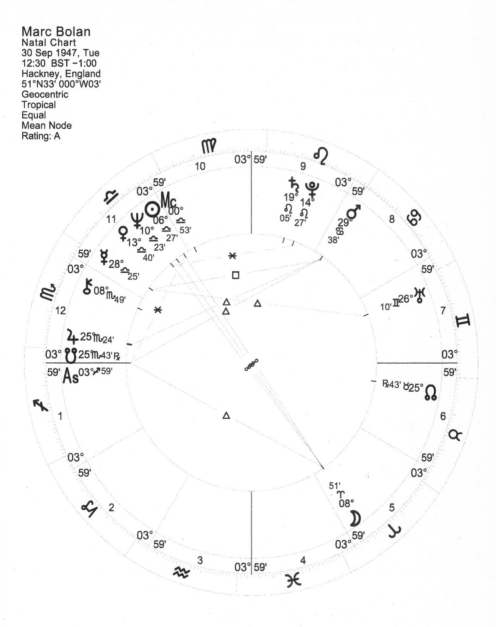

Marc Bolan's chart

goes from 15° Taurus to the end of Gemini, which would become 0° Cancer. And so on. You count 30 degrees from the Moon's position, which brings you to the same degree of the next sign, and then add another 15 degrees.

You can also apply this system to working out aspects on a chart such as semi-squares (45-degree aspects), or sesquiquadrates (135-degree aspects – count four signs round the circle and add half a sign to find sesquiquadrates).

Here are the degree differences to make it easier to see each phase:

Waxing (Moon ahead of Sun by sign)
New: 0–45
Crescent: 45–90
First Quarter: 90–135
Gibbous: 135–180

Waning (Moon behind Sun by sign)
Full: 180–135
Disseminating: 135–90
Last Quarter: 90–45
Balsamic: 45–0

As we go through these natal phases, I'll be referring to both Leon and Elaina's Moon positions and the meanings of these. Let's begin with the basics, as illustrated by their natal charts:

- Leon was born at a couple of degrees past the exact Full Moon, so this is clearly his lunar phase at birth. Leon's

Moon is at 15° 50′ Cancer in the second house, with the Sun opposite on the other side of his chart at 13° 09′ Capricorn in the 8th house. So he has Sun opposite Moon, which means he is a Full Moon individual – with a sense of achievement built in. Interestingly, Leon's Moon and Sun are closely similar, just in terms of the amount of separation, to Marc Bolan's (though of course the signs and houses are different). See further information below.

- Elaina was born in what is known astrologically as the Balsamic phase, less than 4 degrees before the Moon conjoins the Sun. (The term 'Balsamic' for this Moon phase was coined by an eloquent American astrologer called Dane Rudhyar in the twentieth century. A less poetic term for this Moon phase is the Waning Crescent. The fact that this Moon phase is known by the same name as balsamic vinegar is coincidental! Or maybe the name came from the healing 'balsam' qualities of some natural medicines.) The astrological Balsamic Moon phase marks a preference, or even a need, for calm or regular retreat.

- Both are therefore born in the waning phase, though both are fairly close to the waxing phase (at either end of it).

Both Leon and Elaina's Moon phases are fairly close to the next one (Elaina) or to the previous one (Leon). You can see the sign/house/ phase etc. as having some qualities of either the next or previous stage as well, although being close to the dividing line of the cusp is where the qualities are likely to be the stronger, with the term 'cusp' simply meaning the dividing line.

Waxing Moon

The lives of those born at any of the waxing stages of the Moon are generally engaged in building, learning, struggling at times, embracing and 'making real' in concrete terms. The waxing-Moon person seeks results for his or her efforts, and wants to experience that his/her contribution to his/her own life or the lives of others is making a difference. The four phases of the waxing Moon are New, Crescent, First Quarter and Gibbous.

I have rounded Sun and Moon up to the nearest degree where appropriate in the following examples.

New Moon

New Moon

Definition: those born with Moon 0–45 degrees ahead of the Sun's position, in terms of the Moon's sign and house. The two luminaries do not have to be conjunct for the chart to be in the New Moon phase, they just have to both be within 45 degrees of each other.

Suppose the Sun is at 2° Taurus on the day of the New Moon, then the Moon can be at any position up to 45 degrees away, so at up to 17° Gemini.

Main meanings: Seed-sower, pace-setter, initiator, subjective approach, innocence/naïvety, newborn.

On the face of it, New Moon people are often to be found at the beginning of things, with a tendency to meet many new situations in their lives. This tendency is sometimes also about holding a vision, which although inspiring, may lack practical detail. They can be delightfully impulsive, spontaneous, yet also rather confused and vague at times.

This person has a subjective orientation to life, and can be naïve. Their inner world, dreams or feelings can become more real than their outer experience, or even their inclination to act. A situation can become symbolic of something else, rather than being accepted for what it is.

The inner world of the New Moon person can be likened to a seed germinating in the darkness. There is something going on in this person that reminds us that this phase incorporates about 3 days of actual 'dark Moon' when the Moon is not visible at all. Astrology is a circular or cyclic art and cycles have no beginning and no end. Balsamic merges into New in the Moon's endless cycle. So too does the New Moon person carry the seeds of another time and place, of something new that is moving towards birth, and that always has the potential to emerge into the daylight. But it may take most of a lifetime, or it may be simply a feeling. The inner world is hidden inside, yet not always fully comprehensible to the individual themselves.

Well-known New Moon person: Queen Victoria
Dates: 24 May 1819–22 January 1901
Sun conjunct Moon and also conjunct Gemini Ascendant
Difference between Sun's and Moon's position to the nearest degree: 1°
New Moon's standard arc 0–45°

Queen Victoria of Great Britain was born at dawn in the early nineteenth century in a New Moon phase, with her Sun tightly conjunct Moon and both very close to her Ascendant in Gemini. She was a strong-minded kind of monarch, with strong emotions, especially for her beloved husband Albert. When Albert died relatively young, Victoria was inconsolably devastated, and neglected her queenly duties

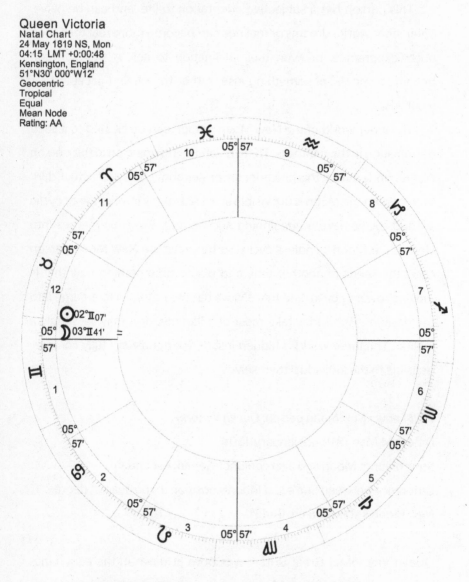

Queen Victoria
Natal Chart
24 May 1819 NS, Mon
04:15 LMT +0:00:48
Kensington, England
51°N30' 000°W12'
Geocentric
Tropical
Equal
Mean Node
Rating: AA

Diagram of Queen Victoria's Sun–Moon conjunction

(which previously she had taken seriously), living in her inner world, which seemed to be more real to her than her day-to-day life. This lasted for about 40 years.

Other famous New Moon people: Mohammed Ali, Edgar Cayce (psychic), Agatha Christie, Sigmund Freud, Billy Graham, Annie Lennox, Karl Marx, Florence Nightingale, Pablo Picasso, Roy Orbison

Waxing Crescent

Definition: those born with Moon's sign and house 45–90 degrees ahead of the Sun.

Crescent Moon

Main meanings: The shoots appear, the plant is not yet established. Willingness to embrace the new and challenge the old, faith in oneself, courage, drive to accomplish or succeed, feeling driven.

No matter what circumstances the Crescent Moon person is born into, there is a feeling of urgency, of something to do or achieve, a sense of mission or purpose. It feels as though the person came into life carrying the memory of a pre-destined situation that needs to be honoured if humanly possible. This can become an obsession for some people.

Many experience a drive to accomplish something during their lifetime, and as such are willing to work hard. But it is by no means a smooth path, and practical support from others is important. This is often forthcoming because the waxing Crescent Moon type of person tends to attract those who are supportive. The Moon has another Crescent phase, but later in its cycle when it is waning, and its shape reverses – see under Balsamic below. The well-known people listed below have gained public recognition in life, but many members of the public born in the phase of the Crescent Moon have equally received support and attention from others in their own private lives.

Well-known Crescent Moon person: 14th Dalai Lama
Date of birth: 6 July 1935
Sun sextile Moon (Sun 13° Cancer, Moon 10° Virgo)
Difference between Sun's and Moon's position to the nearest degree: 56°
Crescent Moon's standard arc: 45–90°

The Dalai Lama was discovered by prominent monks to be the 14th reincarnation of the Tibetan spiritual and political leader when he was a small child, and was installed in the Potala Palace in Lhasa, the Tibetan capital. In 1950, when the Dalai Lama was 15 years old, Tibet was invaded by the Chinese, and a few years afterwards the Dalai Lama escaped across the Himalayas to India, where he has lived in exile in a Tibetan community until the present day. He is now in his 80s but has spent much time travelling the world bringing hope and inspiration to many. He has also written a number of books. The Chinese continue to occupy Tibet. The Dalai Lama was awarded the Nobel Peace Prize in 1989 for his efforts for a peaceful solution to liberate Tibet. Like many Crescent Moon people, he is a pioneer, with a sense of 'destiny', a mission to accomplish something.

Other famous Crescent Moon people: Warren Buffett, Charles Carter (astrologer), Anne Frank, Bob Geldof, Paul McCartney, Maria Montessori, J.R.R. Tolkien

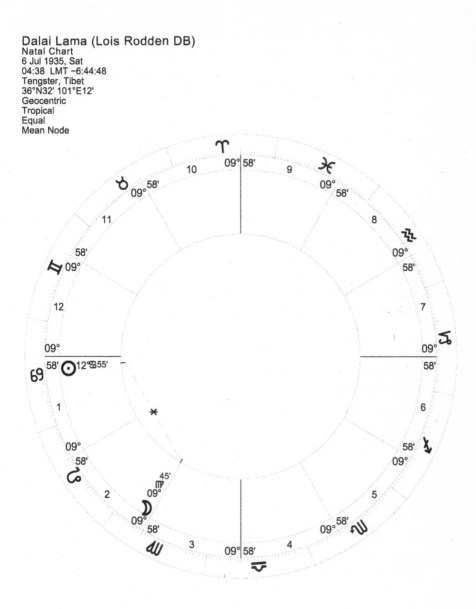

Dalai Lama (Lois Rodden DB)
Natal Chart
6 Jul 1935, Sat
04:38 LMT −6:44:48
Tengster, Tibet
36°N32' 101°E12'
Geocentric
Tropical
Equal
Mean Node

Dalai Lama's Sun – Moon 'mini'-chart

Waxing First Quarter

Definition: those born with Moon's sign and house 90–135 degrees ahead of the Sun's position.

First Quarter Moon

Main meanings: Roots become established, the plant is strengthened. Activist, builder, rebuilding outmoded ideas and structures, pursues own agenda, frustration, sometimes can be rather stubbornly opinionated.

The First Quarter Moon person often displays willingness to make a stand, to follow a principle. These people are often convinced of their rightness, but can lack tolerance for the opinions of others. Likely to be no stranger to battles, the First Quarter Moon person has strong opinions and may feel he or she carries important knowledge but that there are sometimes too many objections from others.

While it is important for them to communicate their values, these individuals must learn that they cannot always win, although they would like to. They can be fired with enthusiasm, and influence people with their ability to transform the thinking of others. They question many things. Some First Quarter people may be bridge burners, always moving on but not always fully appreciating that which is past.

Well-known First Quarter Moon person: John Lennon
Dates: 9 October 1940–8 December 1980
Sun 16° Libra, Moon 4° Aquarius
Difference between Sun's and Moon's position to the nearest degree: 107°
First Quarter Moon's standard arc: 90–135°

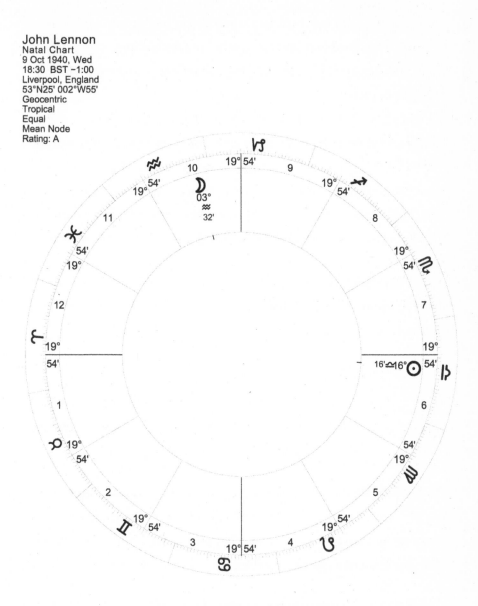

John Lennon
Natal Chart
9 Oct 1940, Wed
18:30 BST −1:00
Liverpool, England
53°N25' 002°W55'
Geocentric
Tropical
Equal
Mean Node
Rating: A

Lennon's 'mini' Sun – Moon chart

The former Beatle was best known for being one of the lead singer-songwriters of the band, and also a rebel and bridge burner, who broke rules and shocked (or delighted) the world. He was well known for his outspokenness.

He released 13 studio albums with the world-famous Beatles in the 1960s, and afterwards several other singles or albums, either alone or with the Plastic Ono band, including the classic song 'Imagine'. He championed equality, peaceful protest, and the importance of constantly striving for your ideals. John Lennon was fatally shot in New York, where he lived with his second wife Yoko Ono and their small child Sean, in December 1980.

Other famous First Quarter Moon people: Carlos Castaneda, Queen Elizabeth II, Aretha Franklin, Charles de Gaulle, John F. Kennedy, Nelson Mandela, Shirley MacLaine

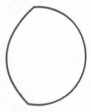

Gibbous Moon

Waxing Gibbous Moon
Definition: those born with Moon's sign and house 135–180 degrees ahead of the Sun.

Main meanings: The buds appear, the plant is nearly at full growth. Perfectionist, principled. Personal growth important, and co-operation with others. Wants to feel part of society, and be of service.

The Gibbous Moon person is essentially a team player, and usually has a goal in sight. Helping others, being of benefit, and learning from other people are traits that come naturally to them. Many are gatherers of information and can put ideas together skilfully. Insight may be gained in this way.

These are 'people persons' who may work for, or be sympathetic to, a cause or ideal of some kind. In the process of clarifying their own objectives, obstacles will need to be overcome. This may sometimes cause them to force issues, which in turn may inspire admiration or even devotion for their courage – or opposition! The Gibbous Moon person is likely to enjoy rewarding relationships with others all their life, which will bring them emotional prosperity.

Well-known Gibbous Moon person: Leonard Cohen
Dates: 21 September 1934–7 November 2016
Sun 28° Virgo, Moon 3° Pisces
Difference between Sun's and Moon's position to the nearest degree: 155°
Crescent Moon's standard arc: 135–180°

This Canadian singer-songwriter, poet and novelist was a kind man who would put himself out for others. Inspired to write songs and poetry in subtle and personal ways, he was a true wordsmith. He was in his thirties when he began to play and sing publicly. He released 14 studio albums, a number of live albums of concerts, and books of poetry and novels. Cohen was robbed by his manager, which inspired him to begin to tour the world extensively, which attracted a large following. Leonard Cohen had a distinctive style of writing and performing, and was known by those close to him as a person who was complex, intense and spiritual, yet with a dry and witty sense of humour. His many fans perceived him as inspirationally generous with his time and understanding. His concerts often lasted more than three hours.

Other famous Gibbous Moon people: Napoleon Bonaparte, Prince Charles, Hillary Clinton, Pope Benedict XVI, Sophia Loren, William Shakespeare

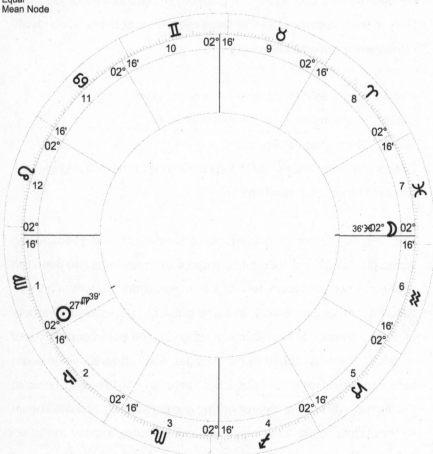

Leonard Cohen
Natal Chart
21 Sep 1934, Fri
04:29 EDT +4:00
Montreal, Canada
45°N31' 073°W34'
Geocentric
Tropical
Equal
Mean Node

Cohen's 'mini' Sun – Moon chart

Waning Moon

When the Sun is opposition Moon on a chart, start to think of the Moon as now **behind** the Sun. Now you are in the waning phase, in any combination beginning at the exact opposition of Sun and Moon.

The Waning Moon (including the Full, Disseminating, Last Quarter and Balsamic phases) is about consolidating, reflecting, absorbing and gathering together. There is a distinct quality of withdrawal as a part of the person's demeanour, which is not operational a large amount of the time, yet is part of the quality of the way they come across to others.

Full Moon

Full Moon phase
Definition: those born with Moon's sign and house 180–135 degrees behind the Sun.

Main meanings: The plant is at full flowering, or the fruit is ripe. Satisfaction, achievement. Seeking the next step, reaching beyond. Inner division, disconnection from reality.

The opposing nature of the luminaries gives the Full Moon person the capacity to stand back and take an overview, to be disconnected from the 'real world', yet also to perceive a situation from the 'outside' in the form of being able to take an overview, or as clairvoyance for a few. This is a common Moon phase for psychics. It is also a position where idealistic love can dominate an individual's life, and there can be a pattern of rising to peak experiences followed by a crisis.

The Full Moon person is likely to have frequent feelings of satisfaction gained through their achievements, which they like to share with others. These individuals have the power to transform themselves in their own lifetime, with a capacity to perceive a continuing potential for new birth, for a new phase, and for rising above difficulties. Very purposeful but not very calm, it is an ongoing quest for them to maintain equilibrium and seek their conscious sense of purpose. Their emotions can be very dominant at times.

Well-known Full Moon person: *Cindy Sherman*
Date of Birth: 19 January 1954
Sun 29° Capricorn, Moon 2° Leo
Difference between Sun's and Moon's position to the nearest degree: 183°
Full Moon standard arc: 180–135°

Cindy Sherman is an American conceptual art photographer who has evolved a way of working on a series of subjects over the years, ranging from 'Bus Riders' in the 1970s to a series of photos of herself in different guises and personas. She has held numerous exhibitions and is very established in her field.

She is often unpredictable, feeling torn in different directions internally, and in terms of where her work is taking her. A close Sun opposition Moon gives Cindy Sherman the unique capacity to stand outside herself and take an impersonal or distant view of the many characters she portrays though her myriad images – she both is and she isn't the central figure in her photographic creations. As she is quoted as saying, 'I feel I'm anonymous in my work. When I look at the pictures, I never see myself: sometimes I disappear.'

Other famous Full Moon people: William Blake, Marc Bolan, Susan Boyle, Thor Heyerdahl, Gene Roddenberry, Rudolf Steiner, Taylor Swift, Tina Turner, Robin Williams

Cindy Sherman
Female Chart
19 Jan 1954, Tue
04:27 EST +5:00
Glen Ridge, NJ
40°N48'19" 074°W12'15"
Geocentric
Tropical
Equal
Mean Node
Rating: AA

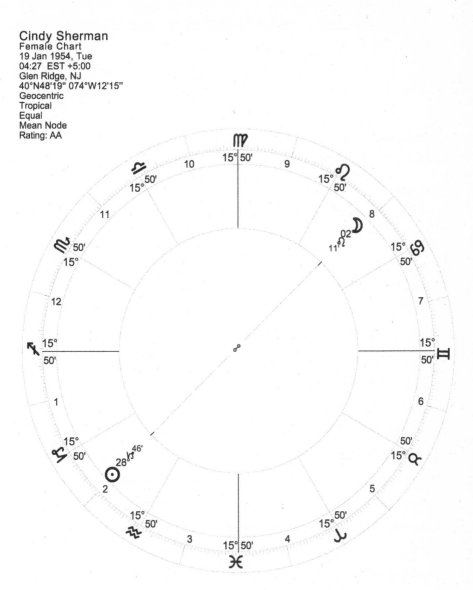

Cindy Sherman's 'mini' Sun – Moon chart

Disseminating phase (alternatively called Waning Gibbous)

Definition: those born with Moon's sign and house 135–90 degrees behind the Sun.

Disseminating Moon, looks like C ¾ Moon

Main meanings: This is the time of harvest, of reaping the bounty previously sown. Communicator, teacher, campaigner. Inspired by a movement, religion, crusade. Can be fanatical. Socially responsible.

Disseminating Moon people generally carry an awareness of participating in the greater whole, and have the capacity to put their visions into action. Some of their own ideas may catch the imagination of others, and inspire expanded thinking. Many are natural teachers or communicators of some kind. They can be very swayed by their emotions or carried away by their passions, and can even be rather fanatical (depending on the rest of the chart).

Those born under a Disseminating Moon want to share that which has made an impression on them, and demonstrate what they have learnt, enhancing people's lives if possible. These individuals have a strong social conscience, but sometimes have difficulty getting the balance right: sometimes they may get too swept up in their enthusiasms, or, at the other extreme, they may feel powerless to change anything. But they nevertheless want to make a significant difference, and will try to do so.

Well-known Disseminating Moon person: Vincent van Gogh
Dates: 30 March 1853–29 July 1890
Sun 10° Aries, Moon 21° Sagittarius

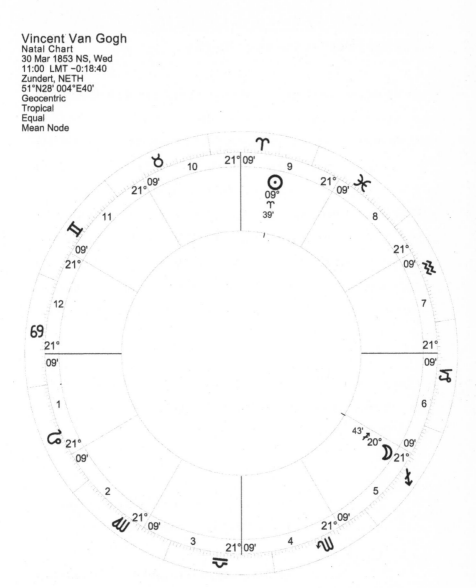

Vincent Van Gogh
Natal Chart
30 Mar 1853 NS, Wed
11:00 LMT −0:18:40
Zundert, NETH
51°N28' 004°E40'
Geocentric
Tropical
Equal
Mean Node

Van Gogh's 'mini' Sun – Moon chart

Difference between Sun's and Moon's degree: 111°
Disseminating Moon standard arc: 135–90°

Much of Vincent van Gogh's painting was created out of his desire to share with others that which had made an impression on him. He could be obsessive or extreme in expressing his strong visions. He was impulsive, and was often influenced by the books he read and by other artists, and sometimes rapidly changed his location and his painting style. His compassion for others, especially poor people, and his love of nature is evident from many of his sketches and paintings. In his short lifetime he completed more than 2,000 works, sometimes producing more than one picture in 1 day. At the age of 37, he shot himself in the chest, and died in his brother Theo's arms.

Other famous Disseminating Moon people: Winston Churchill, Princess Diana, George Harrison, Steven Hawking, Adolf Hitler, Peter Jackson, Vladimir Putin, Mother Theresa

Last Quarter Moon

Last Quarter
Definition: those born with Moon's sign and house 90–45 degrees behind the Sun.

Main meanings: The plant is declining and in its autumn, coming to its end for this year. Principles must be upheld. Bitter-sweetness. Endings in the midst of hope for the future. Reformer, tempering with wisdom. Leaving your legacy.

Those born in Last Quarter Moon phase carry an awareness of the beginning of endings. They are usually aware too, especially when they grow older, that they have a need to 'make their mark', to leave behind some kind of legacy that reflects something about them. Not that Last Quarter Moon people dwell on their 'legacy'! It is more about becoming easy with the concept of the impermanence of life, and the insistent need to look back on what they have done.

These individuals can feel as if they are geared towards a future that they can see in outline, if not in detail, detecting an unclearly defined kind of 'seed future'. Even within new situations or relationships, they sense the ending or the changing. The Last Quarter Moon person senses that longstanding unresolved issues ought to be faced and dealt with if possible. They tend to reflect on ideas of loss, or on rising from the ashes like a phoenix. They have a dry, ironic sense of humour, for they have a unique take on life.

Well-known Last Quarter Moon person: Carl Jung
Dates: 26 July 1875–6 June 1961
Sun 4° Leo, Moon 16° Taurus
Difference between Sun and Moon's degree: 78°
Last Quarter standard arc: 90–45°

Swiss-born Carl Jung was the well-known psychiatrist and psychoanalyst who founded analytical psychology. His life has been well documented in many publications, and many students undertake Jungian psychoanalytical training. He was influenced initially by Sigmund Freud, and collaborated with him for about 5 years before they disagreed and parted ways. His great body of writings preserved

Carl Jung
Natal Chart
26 Jul 1875 NS, Mon
19:29 −0:29:44
Kesswil, Switzerland
47°N36' 009°E20'
Geocentric
Tropical
Equal
Mean Node
Rating: C

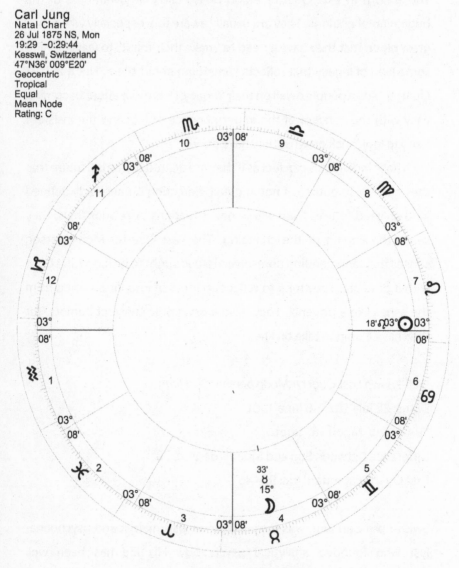

Jung's 'mini' Sun – Moon chart

his legacy of ideas, which in turn influenced the fields of psychiatry, anthropology, archaeology, literature, philosophy and religious studies for generations to come after him. Jung was open to all kinds of ideas, and also wrote on astrology, the I Ching, and flying saucers, amongst other controversial subjects. He was an intensely profound thinker, and had the courage to face his darker self, some of which experience he revealed in his book *Memories, Dreams, Reflections*.

Other famous Last Quarter Moon people: Amelia Earhart, Mahatma Gandhi, Angelina Jolie, Lenin, Van Morrison, Mussolini, Barack Obama, Leon Trotsky, Leonardo da Vinci

Balsamic Moon

Balsamic (Waning Crescent)
Definition: those born with Moon's sign and house 45–0 degrees behind the Sun.

Main meanings: The buried seed, deep below the earth. A melting pot. Can be extremist. Sacrifice, martyrdom. Prophetic vision, psychic sensitivity. Awareness of self-birth. Creative imagination, sometimes an illusory imagination.

The Balsamic Moon individual can feel like a product of the past, yet keeps moving. It is as if these people sense that profound changes are happening in the deeper parts of their minds that they cannot define clearly. They can have a kind of 'prophetic vision' of the future, and will accept martyrdom or self-sacrifice as the price to be paid for something bigger than the self to be born. Metaphorically speaking, they traverse the darkness in the space between the Balsamic and New Moons.

These individuals may feel guided by a 'higher power' and often possess a wisdom that is not dependent on physical age or even life experience, being 'old' in understanding beyond their years. They can be deluded perhaps in youth, but are also intuitively insightful. They may feel the call of the Mystic and need time alone to maintain their sanity; they need some form of spiritual practice to counteract the too-busy outer world.

Well-known Balsamic Moon person: Mia Farrow
Born: 9 February 1945
Sun 21° Aquarius, Moon 12° Capricorn
Difference between Sun's and Moon's position to the nearest degree: 39°
Balsamic Moon standard arc: 45–0°

Mia Farrow is best known as an actress and an activist, who campaigns for children's rights on behalf of UNICEF, and also supports environmental issues. She has famously been married to Frank Sinatra, André Previn and Woody Allen. Farrow has received 3 BAFTA nominations for her roles in various films, for example *Rosemary's Baby,* which also received a Golden Globe award. She appeared in no less than 13 of Woody Allen's films. She has a number of children, both biological and adopted, and has controversially been involved in legal battles to do with some of the children with Allen, from whom she was divorced in 1992. Mia Farrow is not afraid to protest publicly about ecological or humanitarian issues, and has publicly said that in some ways she feels guided by a higher power.

Other famous Balsamic (Waning Crescent) Moon people: Beethoven, Niels Bohr, Leonardo DiCaprio, Bob Dylan, Uri Geller, Whoopi Goldberg, Robert Hand (astrologer), Frida Kahlo, Dane Rudhyar

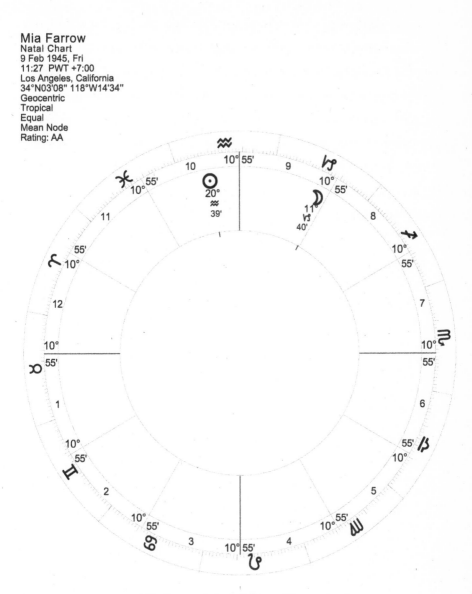

Mia Farrow
Natal Chart
9 Feb 1945, Fri
11:27 PWT +7:00
Los Angeles, California
34°N03'08" 118°W14'34"
Geocentric
Tropical
Equal
Mean Node
Rating: AA

Mia Farrow's 'mini' Sun – Moon chart

Knowing your natal Moon phase will enhance your sensitive under-standing of the Moon in astrology, which is a central key to connecting with the emotional life and experiences of not only yourself, but a basic part of anyone whose chart you read. Having explored the natal Moon on birth charts, the logical next subject has to be looking at the progressed Moon, which follows straight on from here. Find out which p Moon phase you are currently in by checking pages 167–73 and look at how that knowledge will explain the background 'note' of your recent life experiences.

10.
THE PROGRESSED MOON

Your emotional life and changing needs

As we saw in earlier chapters, all secondary progressions show the unfolding meaning of your inner life. With reference specifically to the cycles of the progressed Moon, this means your emotional experiences. The progressed Moon indicates the reactions, instincts and the type of memories we have, as well as reflecting our parental and early family-life experiences, and also ourselves as parents of actual children or the 'children' of our fertile minds. Your changing p Moon position will incorporate and evoke the child you once were, and often will offer you opportunities to help that child mature some more. Your changing security needs, what makes you feel good and comfortable in yourself, and how you orient your life will be met in different ways as your Moon moves from one house or sign to another.

This 'chance to be different' shown by progressions over the years is particularly key with respect to the Moon. As with all forms of astrological forecasting, the natal chart remains the symbolic basis of your character. Your natal Moon phase describes a part of your overall approach to life in general, and your emotional responses. Learning the meaning of the progressed Moon, and in particular which phase you are currently in, and in which p lunation cycle you are too, will expand your astrological understanding. (This chapter will also look at the progressed lunation cycle, also known as the progressed lunation phase, which is not the same as your progressed Moon phase.)

There are several ways to assess the most significant features of the progressed Moon:

- *Changing sign or house*: the p Moon changing sign or house will bring noticeable changes in terms of your personal experiences and preoccupations.
- *Making aspects*: over the course of a year, there will be a variable number of aspects made from the p Moon to both the natal and the progressed chart over the period of twelve months represented. Each p Moon aspect will usually last approximately one month on either side of exactitude.
- *Aspects from other progressed planets,* notably the Sun, to the natal or to the progressed planets/angles.
- *The lunation cycle – also known as the lunar phase cycle*: the difference between this cycle and the p Moon's phase is whether the p Moon is progressing and aspecting the natal Sun (p Moon phase) or the progressed Sun (p lunation cycle).

This provides a comprehensive way to explore someone's emotional life in a given time period. As examples of this in practice, I will be assessing the progressed Moon in the charts of Leon and Elaina towards the end of the chapter to show you how to put the various parts together.

THE PROGRESSED MOON RETURN

The complete cycle of the progressed Moon when it returns to its natal place is 27 to 28 years. Which means that at this age, everyone will experience their progressed Moon return. You'll no doubt notice that the length of this cycle is very close to the length of the Saturn return by transit, which takes place for all at the age of 28 to 29 years. The p Moon return acts as a kind of forerunner to Saturn. The years between the ages of 27 and 30 are known as the period of astrological maturity to astrologers (somewhat later than the commonly accepted age of maturity in many countries, of 18 or 21). We will have our second progressed Moon return at about age 55 and our third, if relevant, at about age 83, not long before the second and third Saturn return at ages about 57–8 and 87.

Your experience of the p Moon return will resonate with the meaning of your natal Moon position – sign, house and aspects – as the Moon return is of course your Moon coming back full cycle to its natal Moon position. Essentially you are likely to feel a 'settling' of your emotional life at the first Moon return, and a feeling of being more comfortable with yourself. The second or third returns are likely to bring an increased capacity for calm reflection or reassessment of your life. However, do remember that this is a generalisation about these periods of life and needs to be individually assessed in relation to the rest of the chart.

The progressed Moon changing sign or house

Because the transiting Moon's average movement is about 12–13 degrees in 24 hours, and it takes 2.5 days to traverse the 30 degrees of each sign or equal house, it takes a little less than two and a half years or so for the Moon to progress through a sign/equal house

(1 day = 1 year). As the Moon's speed of orbit is variable, this is not an exact figure. Many people begin to experience the approach of the p Moon's change to the next house (or sign) at least two or three months beforehand. The position of the p Moon during any given time period essentially reflects what is mainly preoccupying your mind. The p Moon shows where your attention is focused, and you are likely to return to this focus over and over again during the period that the p Moon remains in a particular house or sign.

Next is a brief interpretation of each house position. Because the houses are more overtly personal to our individual charts, based as they are on our time and place of birth, it is common to find that we respond more readily to the changing of the p Moon's house position than to its change of sign, though many people will notice this shift too. Significant meetings and events will often occur when the Moon is moving from one house to the next, or maybe when it aspects a relevant personal planet, as well as of course a shift of feelings.

Below is a list of the meanings of the progressed Moon as it moves through the natal houses. Considering the natural element of the house can also be helpful in chart interpretation.

Progressed Moon through the houses
Fire Houses (Houses 1, 5, 9): feeling as if you have been released emotionally (the p Moon will be emerging from a water house). You might also feel inclined to act spontaneously, perhaps uncharacteristically, depending on the rest of the chart. You could have bursts of creative inspiration. Your confidence is likely to be enhanced.

Earth Houses (Houses 2, 6, 10): feeling oriented to consolidating your inner and material security. Feeling the need to set up a pattern of work or organising practical living matters. Deepening the values that are important to you, living them more, and expanding into a new path, feeling that you are heading somewhere. Developing greater bodily awareness, feeling inclined to develop a health routine. Awareness of your financial position.

Air Houses (Houses 3, 7, 11): gaining perspective, planning ahead, sometimes feeling detached. Here, the p Moon is going through a 'people' phase and when in these houses, there are likely to be more significant meetings and encounters than usual, as well as the working out of relationship concerns. There might be heightened mental stimulation from others, and a noticeably active mind and new ideas.

Water Houses (Houses 4, 8, 12): a reflective time, feeling the need for inner space and a period of overall retreat, even when life is busy. Memories may surface, or past experiences/people may return to your life. Your dream life and your intuition may be active, and you may undertake some kind of in-depth study or some personal growth activity. Enhanced sensitivity to your needs and those of others.

As the Moon progresses to the next natal house, so we will find that the focus in our lives is likely to switch orientation. What occupies our attention much of the time, during the couple of years or so that the Moon is in each house as a background influence, will be largely reflective of the position of our progressed Moon, its house, sign and p lunation phase (addressed later in this chapter); remembering of course that the astrological Moon mirrors the changing ways and areas of life in which we seek emotional security. The states of mind and main interests of the p Moon in each house will be part of our experience no matter what other transits etc. we might have going on in this time period.

1st house

The p Moon has just emerged from its relatively 'quiet period' in the 12th house. As it crosses the Ascendant there may be a greater sense of freedom or of release, and the sign on the Ascendant will have an influence. It is like having an emerging new sense of self, and nourishing your self-image. There is a marked tendency to act spontaneously, and in more immediate ways. Depending on the Moon or the Ascendant's sign, you may find yourself feeling more impatient than you usually would be, or you may be more inclined to act out of self-interest. A bit like being awakened.

2nd house

Feeling motivated to consolidate your inner and material security. Setting up more regular ways of earning a living, and being resourceful, identifying where your talents lie and how to utilise those natural abilities. Feeling a more conscious connectedness with the Earth, wanting to spend more time in nature, and trusting yourself to generate that which makes you secure. Thinking a lot about qualities that you value, and about how you generate, spend or save money. Developing a kind of rhythm in your life with regular activities, and planning ahead, sorting things out.

3rd house

Life begins to open up to a variety of experience and may bring meetings with like-minded others who share some of your interests. Seeking new knowledge or stimulating conversations and mental inspiration.

Sometimes feels like your mind is working overtime. '3rd house' relationships may become a focus: your connections and relationship with your siblings, neighbours, people in your vicinity or in your daily dealings. Orienting your thoughts towards the future and where your life is going.

4th house

The passage of the p Moon through this house may bring an inner re-orientation towards a more private life, including feeling the need to retreat and become more home-oriented. It is possible for some that there could literally be a house move, or a connection with the past, even beyond your personal past. Family, father, culture, country and history itself will preoccupy your mind. This is likely to be a time of reflection and possibly of preparation for an unknown future. Privacy and withdrawal are likely to foster a new sense of inner nourishment and peace.

5th house

As the p Moon approaches the cusp of house 5, your mood is generally likely to lighten and open up. It feels increasingly important to step out of inward reflection and express yourself in some way, to risk being seen and to exercise your creative spirit. In the process, you may well discover hidden talents that might even surprise you. You may also become more geared towards finding pleasure, receiving recognition from others, and feeling enjoyment in your life and your abilities. An exciting time.

6th house

Finding ways to bring your mind and body into better connection – you are becoming more conscious of maintaining a healthy lifestyle, which can become an obsession for some people. Taking up regular activities or practices, which may vary widely from individual to individual. Adjusting your diet, taking up yoga or meditation or a physical activity are a few examples. Dealing with any health issues, or personal development, in a disciplined way. Gaining pleasurable satisfaction from helping or serving others. Making the most of the work and activities that you do.

7th house

This period is mainly about your social life, specifically one-to-one friendships or relationships. You may well meet someone to whom you are attracted and fall in love, or out of love. You think a lot about your love life, and you have an awareness of whether you feel nourished or starved by your emotional life, and reflect on what, if anything, needs to change. Social interactions of all kinds, as well as possible romantic liaisons, are key to this time. For some of us, this is when we might marry, or separate from our partner.

8th house

The years when the p Moon is travelling through the 8th house are often seen as a particularly difficult time. People in your life may leave or die, and you may find yourself thinking about the nature of death, what that means to you and the effect that the death of someone has on your life. Deep and profound thoughts may obsess you as you plumb the depths. Some of these thoughts can become extreme, often depending on the rest of the chart. Issues around sexuality, inheritance, power trips or passionate feelings and/or deception may preoccupy your life at times. Some have likened this period to Moses in the wilderness, or like being naked in public. But the opportunity for gaining understanding and self-knowledge stretches and broadens you, and you could experience intense feelings for someone, or have an in-depth relationship.

9th house

The p Moon emerging from the 8th house and entering the fiery 9th house often feels like a load off your back, and renews your sense of freedom and adventure. Working on making sense of some of your experiences during the passage of the 8th, you are oriented to seeking deeper but not such intense meaning for those recent experiences. As such, you may feel inspired to expand your knowledge, perhaps by undertaking a course of study, or far-flung travelling if circumstances permit. Possibilities may arise, if this not already the case, for speaking in public, or having a piece of writing published. This whole period is generally a time of exploration and of searching for more answers to the mysteries of life. It is almost as if you are learning to see with a stranger's eyes, gaining a bigger perspective.

10th house

The earthy 10th house is usually interpreted as being mainly about work (in the world). There is a definite truth to this interpretation, but the p Moon crossing here sees you reflecting on whether the work you do fulfils you and feels like the right 'fit'; it can be a source of dissatisfaction for quite a few people. Ambition, a desire for recognition, and making efforts to achieve success are all manifest during the p Moon's traversing of the 10th house. If you are fairly young, perhaps under 40 when the p Moon is in this position, you may still be searching to attain clear answers to these important questions. If you are in an older age group, this p Moon can reflect your actually gaining recognition and a sense of achievement, although it is possible that some may realise there is another path waiting for them.

11th house

This period is about taking the larger view, and assessing how you can be of service to groups and humanity in general. Carrying a sense of involvement, duty and what your purpose is in terms of how you can contribute in the best way for the most people, you often have visionary ideas that inspire others. A forward planner, a networker. Sensitivity to being rejected or accepted by the group. Needs some time alone as well as in the group.

12th house

The progressed Moon comes full circle here and you now reach down to the essence of your experiences, paring away that which is not needed. This period represents a retreat from achievement or material desire. With your p Moon in this place, you need to rely on your own resources and inner journey, whatever that is at this time for you. You may be drawn to institutions or to having time alone. You may also be drawn to 'tidying up': this may mean literally sorting things out at home or work, or psychologically getting your thoughts in order. You are inclined to want to 'let go'.

THE PROGRESSED MOON ASPECTING OTHER PARTS OF THE CHART

As the Moon orbits the Earth, so it will aspect every other planet or angle. This sometimes creates so many aspects that there needs to be a limit. Not every minor aspect to the p Moon will be experienced by an individual, unless they are extremely sensitive to emotional nuances! I tend only to look at the 5 major aspects – conjunction, opposition, trine, square, sextile (☌☍△□⚹). Some astrologers only consider p Moon aspects to the natal Sun, inner planets and angles, or only consider conjunctions. I do consider major aspects to all the natal and progressed planets, but nonetheless you still have to use discretion. I am often asked if there is a difference in interpretation between progressions to natal planets or angles; or progressions to other progressed planets or angles. In my experience, if there is a difference it must be a subtle one – I have not noticed it. I do frequently stick just to conjunctions or oppositions in forecasting to keep it simple.

In principle, no matter what technique is being discussed, the combination of two planets has a similar interpretation to it. Here follow some brief examples, in the context of progressed conjunctions, although the sign and house in which a conjunction is based will make a difference to the interpretation, too. For the purpose of this short list of planetary combinations, I am considering only the particular aspect, for clarity.

Moon–Sun: wants and needs are strong in that combined sign; tendency to react or take things personally; may experience inner security issues; may frequently feel 'split' and aware of indecision; direction very influenced by the past.

Moon–Mercury: desire for knowledge, and development of the intellect; curiosity, talkative; the challenge is to listen.

Moon–Venus: peacekeeper, seeker of harmony; seeks love and approval; likes women; needs and desires sometimes at odds.

Moon–Mars: direct in speech or action; inclined to competitiveness and impatience; courageous fighter.

Moon–Jupiter: reaches high; expansive nature; philosophical, spiritual seeker; adventurous, open-minded and generous; can overreach self.

Moon–Saturn: structured and focused; can be depressive or fearful; emotionally serious; self-disciplined; ironic humour.

Further interpretations are in Appendix 1 in the Planetary Combinations list.

THE PROGRESSED LUNATION PHASE CYCLE

The progressed lunation phase cycle is a particularly important cycle of the Moon to take into account. I have found this cycle exceptionally useful over the years, and I consider it with every new chart I look at. This cycle is, in my opinion, a remarkably accurate description of the stages in life, and provides us with an overview of the shift of one period of life into the next. There are eight stages in this system, each lasting quite a long time: between 3.5 and 5 years. What this means in practice is that we sometimes can't see the period of life we are in very clearly, and we may see it better in retrospect.

I once had to deliver a talk about my stages as an astrologer, and as a person. I chose to base this on my p lunation cycle. It wasn't until I explored my p Balsamic lunation phase that I realised how a particular period of my life had reflected my experience very aptly. As you will discover as you read on, that particular phase is about a kind of withdrawal, which is exactly what I had done. During that phase of my life, although I was a qualified astrologer, I was living abroad in a place where there was no call for my astrology, so I stopped practising for 3 to 4 years. The circumstances simply did not come together until I returned to the

UK and my p lunation phase changed into New Moon. This was quite unplanned!

Obviously, we can't remain aware of such a long-term cycle constantly, but when we make a note of it, it is remarkable how frequently activities, experiences and events occur that are relevant to the phase we are in. Transits, progressions and solar arc directions pick up relevant triggers, but in the end they last less time than the lunar phase, so may be seen as focusing the energy of the phase during their period of aspecting the chart.

As a reminder, the progressed lunation phase combines the cycle of the progressed Moon with the cycle of the progressed Sun, from birth to the return of the two progressed luminaries to their natal positions, and then continuing. The whole cycle takes approximately 30 years to complete. This p lunation phase cycle therefore lasts for longer than the progressed Moon cycle to the natal chart, which lasts about 27 to 28 years, as we know that the p Moon return manifests for everyone at the age of 27 to 28 years. The progressed lunation phase cycle lasts for 30 years. The difference in length is because the Moon as seen from here is tied to the Sun by gravity, and astrologically by the changing aspects, as it is in the normal 27- to 28-year Sun–Moon cycle. But the cycle we are discussing has to take into account the fact that the p Moon is not aspecting a passive stationary natal Sun, but is aspecting a *moving* progressed Sun, so the cycle takes longer for the Moon to 'catch up'.

The meaning of the progressed lunation phase

New Moon: EMERGENCE

Definition: from the conjunction (*0 degrees*) to the waxing p semi-square (*45 degrees*) of p Moon and p Sun, with the p Moon **ahead** of the p Sun.

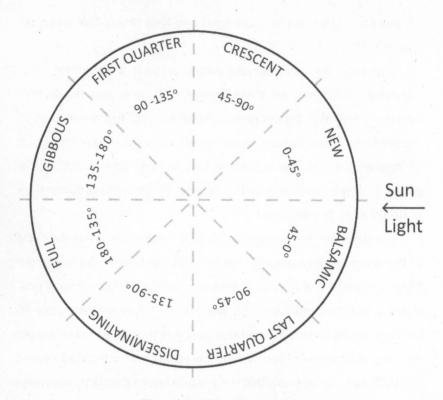

The p lunation phase cycle

Main meanings: New phase/chapter

During this time, the awareness of the new is becoming conscious, and all the lunation phases for the next 30 or so years will stem from this initiation stage. This new beginning, which may take many forms in an individual's life, needs time to take root; like the natal New Moon, it emerges from the Balsamic phase into darkness at first. This period of your life may be better understood when looking back. There is a sense of something innovative and original that is happening, or needs to happen, but which is rather unclear. In his book *The Lunation Cycle* (first published in the 1940s), the astrologer Dane Rudhyar calls this phase 'a time of inner re-orientation'. It asks you to be willing to open to whatever is coming next. The age at which you experience any of these lunar phases is obviously relevant: if you are 4, you won't have much conscious awareness of it, but you are likely to be far more so at the age of 24 and so on. If you are old enough, it can be useful to compare a second or third progressed New Moon phase with the first.

Crescent: EXPANSION

Definition: from the waxing semi-square (45 degrees) to the p square (90 degrees), through the sextile (60 degrees) of p Moon to p Sun, with the p Moon **ahead** of the p Sun.

Main meanings: Challenges to progress; adjustments; needs persever-ance and courage.

The sense of newness is beginning to wear off, and the first lucidity appears. The sense of purpose being generated is still a bit delicate, but cannot now be totally changed. The new cycle's message is coming to your awareness, coming to light and clarifying itself. There is a sense of building slowly, or heading somewhere. Your life is in the process of revealing the direction in which it is heading, and you feel you are expanding into the new path. At the beginning of the phase, at the semi-square, you may experience doubts about where you are going, or you may feel a sense of being held back by the past in some way. You realise you need to overcome this feeling in order to use the time well. As the phase advances towards the sextile aspect, you are likely to begin to experience more certainty, and may feel a sense of urgency to 'get on with it', whatever that means.

First Quarter: ACTION
Definition: From the waxing p square (90 degrees) to the progressed sesquiquadrate (135 degrees) through the trine aspect (120 degrees) of p Moon and p Sun, with the p Moon **ahead** of the p Sun.

Main meanings: action, building and rebuilding, standing up for your principles, putting down roots.

This lunation phase feels like hard work at times, and you are likely to experience a certain amount of struggle. Your projects and ideas need to be nurtured and you may feel at times like giving up. You know, though, that if you do, the energy of what has already been built will be lost; challenges need to be dealt with, and it benefits you to be steadfast and tenacious. The First Quarter phase teaches you to keep going in the face of obstacles. This is a pushing-forward period, and you need to experience personal achievement. This is likely to be seen by others too. The square pushes you; you are in positions where you are forced to make decisions. During this phase you may go through a turning point or a crisis of confidence. With the trine, often the pressure eases and you are settling into your chosen direction, and hopefully enjoying it!

Gibbous: OVERCOMING
Definition: From the waxing p sesquiquadrate (135 degrees) through to p opposition (180 degrees) of p Moon and p Sun, with the p Moon **ahead** of the p Sun.

Main meanings: refining and fine-tuning.

You need to remain flexible and to persevere. You are confident and working productively to establish yourself and your goals. The feeling of growth is tangible and whatever you have been working on or building towards is really blossoming now. You generally trust yourself and your experience, and you can maintain your own opinions even in the face of opposition. Some adjustment may be necessary if you are worried that you may be on the wrong path, but your direction cannot essentially be changed at this stage. You may need to question yourself about what your doubts are. Being true to yourself is your best guideline.

The Waning Phase

The waning phase of the progressed and visible Moon in the sky begins with the Full Moon, even as she figuratively reaches her highest point. Having reached this aspirational point of achievement, and now at the beginning of the waning stage, it is time to share with others what has been learnt. To pass the learning on to the world, to distribute knowledge and experience, which is what the waning phase is about. So the following waning phase is called Disseminating, as the fullness fades from the Full Moon, and the waning shape emerges: in the northern hemisphere the Moon's shape becomes halfway between the Full Moon and the Last Quarter, and in the southern hemisphere section of the world, it is the reverse. The Last (or Third) Quarter has the shape of a half Moon curved to the left, and Balsamic looks like a 'C'.

Full Moon: FULFILMENT

Definition: From the waning p opposition (180 degrees) to the p sesquiquadrate (135 degrees) with the p Moon **behind** the p Sun.

Main meanings: Letting go, coming to fruition, accomplishment.

Highest achievement can be attained in the Full Moon phase – this is when you have the chance to establish yourself or make your mark. This is a period in your life when the promotion takes place, the personal goal is achieved. You feel inclined to take the time to review the past, or examine where you are at this point. You are likely to be aware of being at a turning point: on the one hand, you can reap the benefits of putting energy into your goals from the last several years; on the other hand, you will no doubt be conscious that you are moving away from a time of gaining achievements, paradoxically even as you gain them. You may not have gained everything you had hoped for, but you start to think more consciously about your life purpose. How much this is valid for you as an individual will depend at some level on your age during this 3- to 4-year period.

Disseminating: DEMONSTRATION
Definition: from the waning p sesquiquadrate (135 degrees) to the p square (90 degrees) with the p Moon **behind** the p Sun.

Main meanings: Sharing, teaching, spreading around.

This is a time of coming to terms with and reflecting on the 15-year-or-so period that has now passed, and of moving on if this is appropriate. It is about the strengthening of that which you have gained and learnt, and about disseminating your experience to others. You are drawn to inspire or to help others. During this period you are teaching, mentoring, perhaps advising, officially or unofficially, and might be recognised as an established figure in your field, or simply in your personal life and with close others. Here you are encouraged to build on the success and experience you have assimilated.

Last Quarter: RE-ORIENTATION
Definition: From the waning p square (90 degrees) to the p semi-square (45 degrees) with the p Moon **behind** the p Sun.

Main meanings: holding principles, reformer, leaving your legacy.

Another period of challenge and productivity at the square, at the beginning of the Last Quarter (also called Third Quarter) phase. You are able to exercise discrimination, taking what is best from what has been gained or learnt and applying it. Using the wisdom acquired through the preceding cycles and utilising your insights based on the experience you have gained, especially at the sextile (60 degrees) phase. Reviewing the past and restructuring that which has been learnt. This is a time of decline and being drawn underground, a time when you are less concerned with building but with consolidation. This cycle may bring a time of final achievement on this path. This phase is not a time for starting new projects that have no connection with the past. One of your chief concerns is to make your mark somehow, to leave behind something meaningful that reflects your input from the period that is ending (such as a book, a piece of personal design or even simply a story).

Balsamic: RELEASE
Definition: From the waning p semi-square (45 degrees) to the p conjunction (0 degrees) of the p Moon **behind** the p Sun. Obviously,

once the p Moon exactly conjuncts or overtakes the p Sun, it becomes a New Moon in the waxing cycle!

Main meanings: going to ground, withdrawal, reflection, releasing.

The Balsamic conjunction between Sun and Moon is likely to take place in the same house and sign as the New Moon. This period of rest and contemplation can be an affirmative or a frustrating time – frustrating if an individual is naturally active and energetic. There could be a move to a quieter environment, or even an illness, or some other cause, which slows down life out of necessity. It can be positive as an antidote to tiredness, too much pressure etc. There is a marked inclination to tidy up, to move along and sort old things out – among them people and lifestyle as well as papers and accumulated debris. In the process there is likely to be a growing feeling of promise for the future as the space is cleared and new space created.

PUTTING IT ALL TOGETHER

To show you how to combine these various Moon progressions I am using the charts of Elaina and Leon for 2017–2020, with a particular focus here on 2018, which – in terms of the Moon's influence and other aspects in their charts – proved to be an interesting year in the lives of both these individuals. When interpreting a chart, it is always best to keep your comments simple as there can be a lot of different factors to consider; the art of simplifying, or weighting information, is very important so that the person whose chart it is does not become overwhelmed! The interpretations for the lists below will be expanded where necessary in Chapter 16, and integrated into overall forecasting for both people.

To recap, I will briefly consider for both Leon's and Elaina's charts in this chapter:

- The house and sign of the progressed Moon.
- Major aspects to the p Moon during the year – looking especially for conjunctions, Moon or Sun aspects if any, repeating points.
- The progressed lunation phase.

Not every progressed aspect mentioned in the list below necessarily needs to be interpreted or included. In the light of the other transits, progressions or directions that we will be considering in Chapter 16, we will discover how some of these progressions can be omitted later in order to focus on the most significant features in the chart.

Elaina

P Moon in Leo 5th house: from March 2017 until August 2019
P lunation phase – Disseminating: throughout 2017; April 2014 to May 2018; followed by *Last Quarter phase:* from May 2018 to May 2022.
P Moon major aspects:

- *Trine Ascendant and square p Ascendant:* March – April
- *Trine p Venus September and square Venus:* December
- *Trine Jupiter September 2017 and trine p Jupiter:* February 2018
- *Sextile Mercury July and square p Mercury:* December

Although they are usually passing influences for a month or so, I have included p Moon's aspects to the Ascendant, Venus, Jupiter and

Mercury, so you can note these repeating aspects. This is because repeating combinations of the p Moon and another planet, when one aspect is to the natal and one is to the progressed position of the same planet, even when the aspect is not the same, not only extends its influence but also emphasises its importance during those months. Repeating aspects usually do happen because of p planets aspecting both natal and progressed positions of planets or angles a few days or a few weeks apart, though not always. For example, in Elaina's case, the echo of Moon and Venus in September and December 2017 brings out her feminine sensitivity and desire to love and be loved.

2018
P Moon in Leo and 5th house: all year (from last year)
P Moon lunar phase change from Disseminating to Last Quarter: May 2018
P Moon major aspects:

- *Trine p Mars:* January
- *Trine Jupiter:* February
- *Square p Sun:* May 2018 (Last Quarter phase – as mentioned above)
- *Square Pluto:* December
- *Enters Virgo and sextile Sun:* late December

The most important p Moon aspect for Elaina in 2018 is p Moon square p Sun in April to May; this is actually the entering of progressed Last Quarter phase in May 2018. Each change of progressed lunar phase is usually noticeable in terms of a shift of mood, attitude, or interests from a couple of months before becoming exact. (See below.)

Overall interpretation

P lunation phase – Disseminating: the satisfaction gained from achieve-ments and recognition from others (important to her during the Full Moon phase that began in 2014) inspires Elaina to pass on her know-ledge, maybe by taking an opportunity to mentor or tutor others, formally or informally.

P lunation phase – Last Quarter: a time of consolidating what she has learnt over the last little while and pulling it together. (Elaina remains a student until at least the summer of 2019.) During the 4-year period of the Last Quarter lunation phase, she is likely to make efforts to have her achievements registered in some way, or to create something of lasting value before she moves on in her life, age 23 years.

P Moon 5th and Leo: liking the idea of being noticed by senior staff members – which she has experienced – and finding satisfaction and pleasure in creative self-expression (instinctively feeling the need to express her creative energy). This might lift her mood if other areas of her life are not fulfilling what she needs. Usually a time when life seems positive and full of meaning and her creative inspiration is generally flowing. But affected by the change of Lunar Phase to Last Quarter, so not always a positive response, depending on her mood.

These feelings colour the life from a background place, but set the overall tone. Do remember that progressed Moon aspects are usually only experienced for a couple of months unless they are repeaters, which will last a little longer (i.e. making the same or a similar aspect to both natal and p planetary positions). We will consider this again in the light of the other forecasting systems later on.

Leon

P Moon in Leo: until December 2018 when it enters Virgo

P Moon in 3rd house: from late October 2015 until May 2018 when it enters 4th house

P lunation phase – Full Moon: July 2017 to September 2021

P Moon major aspects:

- *Square Pluto, p Pluto:* June – July
- *Opposition p Sun:* July (entering progressed Full Moon phase – as above)
- *Opposition Venus:* October
- *Opposition MC (conjunct IC) at 17° Leo, 3rd house:* November/December

P Moon aspecting Pluto may embody issues of power and control, which might cause upset (the Moon is of course about our emotional life), and p Moon opposition Venus could indicate a meeting with a friend or lover, amongst other meanings. Generally, Leon wasn't in a serious relationship during this period. He was preoccupied with his own life and his studies, training and self-development.

P Moon conjunct IC may trigger feelings towards his family of origin, which could result in a visit; or he might have thoughts about changing his current living situation or his work/study direction. Perhaps he is simply caught up in memories from the past, or may encounter a person or situation from his past.

2018

A particularly busy year as far as p Moon aspects are concerned, with many changes and consequent emotional fluctuations.

P Moon in Leo: until December 2018 when it enters Virgo (as 2017)

P Moon in 3rd: until May 2018 when it enters 4th house (as 2017)

P lunation phase – Full Moon: from July 2017 to 2021 (as 2017)

P Moon major aspects:

- *Sextile p Ascendant, square Ascendant:* February, May
- *Trine Jupiter, trine p Jupiter:* March, May
- *Sextile p Chiron, sextile Chiron:* June, July
- *Trine Saturn, trine p Saturn:* Aug, November-December
- *Square Mars:* September, October
- *Opposition p Mercury:* October
- *Trine Uranus, trine p Uranus:* October, December

The p Moon–Chiron aspect triggers the generational natal aspect of Saturn conjunct Uranus opposition Chiron on Leon's chart, followed by Leon's p Moon in the 4th house, which also aspects the Saturn and Uranus conjunction over the next 6 months.

The natal opposition of Uranus opposition Chiron is an aspect that can truly be called generational, occurring as it does on and off over about 40 years from the 1950s to the 1990s in different sets of opposing signs. Sometimes T Saturn is part of the pattern too, as in Leon's chart. Planets or angles triggered by p Moon bring our attention during that period to any other planets or points that are linked into the opposition. On Leon's chart, it links into the Nodal axis, also the meaning of the two opposing houses and to a lesser extent to the opposing signs.

Overall interpretation

Progressed lunation phase – Full Moon: Leon is 30 years old in 2018, just after his 'Saturn Return year'. This is an interesting cycle to be experiencing in the middle of his Full Moon lunation phase, as Saturn returning to its natal place also brings the likelihood of achievements of some kind, and a tendency to look back and reflect before moving on. Looking at Leon's chart, you will see that Leon was born at Full Moon phase with a close Sun opposite Moon, both of which are also aspecting Neptune and Jupiter, though by hard aspects which suggests some periods of spiritual or philosophical challenge. So he has lived through the whole progressed lunation cycle in 30 years. He was studying an MA in Religious Studies at university in Britain for 4 years, now completed, and during his Full Moon phase feels he is in the process of finding his purpose in life through various further studies and travels. This is engaging his heart as well as his head, reflecting his p Moon.

P Moon in 3rd house and p Moon in Leo: since the beginning of the p Moon's progress through the natal 3rd house in late 2015, until its entry into the 4th house, Leon has been a student in the UK, which is a nice endorsement of his acquiring new information at university over this period. The Moon's passage through Leo further suggests that he gained enjoyment from his life overall, and has also gained some acknowledgement or praise from others.

11.
SOLAR ARC DIRECTIONS

Following the Sun

When we use solar arc directions in forecasting, we are symbolically following the Sun. This predictive method works by taking the movement in degrees of the Sun per day, as seen from Earth, and applying this same figure to every other natal planet and angle in the chart, including the Nodal axis. This means that the whole chart moves forward by the amount of space that the Sun moves, which is on average 1 degree per day. Each 24-hour day then symbolically corresponds to 1 year of life. Like progressions, solar arc directions provide another significantly symbolic method for looking at different years astrologically.

How to write it? A solar arc direction can be written as either SA or d. So as an example, solar arc Mercury making an aspect to the natal chart can be written as SA Mercury or d Mercury. Both ways of expressing this are acceptable.

Incidentally, it is worth also noting that in both progressions and in solar arcs the movement of the Sun is the same. So progressed Sun and solar arc directed Sun each move at the same rate, so p Sun is in the same place as the d Sun, because in both systems the Sun moves at its natural rate. This does not apply to any other planet, though it does apply to the MC, which also moves at the same rate per day/year as the

Sun, whether it is progressed or directed (due to the way the calculations work for finding the MC in both methods).

As every planet – including all the outer and 'social' planets, Pluto, Neptune, Uranus, Saturn, and Jupiter, as well as all the inner planets and the angles and nodes – moves forward round the natal chart by an average of a degree for each year, this means that the relationships between the natal planets etc. remain exactly the same as those in the natal chart. Even the nodes, and any natal retrograde planets, always move *forwards*. It is like looking at your own familiar birth chart but with every planetary placement, aspect and aspect pattern moving slowly round through the signs and houses, while remaining in the exact same relationship to each other.

As time goes on, each planet or angle inevitably moves into a different house or sign, and these changes are regarded as highly significant when interpreting solar arcs. When a directed planet or angle aspects the positions shown in the natal chart, it is these aspects that form the solar arc directions. The solar arc chart in itself is not interpreted, as none of its aspects change. What is very noticeable is the difference between advancing the progressed Moon, as an example, by the solar arc Sun's movement of about 1 degree per year, compared to secondary progressions when the Moon progresses at its own natural movement of between about 12 and 15 degrees a day, which then, as we know, equals a year in solar arc forecasting.

If you are born during the winter months in the northern hemisphere, the Sun 'moves' at its fastest rate (at 1 degree 1 minute per day) as seen from Earth: this is the time of year that the Sun advances to *perihelion* (its closest position to Earth). In the summer months, from May to August, the Sun moves at its slowest rate per day (57 minutes of arc in a day) as the Sun reaches *aphelion* (furthest from Earth).

The seasons of the year are of course reversed in the southern hemisphere, so the above example occurs during the southern summer months.

Many people use this highly symbolic but effective forecasting method because of its simplicity. In a rough-and-ready way, solar arc directions can easily be estimated for any given year, even if you are working without an ephemeris or an astrology software program.

One-degree method

There is an even easier method to work with than solar arc directions, which is known as the 1-degree method. This is not based on actual solar arc directions but on an approximation of them. The 1-degree method simply involves moving everything forward in the chart by exactly 1 degree per year. This could be called the lazy person's method, as it has no basis whatsoever in any kind of reality; while solar arcs might be a symbolic method, they do have some basis in fact: that is the actual daily movement of the Sun. But there are advantages to using the 1-degree method as a fast way to count forward, mainly because it's quicker to calculate! You can, for instance, count forward at 1 degree a day/year to get an estimated idea of the age at which someone will experience a conjunction from a SA planet to a natal planet or angle.

As we have seen, the Sun's daily motion varies up to about 4 minutes a day at different times of the year – not much, you might think, but over the course of an average lifetime, this means there is a notable difference between the 1-degree method and solar movement used in solar arc directions, as we grow older. The disadvantage of using the approximation of 1 degree for the Sun's movement instead of the actual movement is that, over the years, the age at which future events or experiences appear to take place according to the 1-degree method will start to diverge from the solar arc measurement, and can be as much as 2 or 3 years out by the time someone reaches their middle years, and therefore the timings will be inaccurate.

WHAT CAN YOU EXPECT TO EXPERIENCE FROM SOLAR ARC DIRECTIONS?

Your most relevant and noticeable solar arcs to natal aspects are the conjunctions, and maybe the oppositions. Other aspects are not much used, or there would be too many to analyse. By all means, experiment with other major aspects – squares or trines – but for many people, these aspects are not much noticed in the course of a life. I would not try to look at the minor aspects, as these will probably hardly be registered by a person.

There is nearly always some psychological component to any changes that take place during a solar arc directed experience. Solar arcs are not always accompanied by an event, though the emotional impact of a major direction can reverberate for quite a while. However, they often *are* event-oriented.

Events that correlate with a solar arc direction do not of course take place in a vacuum. Our inner and outer worlds are not separate from each other, though it may sometimes be hard to see the immediate connection between them. The rise of psychological astrology in the

West in the latter part of the twentieth century went through a phase of approaching forecasting by placing personal responsibility on the individual for every important event that took place in their life (no matter how disconnected from it they appeared to be). For example, an accident that affected your life, even when it was apparently the fault of someone else, was deemed to be because you were out of balance in your inner life; similarly, the death of someone close to you was believed to be caused at some deeply unconscious level by your need to experience loss, and so on. This way of thinking is not so prevalent in the first two or three decades of the twenty-first century, which is a good thing as some people started to accept the blame for virtually any event that took place around them.

Life events can certainly be symbolised by this forecasting method. Perhaps the quality that distinguishes solar arcs the most from the manifestation of secondary progressions is that, broadly speaking, we are more likely to experience some concrete change during the passage of a solar arc direction than we are during a progression. As stated earlier, when it comes to secondary progressions, we are more likely to go through an inner shift, or a change of attitude/orientation – depending on the nature of a given progression – than an obvious event, though it is impossible to accurately predict precisely how it will manifest.

Take, for example, the natal chart of a young man called Ian, whose Moon is at 11° Aries while his Mars is at 21° Aries. When Ian is between 10 and 11 years old he experiences an important solar arc direction in the form of SA Moon conjunct natal Mars, an active yet sensitive combination. Bearing in mind the properties associated with Moon and Mars, perhaps the young Ian experienced a major difference of opinion, or his feelings were hurt, at home or at school; or he started self-defence classes; or maybe he did something scary like stand up on a stage and address others ... Because of the active nature of the planets involved, an event is likely to have occurred that seemed in some way to test his courage (Mars), gave him a way to express his feelings (Moon) and enhanced his ability to stand up and demonstrate what he could do. His experience was a combination of events and an inner learning.

PUTTING IT INTO PRACTICE

To get a sense of how this works in practice, check out an upcoming SA for yourself, if you can, and observe whether you can feel the influence in advance of exactness. Choose a past year to look at, and either search for your directions for that year using an online program (see Further Reading on page 326) or use the 'rough-and-ready' one-degree method of counting from the year of your birth to the year you are wanting to research. With regard to the question of how long the effect of a major direction lasts, I suggest you work with tight orbs; I use 0.5 degree (30 minutes of arc) before the solar arc direction of the approaching planet to the natal planet becomes exact, and the same as the directed planet moves on. Don't forget to look up to 6 months or so before and afterwards, to see which solar arc aspects were operating that year.

Start with the Sun – and count the number of degrees forward until the Sun reaches the next planet or angle (or one that is further away) round the natal chart. This rough calculation means of course that you are using the 1-degree method to direct the chart. If you can access the actual SA planetary movement and if the birth time is accurately known, then you will be able to see the effects of Sun conjunct the chosen planet were occurring more or less at whatever age.

There can be a 3- to 6-month run-up before exactitude. For instance, if an exact direction takes place in June, then you may start experiencing the feelings that accompany the particular direction – something is about to change – from the spring onwards, and for a similar period afterwards until, say, late autumn. This can even extend longer depending on the particular directed planet. Another example may help to illustrate this:

Take the chart of Bob Dylan, the singer-songwriter who has penned a vast library of songs over many years, and who has been awarded many honours, such as a number of Grammys, a Golden Globe, and an Academy Award. Perhaps his most respected award was the Nobel Prize for Literature, which he was awarded in Sweden in October 2016. This is the only time a musician has been honoured with this prestigious prize. Keeping this in mind, I looked at his chart to see if there was a solar arc direction to indicate an event of note and, indeed, there is one.

In November 2016, Dylan's directed MC entered Capricorn, a sign that contains no planets on his natal chart. The changing of a sign or an angle indicates a rare, once-in-30-years occurrence. So this direction was picking up on Dylan's career path – his latest new departure from his many previous musical styles, which had begun on a slow burner a year or two earlier. The fact too that the sign is Capricorn is like symbolically joining the serious, grown-up world of literature with 'serious music' – symbolised by his parallel shift towards the classic musical style of the timeless American singers of the 30s/40s such as Sinatra. The extraordinary creative ability for which Dylan is honoured is surely also shown by a six-planet stellium in Leo on the same date of the entrance of the directed MC into Capricorn (28 November).

Interestingly, Bob Dylan's directed Pluto crosses his natal MC (conjunction) in May 2020, which is also a powerful solar arc direction . . .

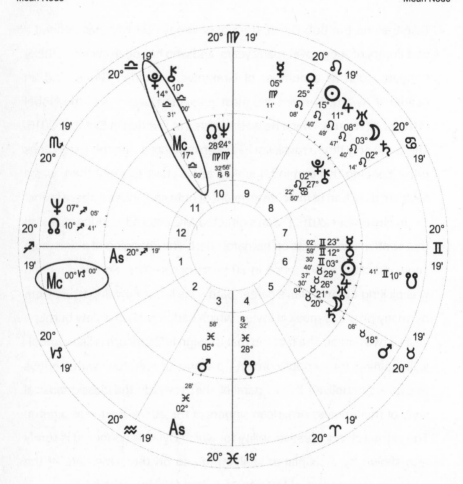

Inner Wheel
Bob Dylan
Natal Chart
24 May 1941, Sat
21:05 +6:00
Duluth, Minnesota
46°N47' 092°W06'23"
Geocentric
Tropical
Equal
Mean Node

Outer Wheel
Bob Dylan
Directed – Solar Arc
28 Nov 2016, Mon
12:00 +6:00
Duluth, Minnesota
46°N47' 092°W06'23"
Geocentric
Tropical
Equal
Mean Node

Bob Dylan's chart and bi-wheel

Although, as we have seen, all the planets and angles move forward every year with directions, the outer or social planets barely move by progression. Therefore there are likely to be more solar arc directions for you to interpret. The exception to this is, of course, the difference between the movement of the p and d Moon, explained earlier. The p Moon, with its relatively rapid movement, will form more aspects to either the natal and/or the progressed chart. There are sometimes years when there are hardly any directions happening, though.

Here is one more example, of a study chart solar arc direction in action: this bi-wheel has Leon's natal chart in the middle, with his directed chart planetary positions round the outside. It shows that in early September 2018, his directed Moon was at 17° Leo, directly opposite his natal MC at 17° Aquarius; that is, d Moon opposite MC, often expressed as d Moon conjunct IC, or SA Moon conjunct IC, which of course means the same thing (the *Imum Coeli* being the point exactly opposite the Midheaven). This is usually an important period, and often has to do with where and in what circumstances the individual feels at home, and in which direction (and where) he wants to head. For Leon, it seems unlikely that he will live in his country of birth, Singapore, in the long term, but he is in the process of searching for where he feels 'at home' in his life, and also where he can viably generate sufficient resources to settle somewhere in the world (d Moon opposite MC and conjunct IC). Or he may always be a traveller. But the emphasis on the MC–IC axis during this period highlights his continuous learning and exploring. This is, in fact, what he was doing during this period – he was travelling and taking courses in yoga and other subjects in India, and in the longer term looking to where he might be able to build a viable base.

Also of importance during the period of this SA, Leon met a woman (Moon) with whom he felt he had a very special connection, sharing

Inner Wheel
Leon FD
Natal Chart
4 Jan 1988, Mon
15:30 AWST −8:00
Singapore, Singapore
01°N17' 103°E51'
Geocentric
Tropical
Equal
Mean Node

Outer Wheel
Leon FD
Directed − Solar Arc
4 Sep 2018, Tue
12:00 AWST −8:00
Singapore, Singapore
01°N17' 103°E51'
Geocentric
Tropical
Equal
Mean Node

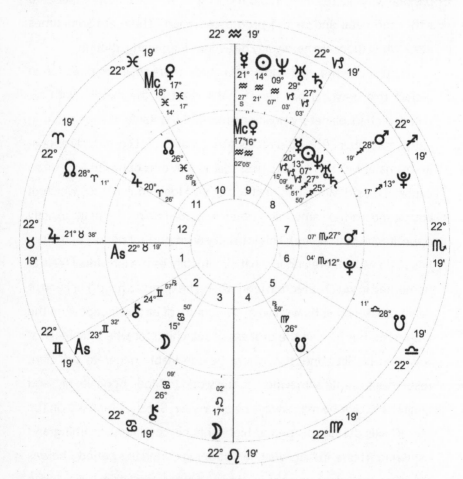

Leon's bi-wheel for 2018 – natal chart and SA

many interests, a taste in the same types of music and a similar spiritual outlook. This caused him to alter some of his plans for his intended voluntary work at a Dharma (teaching) centre, and decide to travel around India with her.

A list of the most important solar arcs to consider

- an SA planet or angle crosses or opposes a natal angle
- the SA Sun changes sign
- the SA Sun changes house (applies to charts with an accurate birth time; if the birth time is inaccurate or unknown, you may not be able to use this criterion)
- the year that an SA planet reaches 29° of a sign (significant because this means it will change signs the following year, and the 29th degree therefore places an emphasis on leaving that sign)
- a planet or angle aspects a natal planet or angle by conjunction or opposition. A soft aspect such as a trine or sextile can be considered if you think it is significant.

This exploration of solar arcs brings us to the end of the focus on the symbolic forecasting techniques, as both progressions and directions have been considered. There is one more method for looking into the future using astrology, and this follows in the next chapter – it is not a symbolic system but is essentially based on the 'reality' of transits, albeit in a different way.

12.
SOLAR RETURNS

Happy birthday, 1 year on!

The reason we say 'many happy returns' to each other on birthdays is that we are, literally, celebrating the return of the Sun after a year. The solar return (SR) chart acts like a birthday card to yourself – a new chart set for your birthday for each passing year. This chart is set for the day the Sun returns to the exact degree and minute of its position at your birth after its annual journey. It is sometimes called the birthday chart.

Essentially, the solar return chart is a snapshot of the current transits at the time of the Sun's return, reflecting our day of birth. There are similar names for the Sun in other languages, such as *sol* in Latin, the basis of many languages, and also adopted verbatim by Danish, Spanish, Portuguese, amongst others. The Sun is truly at the centre of each person's life, and as such, it is a central and powerful symbol. As well as being essential for human life, its light is embodied within us, even if we cannot see it.

The solar return chart does not necessarily fall on your actual birthday date, but may be the day before or the day after the birthday. The day you celebrate as your birthday does not change, though. For example, if your birthday is 28 March, it remains 28 March each year. However, your solar return chart for any given year may sometimes fall on your birthday, or it may fall on 27 March or 29 March. It is rarely more than 1 day different, in fact only in a leap year can the SR day be up to two days different from the birthday and this is not common. If you are born in a leap year, this will not alter the above.

KEY FACTS ABOUT THE SOLAR RETURN CHART

- You get a new solar return (SR) chart every year, which is valid for the year to come only.
- Tighter orbs than for a natal chart are used in SR calculations, so that the main aspects are easy to spot.
- I use only the 5 major aspects for SR charts – conjunction, opposition, trine, square, sextile (☌☍△□✶) – and not minor aspects – semi-square, sesquiquadrate, the quincunx or semi-sextile (∠⯑⚻⚺). It is your choice, of course – you can use the minor aspect if you wish, but do check recommended orbs, below.
- The solar return chart does not replace the natal chart, but 'overlays' it in meaning. You do not get a new birth chart once a year! Your natal chart remains key to your fundamental character.
- This chart is set for the Sun's return, but not necessarily set for the birth place (see below).
- This yearly chart can be read by itself, or in relation to the natal chart.

The benefits of consulting the SR chart each year as your birthday comes around are that the chart highlights specific areas of experience you are likely to encounter in the coming year. Basically, the important factors are picked out. The occupied houses suggest the areas of life that will be a focus of experience in the coming year. This is very helpful as an outstanding feature as there is quite a lot of other forecasting to consider. Continuing transits to the solar return chart as well as to the natal chart may trigger some noticeable further changes during the relevant year.

To use or not to use the solar return chart

Generally speaking, astrologers fall into one of two camps: they always use the solar return chart when forecasting and feel a lot of understanding can be gained through it, especially in combination with other forecasting techniques; or they tend not to use it at all, relying instead mainly on transits, progressions and/or solar arc directions. As a reminder, it's always worth experimenting with all the forecasting techniques to see which ones you like and which resonate with you the most. However, personally I believe transits should always be the first choice, as they are of course usually the most obvious in their effects. In this respect, a solar return chart is actually a 'picture' of the transits for that day when the Sun's exact return becomes significant for that individual in forming the return chart. This is true also of your natal chart – a very special picture of the day's transiting planets.

The SR chart is a powerful forecasting method that describes our solar journey towards deepening our sense of who we are, and our purpose in this lifetime. Differences may be found in any area of the SR chart when compared to the natal chart, except in the sign and degree of the SR Sun, which always remains the same as the natal Sun. Its house position may change, however, which is often where you might start with studying the chart.

Keep it simple

So, you decided for now to use this chart! When working with it, remember to *keep it simple*! While a great deal of insight can be gained from these charts, some of which is not so obvious in the other fore-casting methods, and you will find that devoting a lot of time to studying the SR chart in depth each year will give you masses of information to combine with the other three methods described in this book, unless you have a great deal of time on your hands, allowing you to spend days dissecting a single chart, it is important to develop a sense of discrimin-ation. With practice, you will discover ways to pick out the most important features. This means not analysing every semi-sextile, assuming minors are being used – an individual might not experience every subtlety anyway.

The orbs you use for an SR chart need to be tighter than those used for the natal chart, because of its ephemeral nature. This will, in turn, reduce the number of aspects in the SR chart in comparison with the natal, and thereby increase the chances of having an unaspected or minimally aspected planet or angle.

I suggest you use the following orbs:

- For conjunctions, oppositions, trines and squares: 5°
- For sextiles: 3°
- For the minor aspects, if using them, i.e. the semi-sextile, semi-square, sesquiquadrate and quincunx: 1°

Chart location

As with which is the best house system or what natal orbs should be allowed, astrologers are not all in agreement about the issue of SR chart location. The question is: should the SR chart be set for the birthplace, or set for where the person is now living or residing on the solar return birthday (remembering this could vary by a day from the actual date of birth).

For those astrologers who do not relocate the chart, even assuming the person has moved location since birth, their reasoning seems sound: no matter where the person travels to, their place of birth has a resonance for them, as it defines their nationality and origins, even if they moved shortly after birth and/or changed their nationality. Remembering that the SR chart does not supersede the natal chart, which remains the basis for all forecasting work; but it adds further information to it.

However, other astrologers make a case for using the place where the person is currently living, if different from the birthplace (or even the place where the person is staying for at least one night on the SR date), as this reflects the changes of energy and atmosphere around that individual.

I personally always relocate the SR chart for the year to come if the person has moved since birth, and have found this to be effective. The angles (particularly important is a changed Ascendant and its different approach to life), the houses including the SR Sun's house, and the Moon are the parts of the chart that will change the most, depending on how far away the relocated chart is from the birthplace. (Remembering that the Ascendant sign changes by 1 degree approximately every 4 minutes as the Earth spins.)

To help you decide, you could try setting two SR charts for 1 year: one for the location of the birthplace, and one for the relocated place, to observe which chart seems to be the most valid. If you don't want to spend the coming year thinking about this, you could pick a busy year from the past in your own or in another person's life instead, in which important changes or experiences occurred, and set an SR chart for that year. Then look at which of the two charts seems to be the most valid.

It's also worth bearing in mind that any transit of significance will be repeated on the SR chart if it falls on or around the birthday, and will therefore last a year, which might be longer than the transit itself, very probably unaffected by the location you use. So the effects will last longer.

The majority of astrologers are highly unlikely to relocate any of the other forecasting techniques. A common given reason for basing the calculations for transits, progressions and solar arc directions at the place of birth for any year is that these techniques could be said to represent an unfoldment of the self or the soul in that year, based on the intrinsic location of where a person was born. Solar return charts are usually the only forecasting method where astrologers will take the option to relocate the chart. The reasoning behind it is whether you will get a 'better' chart if you set the SR chart to where you live now (assuming you are not living at your birthplace); some astrologers choose to go somewhere else on the day of the SR to try to 'improve' their chart for the next year; if you perceive the current place of residence as having influence on your life experience, relocate the SR chart to your residence. You will no doubt be influenced in your decision by whether or not you are settled for the long term in the place you are currently living – if not, maybe use your birthplace. This debate has been going on online for some time, and there are no definitive answers!

Opportunities

If you have a challenging T-square on your natal chart, it might not be there on your SR chart for the coming year. Conversely, you might find that a new planetary pattern has appeared that you like the look of, or that you don't really like! The best way to deal with reactions like these is to try to see the positive opportunities that a focus on some new experience of yourself may bring. It goes without saying that most people would like to see what they consider to be their positive potentials for the next year!

Looking at your next year's birthday chart can be a little nerve-racking if there are configurations on the chart that you interpret in a negative way. (This can be the case too for those who worry about an upcoming transit.) It is so important not to let anxiety dominate. What will be will be, and at least next year's solar return chart allows you to be forearmed. It is also useful to remember that transits don't always manifest in the ways that we expect. As none of us can stop the lining up of the planets, then looking for the positive side to SR Pluto square Moon or SR Neptune opposition Venus, to name a couple of possibilities, can help us to put our reactions into perspective.

WHAT ARE YOU LOOKING AT ON THE SR CHART?

As with a natal chart, you can start by simply contemplating the SR chart, which can be read in its own right. You are (of course!) going to approach it in a simpler way than you would treat the natal. Because of the reduced orbs, there are naturally fewer aspects, and you will probably quite easily get an overall impression. You are not looking to make a fully comprehensive analysis of the SR chart, but to pick out and highlight the parts that stand out. You can use this list also to compare natal with the current SR. The list below shows you what you are looking at in particular (although not all of the list will be relevant for every SR chart).

- *a planetary emphasis* in signs or in houses.
- *hemisphere or quadrant balance.*

- *the SR rising sign, any rising planets and the chart ruler's position* are all significant, and all of these offer clues as to the theme of the SR chart for that year, thus the theme of the person's major experiences to come.

- *elements, modes and polarity:* compare the result with the natal balance – there may very often be a difference, sometimes quite marked, which will of course give you a sense of which of these is missing, or notable, and is therefore noteworthy.

- *the Sun's house position* in the chart is a very important key, and gives an overall focus to the year.

- *the Moon's sign, house and major aspects, plus the SR Moon's phase* – can add an overall assessment of the emotional orientation of the year.

- *Angular, unaspected or notably multi-aspected planets* can throw an important emphasis on those planets. This is particularly so in the case of differences between the natal and SR chart's emphases.

- *any outstanding patterns or busy areas,* showing which areas of life will be a focus for your attention in the year to come. For example, a SR chart with a concentration of planets in the 7th house would indicate that a focus of the person's attention is likely to be on relationships and interactions with others in the following year, perhaps more than is usually the case. With a focus of planets in the 3rd, learning and sharing of ideas will stand out, and in the 8th, secrets and hidden issues may be a prominent part of experience, or there may be endings, major changes or even encounters with death; and so on. Obviously the actual experience of the SR chart's emphases does depend on which planets are featured but not every chart has a clear emphasis on any particular house or sign – the planetary spread may be fairly balanced.

- *empty sections* of the SR chart do not of course mean that the person will have no experience of these areas of life in the coming year, but simply that the focus of the year is unlikely to be in those areas of his or her life. This is true of the natal chart too, unless empty sections are challenged by the transiting planets at some point.

Making a direct comparison between features on the solar return chart and the differences or similarities with the natal chart is also usually quite revealing. The best way to show you how valuable the SR chart can be is to demonstrate this by looking at one of our case-study people's charts.

Elaina's Solar Return chart October 2018

DOB 23 Oct 1995, 17.38, Rockledge, Florida

Set for Eugene, Oregon

Elaina was born in Rockledge, Florida, but on her birthday in 2018, when she was 23 years old, she was in Eugene, Oregon – a very different part of the States. So, using relocation, Elaina's solar return chart is set for Eugene. This is an example of an SR chart from a past year, to illustrate how effective the SR chart can be. There is an SR chart for her set for 2019 in Chapter 16 – and although that year will also become a past year, hopefully the principles of the SR chart will enable you to look

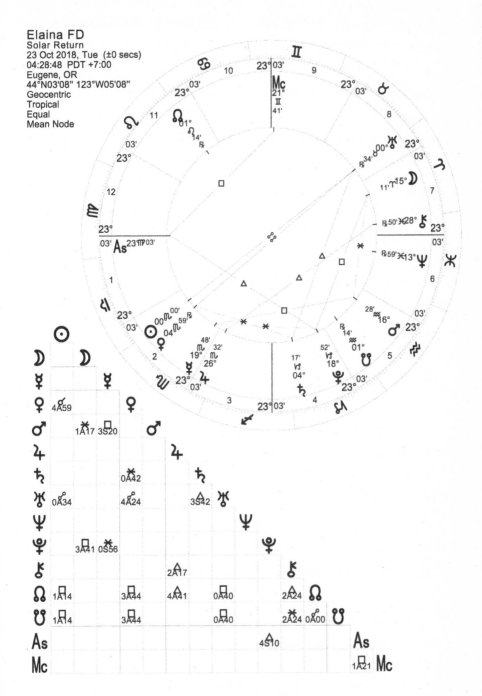

Elaina FD
Solar Return
23 Oct 2018, Tue (±0 secs)
04:28:48 PDT +7:00
Eugene, OR
44°N03'08" 123°W05'08"
Geocentric
Tropical
Equal
Mean Node

Elaina's SR chart 2018

at SR charts for 2020 and beyond. I have set the orbs of the aspects to the suggested smaller orbs, above, for solar return charts.

Notes on SR chart and comparison with natal – 23 October 2018
Her Scorpio Sun is in the 2nd house in 2018. The Sun's closest important aspects on her twenty-third birthday for her year to come are Sun opposition Uranus (☉☍♅ – exact at 0° Taurus) and square the Nodes. You can see Sun conjunct Venus too (☉☌♀ – which is nearly at the maximum orb of 5° for a conjunction) but Sun opposition Uranus is dominant because it is exact.

- *House and sign emphasis:* stellium in Scorpio and 2nd house
- *Quadrant emphasis:* 1st Self-development,* 4 planets – Sun, Venus, Mercury, Jupiter (3 personal planets)
- *Secondary quadrant emphasis:* 2nd Self-expression,* 4 planets – Saturn, Pluto, Mars, Neptune (just one personal planet)
- *Majority of planets west* (as natal)
- *Water–Fixed chart*
- *Lack of fire* – natal has 2 planets and Ascendant in fire
- *Moon Aries,* only fire planet, 7th house, Moon sextile Mars
- *Saturn and Ascendant earth* (no natal planets in earth)
- *Sun conjunct Venus 2nd* – no natal aspect
- *Ascendant Virgo* – Chart Ruler: Mercury in Scorpio 2nd house
- *MC Gemini* – Ruler: Mercury in Scorpio 2nd house

*With thanks to the late Howard Sasportas for coining these phrases for the quadrants.

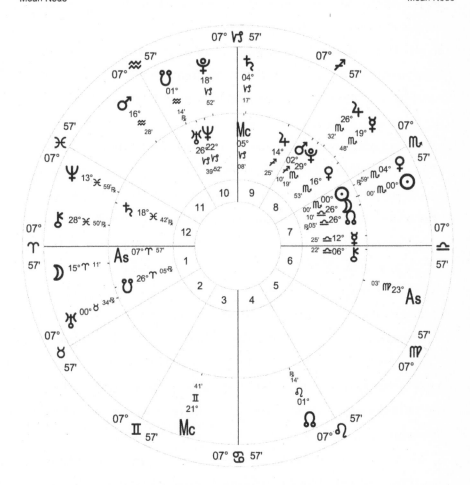

Inner Wheel
Elaina FD
Natal Chart
23 Oct 1995, Mon
17:38 EDT +4:00
Rockledge, Florida
28°N21'02" 080°W43'32"
Geocentric
Tropical
Equal
Mean Node

Outer Wheel
Elaina FD
Solar Return
23 Oct 2018, Tue (±0 secs)
04:28:48 PDT +7:00
Eugene, OR
44°N03'08" 123°W05'08"
Geocentric
Tropical
Equal
Mean Node

Elaina's bi-wheel – natal chart with SR 2018

Summary:

Themes beginning to emerge: 2nd house – mentioned several times, including the SR Sun's house. A year when Elaina would be reassessing what she is good at, and what she really values, where she wants to go and what purpose she is seeking to fulfil in her life. She would likely have been focused on her own future (1st quadrant) and her studies at university (strong Mercury). Financial arrangements may have needed to be adjusted (SR 2nd house emphasis) – she undertook no less than 3 part-time jobs during this period as well as her studies, for financial reasons – and she was likely to encounter situations in which she needed to be very grounded and organised (natal lack of earth, and SR 2nd house).

Uranus opposite Sun is a transit which has been 'captured' by the SR chart, so instead of transiting Uranus ending the opposition after 3 passes across the Sun in her natal chart in March 2019, it continues having an effect until her next solar return chart in October 2019. Many aspects in the SR chart are the transits of the moment and will be extended as a result of being held in the chart. This is the case, for example, with Sun conjunct Venus opposite Uranus, which is a brief, passing, minor transit of Venus. Yet with Uranus continuing to oppose Venus too on her SR year 2018–2019 chart, even though it is not tight, Elaina is likely to have had some lively, exciting, or disruptive, experiences in the area of romance – which she did experience, albeit a rather short-lived affair (Uranus does not bode well for long-term commitments).

Elaina may have found herself being more outspoken than is her usual style (her natal Moon is in the opposite sign, Libra), and she may have found it easier to express her honest opinion when she thought a situation called for it (or even occasionally out of turn)! (SR Mercury square Mars, Moon Aries.)

Hard-aspected Uranus is not an easy transit or aspect, but one of its names is the 'awakener'. Sometimes it opens our eyes to what we are really looking for, even though it can bring the end of a relationship that causes pain, perhaps because it was the 'wrong person' or the 'wrong time', which we needed to understand a bit better. For Elaina, her SR chart also has Uranus in Taurus trine Saturn in Capricorn (an earth trine that balances the natal lack of earth), which is very helpful in grounding and mitigating negative feelings, once taken on board. Elaina has already experienced something of this! Other thoughts:

- *Mercury* is an important planet in this chart – it is not only the chart ruler of the Virgo Ascendant, but also rules the other angle, the MC in Gemini, plus Mercury sextiles Pluto, Scorpio's ruler. This sets a tone for the year.
- *Scorpio* is represented by four planets, including the Sun, which means the chart is more Scorpionic than the natal chart. Life is lived very intensely.
- *Moon–Sun*: natally the Sun and Moon are conjunct, and in the SR chart they are on opposite sides of the chart – although the lunar phases are not quite opposite one another. Instead of natal Balsamic phase, this SR chart is Gibbous phase.

The elemental balance compared across the natal chart and the SR chart results in a strong dominance in both charts of the water element, the feeling and intuitive realm. Especially with so many Scorpio planets! This shows she has a marked sensitivity and a compassionate nature, as well as the capacity to experience intense feelings. It is likely that Elaina is mindful of the monthly Moon phases as these appear in the sky, perhaps being especially aware of the Full Moon every month. Her natal chart shows the Balsamic Moon phase; she needs a certain amount of quiet space to absorb her experiences, and to protect herself from the busy world at times. She has found the pressure of the three jobs plus her studies, exams and projects almost too much to cope with. Her 2018 SR chart has a different emphasis, as the chart has a Gibbous Moon, which may have helped her as it is a phase which usually has a goal in sight. Elaina is probably very aware of needing to persevere towards her goal to graduate successfully. Helping others and being of benefit probably provided her with a sense of purpose in the midst of being busy. Even though the SR chart is ephemeral, the current SR Moon phase is valid during each birthday year.

The emphasis on Mercury this year points towards the focus on using her mind, and augurs well for success in her studies if she continues to work hard. If I include a minor aspect or two, natal Mercury is tightly semi-square Saturn in Capricorn and sextile Pluto. These are both very useful aspects that will add to her determination to do well at university, although the work is hard and challenging. (She probably would not value her achievements when they come if this were not the case!) The exact (up to 1 degree) Mercury sextile Pluto in particular echoes all her Scorpio passion, and brings a certain rewarding satisfaction if her aims are fulfilled.

Mercury natally is in Libra in the 7th house conjunct Chiron across the Descendant, suggesting that either there was perhaps an issue for Elaina feeling inadequate mentally in youth, or there was some other obstacle to her acquiring confidence in her mental activities, which she is now trying to compensate for, as suggested in this year's SR chart. This emphasis on Mercury over a couple of years in her SR chart is revealing what stands out.

As happens with every bi-wheel, because the natal chart is in the inner circle, using the natal Ascendant, with the solar return (or whatever chart is being compared) arranged round the outer circle, the comparison looks different in terms of where the SR planets fall. So in this comparison 'wheel' the SR Sun–Venus conjunction falls in the 7th house of the natal chart. Its position in the actual SR chart is valid as well. That conjunction is in the 2nd house of the SR chart but in the 7th of the bi-wheel and is emphasising Elaina's relationships with close others during the year October 2018–October 2019. And so on with the other planetary and angular placements. Both the SR chart itself, and the comparison with the natal chart, are valid.

We could go on, and before you'd know it we would have a full-blown written solar return chart analysis, which of course is not the point! But my intention is to leave you to work out whether there are other points to be made. I hope you get the picture of how to do this, even though it is not comprehensive. As we have seen, solar return work is best kept as simple as possible. You just need to touch upon the essence of what is important and what can be left out.

Elaina's SR for the following year, 2019, will be explored succinctly in Chapter 16 with the rest of her forecasting for the year, along with Leon's 2020 SR chart and his other forecasting.

OTHER TYPES OF RETURN

We looked at two other important returns in astrology in Chapter 7: the Saturn return, which occurs every 29 years or so, and the Jupiter return, which happens every 12 years. Each return occurs of course as often as it takes the relevant planet to go round the Earth as seen from our planet – or, in reality, around the Sun.

Logically, this means that it is perfectly possible to draw up charts for the other returning planets. If you work out the length of time it takes for Mars or Venus or Mercury to orbit, which varies from year to year, you can then calculate a return chart for each planet for any particular year that you might want to study – assuming a return of that planet occurs in that year! A Mars return, for example, does not occur every year as its orbit takes somewhere between 1 and 2 years to complete and is a little variable.

Such a chart would naturally emphasise the qualities associated with the returning planet. So, for instance, a Mars return might indicate your capacity to show courage or fight for yourself; whereas a Venus return of approximately 1 year would illustrate matters of the heart and relationships; a Mercury return, also of about 1 year, would focus on your intellect or on your communication skills. The returns of these three personal planets are somewhat complicated by the fact that all three have retrograde periods, which could occur as the return period approaches, thus lengthening or moving the cycle. Mercury, for example, turns retrograde at least three times a year, and occasionally four times.

In practice, the only other return chart that is regularly used by some astrologers is the **Lunar Return**, which of course focuses on the Moon's return after about 28 days. A new chart is calculated at the lunar return for each month to come. There is a book recommended in the Further Reading list that covers the returns of the Moon, as well as solar returns, but in this chapter I have kept the focus on how best to utilise solar returns, these being by far the most commonly used of return charts by most astrologers.

Utilising the Lunar Return chart, the professional astrologer can consider the changing inner emotional life of a client, which in some situations is very useful to explore. However, it requires a lot of consultations. As far as I am aware, the Lunar Return is not very commonly used.

Part III follows – which considers less obvious astrological features, ties up some loose ends and pulls most of the earlier information all together, including exploring the charts and some more forecasting for our two example charts, those of Leon and Elaina.

PART III
PUTTING IT TOGETHER

13.
TIME TRIGGERS

Eclipses and the minor cycles of the inner planets

We have now covered the four main methods of forecasting in modern Western astrology. But we can't really leave it there. Other considerations remain to be explored in this third part of the book, such as the returns of the Nodal axis and of the planetoid Chiron: of what significance are these in comparison with the transits of the slow-moving planets, Jupiter out to Pluto? The Nodes and Chiron do also, of course, form transiting aspects to natal charts. However, as we have seen, in order to avoid being overwhelmed by information, we must learn to discriminate between bodies in space, make choices and pick those that have the most obvious and noticeable effects.

The movements of the planets, whether making transits to a natal chart, or forming a solar return chart, do not vary from their predicted passage, as foretold by an ephemeris. We cannot control what is coming, whether we wanted this or not. This much is fated. What we *can* control (to some extent!), however, are the ways in which we respond to our transits or other features affecting the chart. Yet when we find ourselves in the midst of a long-running transit, for instance, it can be hard to pin it down and to say precisely when we are most affected by the qualities that the transit represents.

In this chapter, we are going to explore 'time triggers', the shorter-term transits and other types of forecasting that can sometimes reveal key periods ahead. As we will see, solar and lunar eclipses both have a part to play in highlighting longer-term transits, or simply affecting the chart, for example, as do the short and passing transits of the personal planets, Mercury, Venus and Mars, as well as the progressed Moon.

ECLIPSES

Solar Eclipse: at New Moon – the Moon's shadow falls across the Sun.
Lunar Eclipse: at Full Moon – the Earth's shadow falls across the Moon.

Have you ever seen a total solar eclipse? Unless you are a person who literally follows solar eclipses, travelling to locations where they take place around the world, sighting a total solar eclipse is a rarity. This astronomical phenomenon is awe-inspiring, even for today's largely educated population, with our scientific knowledge and sophisticated attitudes. The way the world goes dark in the middle of the day, sensors activate the street-lights at the apparent arrival of night time, and the quiet that descends as birds stop singing is extraordinary. You may already know what causes a solar eclipse, but that knowledge does not entirely take away the 'magic' of the experience.

Solar eclipses are not visible to many people at a time, as the location from which they are visible on Earth is very limited. To get a clear view of the darkening of the Sun when the eclipse takes place will probably take you round the world. If, for example, you lived in certain parts of Indonesia or Borneo or were on a boat on the Pacific Ocean in the eclipse path of 9 March 2016, and the sky had been free of clouds, you would have been a witness to the total solar eclipse that took place there on that occasion. (As happened to me in Cornwall, UK in August

1999, when cloud covered the total eclipse, with just a tantalising glimpse for a few seconds. The next total eclipse for Britons will not be until 2026.) In the United States of America in the summer of 2018, there appeared a partial solar eclipse path across large swathes of the country, causing great excitement. Even a partial eclipse of the Sun stirs emotional reactions from those watching. Indeed, the eclipse followers who are so moved, or scientifically inspired, by the sight will literally follow the Sun in the eclipse seasons, which occur approximately every 6 months.

It is not surprising that people from earlier centuries, with no knowledge of the actual causes of eclipses, were amazed if they witnessed a solar eclipse. It might have been the only time many people had ever seen one, or indeed would ever see another. The sheer unexplained awesomeness of the Sun going black was terrifying to our ancestors, as you may imagine, and the stories that emerged from such a sighting varied according to the culture and beliefs of those watching. After all, the celestial body they most depended on for light and warmth suddenly disappeared in daytime! One such story from ancient China was that a dragon had swallowed the Sun. There is still a lot of superstition around a solar eclipse – especially as the event is so relatively rare that there are still many people who have never seen one.

You are far more likely to have seen a lunar eclipse, which also occurs every 6 months, and is visible across an entire hemisphere of the Earth when it happens during the night hours. The media usually tells us when the next one will be, but I have given you a short list of upcoming eclipses and the dates, in the table below. In fact, you might have seen many lunar eclipses, perhaps without always being aware that you were witnessing one. These occur at Full Moon every 6 months or so, and are usually characterised in appearance by the darkening of the brightness of a Full Moon, and often by a reddish or coppery tinge to the Moon as the Earth's shadow crosses it when the Moon and Sun are in opposition on either side of the Earth. The event is not as obvious as a solar eclipse, but still impressive.

Solar eclipses always take place at New Moon, when the Moon and the Sun are next to each other in conjunction as viewed from Earth, and the Moon sits in the way of the Sun, blocking its light. The cycles of the Sun and Moon, with or without an eclipse, are collectively known as *lunations*.

How eclipses work

There is of course a New Moon and a Full Moon every month, but only one in six become eclipses. This is because of the involvement of the Nodal axis. An eclipse, solar or lunar, must be fairly widely conjunct the position of one of the Nodes, otherwise there will simply be a New Moon or Full Moon as usual. A solar eclipse can be conjunct one of the Nodes by a maximum of 18 degrees, which distance will create a partial solar eclipse. The tighter the conjunction is (up to 10 degrees), the more of the Sun can be covered by the Moon and the eclipse will be total.

Every Full Moon, whether or not there is a lunar eclipse, occurs because as the Sun sets in the west, so the Moon rises in the opposite part of the sky, in the east; meaning that we find ourselves in the middle between both luminaries. So moonrise at Full Moon takes place in the approaching dark in the east, as sunrise occurs in the east at dawn. Because the Moon's orbit of the earth is angled to the Earth's orbit of the Sun by 5 degrees, it works out that an eclipse only lines up about every 6 months. If the Moon and the Earth were on the same plane, every New and Full Moon would be an eclipse. The Nodal axis is active in creating a lunar eclipse of the Moon at Full Moon as well as at New Moon for a solar eclipse by its proximity to the luminaries. For further astronomical information, I refer you to a little book by Robin Heath, called *Sun, Moon & Earth*. The movements of the Sun and Moon are complex, so I won't be going into this in more detail here; however, in terms of forecasting, it is important to know what eclipses may mean for us from an astrological perspective.

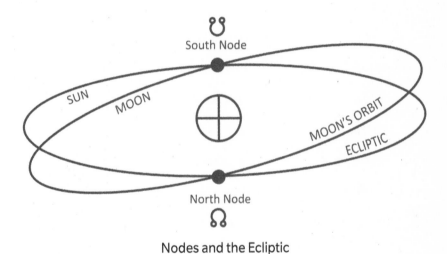

Nodes and the Ecliptic

Table of upcoming eclipse dates 2019–2024

Date	Type of Eclipse	Degree + sign
26 Dec 19	Annular solar	4 ♑
10 Jan 20	Annular lunar	20 ♋
5 June 20	Annular lunar	16 ♐

Date	Type of Eclipse	Degree + sign
21 June 20	Annular solar	0 ♋
5 July 20	Annular lunar	14 ♑
30 Nov 20	Annular lunar	9 ♊
14 Dec 20	**Total solar**	23 ♐
26 May 21	Total lunar	5 ♐
10 June 21	Annular solar	20 ♊
19 Nov 21	Partial lunar	27 ♉
4 Dec 21	**Total solar**	12 ♐
30 Apr 22	Partial solar	10 ♉
16 May 22	Total lunar	26 ♏
25 Oct 22	Partial solar	2 ♏
8 Nov 22	Total lunar	17 ♉
20 Apr 23	Annular solar	0 ♉
5 May 23	Annular lunar	15 ♏
14 Oct 23	Annular solar	21 ♎
28 Oct 23	Partial lunar	6 ♉
25 Mar 24	Annular lunar	5 ♎
8 Apr 24	**Total solar**	19 ♈
18 Sept 24	Partial lunar	26 ♓
2 Oct 24	Annular solar	10 ♎

Solar eclipse

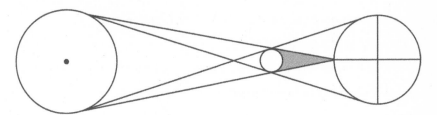

Diagram of a solar eclipse

There are three main types of solar eclipse: total, partial and annular. Certain sets of criteria are needed for a lunation to become an eclipse. The astronomy of a total eclipse of the Sun is when:

- At New Moon, the Moon's orbit of the Earth crosses the path of the Ecliptic at the Moon's Nodes – that is, at two crossing points, as we are talking about two interlocking circles/ellipses. The North Node on the chart is where the Moon is crossing the Ecliptic north and at the South Node where it is crossing south, so the Nodes form an axis and always move together. (See the diagram above.)

- The Moon is at *perigee* (closest to the Earth in its orbit), which means that its maximum diameter as seen from Earth covers the apparent size of the Sun, even though obviously these bodies are vastly different in size. It is indeed a neat arrangement whereby the Moon is 400 times smaller than the Sun, yet because it is also 400 times closer to us than the Sun, the discrepancy balances itself out, and they appear, as seen from here, to be the same size. This is a perfect 'cosmic serendipity'.

The astronomy of a partial solar eclipse is when:

- Either the Moon and Sun are not fully aligned with each other at New Moon *or*
- the Moon is not completely lined up with the Sun so that it only partially blocks it out.

The astronomy of an annular eclipse is when:

- The Moon is at *apogee* (its furthest point from the Earth), so it is at its apparent smallest as viewed from Earth and its diameter does not fully cover the Sun. It only covers the central part of the Sun at this stage in its orbit, thus leaving a ring of fire – the corona, which shines out from behind the black disc of the Moon.

A total eclipse, in which the Moon's disc covers the Sun, might last only for a few minutes, yet is so impressive that it seems longer.

Lunar eclipse

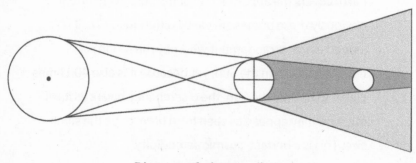

Diagram of a lunar eclipse

There are really only two main types of lunar eclipse – total and partial:

- A total lunar eclipse occurs when not only are the Sun and Moon on opposite sides of the Earth, but the Full Moon is totally in the shadow (or *umbra*) of the Earth *and* aligned with the Nodes. All other Full Moons do not have one or other of these requirements, so are not an eclipse of the Moon, owing to the angle of the Moon's orbit at 5 degrees to the ecliptic.

- A partial lunar eclipse occurs when the umbra of the Earth blocks the Sun's powerful light from reaching the Moon, but not fully. Only a part of the Moon's disc is in the Earth's shadow.

- The Moon can be at apogee or perigee during a lunar eclipse; if it is at apogee, thus smaller from the Earth's point of view, the eclipse will last longer as it will take longer to pass through the Earth's shadow.

A total lunar eclipse can last up to an hour and a half or even a little longer (which means there is plenty of time to observe it, unlike its solar equivalent), and, depending on cloud cover, it is usually visible to everyone on the hemisphere on the night side of the Earth. Those in the daytime half of the Earth at the time of the eclipse will not see it.

When the Moon is at perigee, it appears bigger in the sky, and it is especially striking when it also turns red during an eclipse. As you might imagine, the sheer unexplained awesomeness of the Moon going red was a terrifying sight for our ancestors. For many, this omen probably presaged war, or at least bloodshed. Not for nothing was this Moon called a Blood Moon. To demystify this, but hopefully not disenchant the specialness of the sight, a red eclipsed Moon occurs because the sunlight falling on the Moon is blocked by the Earth's shadow and any sunlight that does get through is refracted by the Earth's atmosphere, thereby making the Moon look red.

Eclipses in mundane astrology

There is a branch of astrology known as 'mundane astrology' ('mundane' meaning of the terrestrial and material world, rather than the heavenly one), as opposed to the natal astrology that is the focus of this book. Its purpose is the astrological study of events in the world beyond the personal, such as the happenings in countries, businesses and organisations, involving prominent members or leaders. It also observes the astrology of natural or man-made disasters, accidents and other extraordinary events such as the changing fortunes of wars, or financial losses and gains in a broad sense.

Those who practise mundane astrology today, of whom there are a surprising number, can be compared with the astrologers who have been advisors to monarchs or leaders in generations past, or who would have practised as wise shamans in tribal cultures, and offered wisdom and insight in the noble courts of history. Their role was often (although not always) to consult the heavens concerning matters of war, to identify enemies, or the likely outcomes of a faction's or a country's strategies of war. The influence of recent or coming eclipses was considered a crucial part of the picture. No self-respecting wise man or woman would ignore the trigger points of eclipses. (Please refer to the Further Reading list on page 326 for a book on mundane astrology.)

According to the findings of mundane astrology, eclipses have indeed proved to be important triggers in worldly affairs. While the mundane astrologer can often only study a natural disaster such as an earthquake or a volcanic eruption after the event, eclipses offer much more predictable markers. If the mundane astrologer is interested in certain issues in particular countries, he or she can keep an eye on major transits or solar arcs to those countries' charts, as well as the close eclipses, solar or lunar, that might bring a situation to a head. With respect to individuals' lives, the principles of their use for forecasting are the same: the short-lived eclipse often highlights a situation.

Meanings of eclipses in natal astrology

Of course, there are generic interpretations that can be given for both solar and lunar eclipses. However, while it is important to have a general understanding of the purpose eclipses play in astrological interpretations (which are actually transits), it is more relevant for our purposes to look at what they might mean for us individually.

Solar eclipse meaning

No matter what type of solar eclipse it is, we know that a solar eclipse always occurs at New Moon, traditionally a time of renewal and new beginnings. This means that the solar eclipse in general has become associated with new starts, and with re-orientation, inception or conception in the broadest sense. The fact that it is an eclipse makes it a much more powerful influence than the monthly New Moon by itself. You do not have to be able to *see* the eclipse for it to be effective; it is enough that it is happening somewhere in the world.

Look at the sign and degree of the next solar eclipse to see if it falls on a significant place for you – does it aspect an angle or a planet on your chart? Check back a few pages to the table of eclipses for the date and position of the next eclipse. I tend only to consider a conjunction, or possibly an opposition, but if it so happens that the eclipse degree connects with a natal planet/angle by any other major aspect then note it and see whether there is any effect. The orb between the degree of the eclipse and whatever it aspects on your chart should be no more than 2 degrees to be valid. If a solar eclipse does fall conjunct a planet or angle on your chart, the natal planet that is being triggered will become particularly sensitive. This could take the form of a spur to start something you have been considering doing, or another form of activating the seed sown by the eclipse.

If (as will often happen) the eclipse degree that is coming up does not aspect anything on your chart, it's worth noting the house the eclipse falls in to see if that area of your life is affected. Some new event or adjustment in that area of your life may occur that brings in change of some kind connected to the affairs of that house. People do have varying responses to eclipses. Some people may not notice anything out of the ordinary even if the eclipse degree aspects their chart. Others are very sensitive to the effects of these astronomical phenomena.

The use of eclipses in timings during longer transits

An event or shift of feelings does not necessarily occur at the actual time of the eclipse but, as will become clear, could occur fairly near that time. In a sense, a solar eclipse is a particularly noticeable New Moon(!) and its length of influence does vary. There is rarely common agreement amongst astrologers as to how long the influence of an eclipse lasts. The general consensus is that if an eclipse aspects the natal chart exactly (or nearly), its effects can last as long as 6 months. However, I usually reckon the immediate effects can easily last for up to a month –

or that some new beginnings seeded at the time of a solar eclipse will lead us in a different direction in due course.

Incidentally, the orb usually used is quite tight. Some astrologers would only allow a degree away from exactness on the natal chart, but I have found that up to 2 degrees on either side of its being exact is effective, as in the example below.

Here's a true story from my records (names have been changed, but the dates are correct). The solar eclipse of 15 February 2018 was at 27° Aquarius, which was conjunct John's Mercury on his Descendant at 25° Aquarius (signifying a connection through a friend). John had been struggling financially for a while with his film-making business. He had a couple of fairly long-lasting transits going on: Saturn conjunct Moon and Uranus conjunct Mars. Through a friend who was also a business colleague, John was introduced to David, who was the CEO of a bedroom furniture business; and after some negotiation (symbolised by Mercury) this man offered John a lucrative deal to make a series of videos advertising his goods. John had been feeling quite irritated, believing that he deserved a better deal from life (T Uranus conjunct Mars), which did not seem to be going anywhere for him – until the eclipse brought David into John's working life.

Then there was a summer solar eclipse at 19° Leo in 2018 that fell conjunct John's Ascendant, at 20° Leo. Since beginning the work with David and his company, John's connections (Ascendant) in the world of advertising have continued to increase greatly, and he is getting more offers of work. This increase in his income has enabled John to move house, which he had not had the funds to do in the previous year. One of the important background transits for John during this period was T Uranus (2nd house) trine Moon (5th house) – unexpected good fortune, and a potential house move. In January 2018, T Saturn had crossed John's 5th house Moon in Capricorn with a short conjunction, suggesting that there might be a concrete (Capricorn) change to come. Interestingly, there was a lunar eclipse in late January in Leo, although it passed by in a week or two, and did not aspect anything on John's natal chart. Maybe it was simply a harbinger of what was to come in 2018.

The two eclipses that connected with John's chart, plus a repeating transit of an outer planet, led to a sequence of events following on each other's heels. In both cases, the orb used for the most important aspects with the eclipses was 2 degrees or less, which is usually recommended. Keep eclipse aspects tight! It is important to note that it's quite normal for nothing to seem to change radically in a person's life when an eclipse takes place, and we might even be tempted think, 'Mmm, I don't see any effects. So maybe eclipses don't have any effect.' But give it time; as in John's case, the after-effects might gradually emerge. Sometimes the effects – which can be life-changing, as they were for John – will emerge more slowly than might be expected.

Eclipse effects do sometimes last up to about 3 months beyond their exact date. It is more usual though, as you might imagine, to perceive an effect when an eclipse actually informs a natal aspect a short while after the date that it aspects the chart in some way.

Lunar eclipse meaning
If the eclipse that triggers your chart is a lunar one, it might mark a high point of whatever you are involved in, or bring closure or an ending of some kind.

A lunar eclipse, occurring usually two weeks later than an accompanying solar eclipse (and occasionally also two weeks before a solar eclipse) represents a culmination, fruition or a high point. The Full

Moon phase of the Moon's cycle takes place about 2 weeks after New Moon, so if you are in what is known as a six-monthly 'eclipse season', then a solar eclipse taking place at the New Moon is very likely to be followed by a lunar eclipse at Full Moon. This can be total or partial. However, it is not inevitable, just usual, for a lunar eclipse to follow automatically on the heels of a solar eclipse, or that a lunar eclipse leads the way for one.

At Full Moon, the Moon reaches the culmination point of the lunar cycle. She shines with full splendour and illuminates the night sky, showing herself at her best. So one could say the monthly Full Moon in its natural cycle is about a result, outcome, an achievement or a letting go. The lunar eclipse, being so much more powerful (as is the solar eclipse) if it falls on a significant planet or angle in your chart, may bring a release of previously held views or feelings from a more objective viewpoint. After all, the Moon has to do with our emotional life and a lunar eclipse may bring matters of the heart to a climax or a closure.

How long do the effects last? That seems to depend on how much a lunar eclipse affects us emotionally. For some people, it seems to pass quite quickly or they don't particularly experience much. However, those who are more attuned to the emotional realm, with strong Cancer, Scorpio, Pisces or 4th house planets, or a multi-aspected Moon, may experience particularly fast-changing moods, deeply sensitive feelings, or an increase in intuitive insights when the Moon is full. This would be enhanced by a lunar eclipse that falls on a resonant natal sign and degree. A sense of achievement, or a feeling that some situation is resolved or can be released at this time, might happen. Or you might simply experience more vivid dreams, or have difficulty sleeping on a Full Moon night.

A royal solar eclipse

It is interesting to note that the second in line to the British crown, Prince William, Duke of Cambridge, was born on the day of a solar eclipse. He was also born very close to the summer solstice, and is the son of Princess Diana and Prince Charles, the heir to the throne.

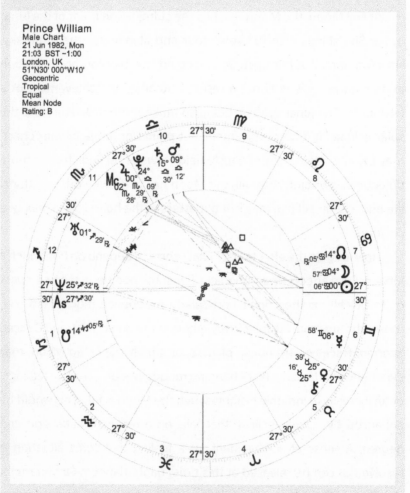

Prince William's chart: 21 June 1982, 21:03, London, England

As the first male child of his famous parents, and given the social position that he was born into, his solar eclipse in Cancer with its accompanying North Node denoting his future destiny, closely conjuncts his mother's Sun and Mercury in Cancer, and sextiles his father's Moon and North Node in Taurus. And that upholder of tradition, his grandmother Queen Elizabeth, is a Taurus. Putting these simple family connections together, it seems that William embodies and combines the tradition of the British Royal family with the warm and generous heart of his mother.

The new beginning shown by his natal solar eclipse suggests that, when he comes into his authority as the future king, either the monarchy might cease to exist as a traditional institution and become something else, or William will build his kingship into a new and very different kind of sovereignty, based perhaps on warmth and emotional connections, with a changed attitude towards what tradition means.

TRANSITS OF THE PERSONAL PLANETS

The orbiting positions of the personal planets – Mercury, Venus and Mars by short-term transit – can sometimes act as triggers that pick out days or weeks and pin them down. The reality is that many astrologers do not consider the transits of these planets because their influence is usually so fleeting. With this in mind, you might like to remind yourself of the length of time these inner planets usually take to pass by a natal planetary/angular placement. (If you need to refer to it, the table is in Chapter 8, page 106, or you could simply look in an ephemeris.) On average,

T Mercury moves about 1.5 degrees in 24 hours, Venus moves almost the same amount with an average of 1 degree 12 minutes per day, and Mars moves even less than 1 degree, at about 30 to 40 minutes per day. So these passing transits are often not going to be experienced, depending on which other astrological transits are going on (if any).

Where these inner planets are perhaps more useful is when trying to identify a day that is particularly suited to a specific event. For example, if you wished to choose the best date for a wedding, you might consider looking for a favourable day with flowing aspects from Venus to other planets (e.g. the other benefic, Jupiter, to Venus, or a good Venus house placement – T Venus). Similarly, if you are thinking of starting a business, you might perhaps look for a date when Mercury is in aspect to Saturn if possible. Obviously check out transiting Venus (along with more long-term forecasting) if you want to go shopping for a new item of clothing!

This approach is actually tapping into a different branch of astrology called 'electional astrology', which is the art of choosing favourable dates – but in doing this, we are still considering future transiting inner planets. Ideally, there should also be some back-up from more major transits as well.

Transits of the Sun and especially the Moon can also be taken into consideration, but only in detailed daily analysis. I don't need to remind you how fleeting the transits of the luminaries are! It is of course also possible that a passing transit of the Sun, or even the Moon, could be used to pin down a day, or part of a day, which is useful if you want to schedule a particular event or consider something specific that has taken place. However, the Sun and the Moon feature so frequently in other transits or progressions that their use in such a specific moment is very limited!

Churchill's speech

Astrology never ceases to amaze me with how specific it can get, even if we aren't around in person on a particular occasion to witness it unfolding. As part of improving your forecasting skills, it's worth looking backwards as well as forwards; to that end, I highly recommend examining important past events to see what was happening astrologically at the time. Have a look at occurrences such as your inner planets in the midst of a longer one. And do look at your progressions, especially the progressed Moon.

When Winston Churchill was the British Prime Minister during the Second World War, he made a number of influential, morale-boosting speeches, some of which have gone down in history. He famously exhorted the nation to 'never surrender' in his 'We shall fight on the beaches' speech, which went on to become more well known than almost any other address that he delivered. (Do check out the radio recording listed on YouTube.)

Churchill first delivered this speech in London on the afternoon of 4 June 1940. As far as I have been able to ascertain, the time was around 15:00. So I have set the chart for that date and time as follows in this bi-wheel, which combines the speech with Churchill's own chart:

You can see that at about 15:30, T Mercury crossed Churchill's MC, so Mercury in the sky was then at 29° Gemini, right on Churchill's natal MC at 29° Gemini. While Churchill was an inspired writer and speechmaker in most circumstances anyway, with his natal Mercury in penetrating Scorpio opposite Pluto, this speech is particularly remembered for its inspirational language

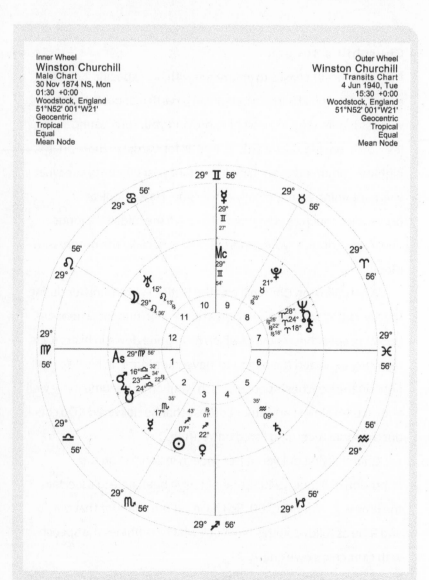

Inner Wheel
Winston Churchill
Male Chart
30 Nov 1874 NS, Mon
01:30 +0:00
Woodstock, England
51°N52' 001°W21'
Geocentric
Tropical
Equal
Mean Node

Outer Wheel
Winston Churchill
Transits Chart
4 Jun 1940, Tue
15:30 +0:00
Woodstock, England
51°N52' 001°W21'
Geocentric
Tropical
Equal
Mean Node

Churchill's chart and speech bi-wheel

and morale-boosting effect, addressed not only to the
government but later to the nation by radio in the first year of the
war. No doubt T Venus and T Mars (addressed briefly in Chapter 7)
had relevant effects too at times.

Progressed Moon

As we saw in Chapter 10, the progressed Moon moves quite quickly, in a couple of weeks, given an orb of a degree or so either side of exactness; however, it could well mark a trigger point in the midst of a longer transit. Given the nature of the Moon, this will very likely concern our inner world and emotional life in some way, whatever else the progression is about.

So the p Moon acts as quite an effective time trigger for identifying an occasion when a culmination is reached during a longer transit, by stirring up an emotional reaction that shifts the energy somehow during the transit – depending what the transit is! The next time you have a reasonably long transit of an outer planet to your chart, check this out by looking from time to time at your p Moon's changing position to see if this is the case for you. It is always worth checking out new ideas or techniques; and apart from anything else, it draws your attention to your Moon progressions themselves.

14.
OTHER RETURNING POINTS OF SIGNIFICANCE

The return of the Dragons and the Wounded Healer

The return of the Moon's Nodal axis to its own position, and the return of the eccentric orbit of Chiron, can be highly noticeable in an individual's life. The Nodal axis and Chiron do of course make other transits across the years to natal planets or the natal angles, just like every orbiting planet does, but their returns and sometimes their half returns are often quite key to a person's life, which is why I'm going to be focusing on them in this chapter. Transits of the other major planets are usually more immediately important in terms of experiencing the effects when it comes to analysing forecasting for a chart, so should be considered first. For further information on transits or returns of the Nodes and Chiron to their natal places, please see books on the Further Reading list that deal more comprehensively with both.

The Moon's Nodes were known as the Dragon's Head (North Node ☊) and the Dragon's Tail (South Node ☋) in some cultures, mostly in India and other Eastern countries, triggered by a popular belief in a heavenly dragon in the sky, which devoured the Sun or Moon during a solar or lunar eclipse: they are always two exactly opposing points in space, forming the Nodal axis. Astronomically, the Nodes are at the two crossing points of the ecliptic and the Moon's orbit round the Earth, so they are points in space (travelling north, that crossing point is the North Node, and travelling south, the opposite point is the South Node). In Vedic astrology, they have other names: Rahu is the North Node, and Ketu the South Node. As we have seen, they are key in the astronomy of solar and lunar eclipses. (See Chapter 13 on the astronomy and meaning of eclipses.)

There have been a lot of books written about the Nodes of the Moon. These have been written both by Western astrologers and by those whose practice is essentially Vedic (Indian astrology). This is because the Nodes are taken seriously as life pointers by most astrologers, in either system.

In a nutshell, the Nodal axis is known to many as the Path of Destiny and indicates our essential individual purpose for this lifetime. The placement of the North Node is said to show where we potentially can grow into this sense of purpose (through its sign, house and aspects), whereas the South Node shows where we have come from, or patterns of behaviour that come easily to us, but through which we do not learn and grow. The axis also gives insight into the nature of our relationships with others.

I refer you to books that offer a more comprehensive explanation or set of interpretations for the Nodes, included in the Further Reading list. There is also a section on the meaning of the Nodes in *Astrology Decoded*.

Vedic – also known as Jyotish – is an Eastern-oriented astrological system that differs in many ways from modern Western systems. However, there is a small but increasing number of Western-trained astrologers who have switched to the type of astrology the Vedic system follows. (If you think what I am describing in this book is complicated, it is probably an even longer process to train to be a Vedic astrologer!) At least the general public in India and some adjacent countries mostly have a positive attitude to astrology, and it is still normal for many people to consult the local astrologer for help for all kinds of reasons – notably to assess a potential marriage partner. In this process, one part of the work is to examine the Nodes in some depth, especially those which aspect the partner's chart. In fact in this Indian branch of astrology, the Nodes of the Moon play a crucial role when an astrologer is advising potential marriage partners.

THE NODAL RETURNS

The Nodal axis has an orbit of 18.5 to 19 years, with recurring returns at multiples of 18.5, i.e. at the approximate ages of 18 to 19, 37, 55, 73, 92 years. The North Node projects us into the future and shows us where we are potentially going and the main purposes of our lives, in terms of our personal growth and life lessons. Its opposite number, the South Node, indicates where we have come from, our past and our early experiences, which formed the essence of ourselves, and what comes naturally to us. You could say that your Path of Destiny, as shown across the Nodes, especially at the Nodal return, needs to be fulfilled by opening up to new untrodden paths, while not rejecting the past but by incorporating valuable experiences gained, even if these were difficult, or if they have been rejected formerly. So the Nodes give clues as to your karmic destiny – you could say, to what you came to this Earth to accomplish.

Think back in your own life to see if anything significant occurred for you at the age of 18 or 19, or at the ages of any of the later Nodal returns, depending of course on how old you are at the time of reading this book! Events that occur at, or very close to, the ages listed above for the Nodal returns may be experienced as having a quality of 'being fated' or 'destiny'. This does not mean that any such events are necessarily linked to each other – though there might be a connection between them. Obviously too the experience of this return will be different depending on what signs and houses your natal Nodes fall in.

For example, one of my clients, Jennifer, left her parental home to live alone at the age of 18 and a half at her first Nodal return, not because she had a bad relationship with her parents, but because she felt restricted by their style of life and was looking for more space to 'do her own thing'. Leaving home is not such an unusual event at that age, but she can still recall the thrill of it – the sense of standing on her own two feet. It was 'time' for her to realise her own independence. This is a feeling that often accompanies the Nodal return, no matter how it manifests for each individual. The type of event or change that manifests will of course vary depending on our age and specific circumstances, but the sense that destiny is at work is a confirmation that the Nodes are involved here.

What particularly stood out for Jennifer at this time was the ability to exercise her freedom to create the rhythm of her own life; indeed, in the early days, she delighted in cooking and eating soup at 3 o'clock in the morning. Her natal Nodal axis falls in North Node Taurus 2nd house, and South Node in Scorpio 8th house, so food symbolised freedom and emotional satisfaction at that time. Significant aspects to the axis include a semi-square (North Node) and sesquiquadrate (South Node) to Uranus (giving her a sense of personal freedom), plus a trine to natal Mars, representing her determination to conduct her life in her own way.

When Jennifer, a whole Nodal cycle later in her life, reached the age of 37, she gave birth to a boy in this return period. It was an unplanned pregnancy and he was the only child she conceived with her partner of the time. She describes how she looked into the eyes of this child in her arms and felt an instant connection with him, as if she had known him over many lifetimes. He was born in late April: yes, he was a Taurus, born on the day his Sun was conjunct her North Node. The child had an Aquarius Ascendant, which echoes the aspects to Uranus of her natal Nodal position. Both of these experiences at the time of a Nodal return could be said to be 'fated': in both cases, the events described above altered Jennifer's life in irrevocable ways.

The workings of fate are mysterious, and the Nodal returns can manifest themselves in all sorts of different ways.

From the perspective of spiritual growth in this life, it does seem plausible that the position of the sign, house and aspects of the natal North Node do point towards lessons a person is destined to learn, or encounters they are destined to have, although these experiences may take many forms, and may be a theme that runs through the life.

Half returns and relationships

Some people are much more sensitive to the Moon in all its guises than others, and might be markedly affected by the Nodal half returns, which occur at approximately the ages of 9, 27–28, 46, and so on. As you might already have noticed, this means that the Half Nodal Return in your late twenties corresponds roughly with the return of both the progressed Moon and the T Saturn. Some of us will recall significant events that occurred at around that age, and there might have been a psychological shift of some kind, while others of us probably didn't notice a great deal. Nevertheless, there might have been a sense, at least in retro-spect, of something that seemed destined which stands out in our memory.

What does make an impact on many people at their Nodal return or half return concerns a major experience that affects most of us at some point – our important relationships. These are very often romantic rela-tionships, but similarly any close connection between ourselves and a close friend can be impactful if the Nodal axis is involved. The Nodes mystically seem to connect us with significant other people; indeed, the partners in many such relationships often share aspects with each other's Nodes and their personal planets or angles. The sense of having known a person before often permeates these relationships. Some-times, however, this can mean that we remain 'tied' to someone through all kinds of misery, feeling we have something to work out with them – but this might not always be the case.

THE RETURN OF THE WOUNDED HEALER

Known as the Wounded Healer, and also as the Maverick, the planetoid Chiron is often astrologically misunderstood on the birth chart. By the time Chiron has orbited back to its natal position, when we are 50 years of age, perhaps our understanding of life has grown enough to allow us to develop a certain tolerance for the process of living. While experi-ence doesn't necessarily bring with it the promise of unmitigated joy, there can be a poignancy that uplifts the spirit. Most of us are more than halfway through our lives by the time we experience the return of Chiron to its natal place.

Chiron's orbit is highly irregular, with its passage through the signs varying widely, taking between 2 and 9 years to traverse one sign. In the signs from Capricorn to Cancer, it traverses each sign in about 4 to 9 years, and from Leo to Sagittarius it passes through in about 2 to 4 years. Its movement through space is irregular too, moving inside the orbit of Saturn and then back inside the orbit of Uranus. No doubt this irregularity has contributed to its name of the Maverick.

And the most frequently used informal epithet of Chiron, the Wounded Healer, has been adopted by many astrologers from the story of the Greek hero Hercules of classical times, who accidently shot his teacher Chiron the centaur with a poisoned arrow. Chiron was immortal so he could not die, so he continued to suffer. But over time he came to realise that he could, in his capacity as a healer and educator of other Greek heroes, relieve his own pain by giving of his experience to others. This is the opportunity Chiron brings as he returns to his natal position: to reconcile himself with that which he cannot change now, and look to his next steps and his future possibilities.

There is no denying that Chiron carries with it a certain amount of regret, sorrow and nostalgia for what has been, or for unrealised potential. This relates to that relatively unconscious part of ourselves which often takes time to come to our attention as we grow older, but which makes more sense to many of us when we experience some of life's ironies, and inevitable loss or pain. At a certain point in life we come face to face with feelings like these, although this can often be experienced far earlier for many than the age of 50, at Chiron's return. It seems for most to be an unavoidable part of living on Earth. No one's life is all peace and joy, although that is what everyone strives for!

Some of these descriptions make the meaning of Chiron in astrology sound like really hard work. But there is also the potential for learning to heal any of your own pain by helping others to find ways to come to terms with theirs. This, of course, is the meaning in myth of the Wounded Healer Chiron the centaur, who found that his suffering could not be healed in another way. There is a deep satisfaction, even a sense of peace, in giving real support to others who need it, in whatever form.

The return period of Chiron often revives memories from the past, and we frequently re-encounter previous experiences or people and are reminded of our vulnerability. At this time we have a chance to heal ourselves and others through coming to terms with our past as far as we can, if this has not yet occurred. At this time, we tend to be reflective, looking back over our successes and achievements so far, whatever that means for us individually; but it is also a period when we, perhaps painfully, remember what we did not achieve and probably never will. We tend as well in this period to plan or imagine what we want to do while we still have relative youth and energy.

This is a chance to let go of whatever needs to be let go, if that is possible, which might extend from as far back as childhood, or even before that, from a previous life, or from our ancestors, depending on how we perceive it. But we are also likely to be aware that we are forging a new destiny that allows for a renewed experience of life. The astrological understanding of this intriguing planetoid has grown since its relatively recent discovery in 1977, and refined meanings have been emerging as more associations surface for it. We are, after all, not yet at the Chiron return of this planetoid's discovery, which will take place in 2027; and while fresh wounds are certainly being created constantly, amongst these there is also the opportunity for healing to take place in the world. As is true of the passage of the outer planets, Saturn and Jupiter, Chiron's passage over important points in the chart of a country can bring damaging circumstances but also potentially indicate ways for reconciliation, or restoration of balance.

I believe the Chiron return marks an important period for many people. There is, however, the possibility for some people that it will pass without much effect, and the energy of this transit may be fairly quiet. Similarly, not every astrologer includes Chiron on the chart.

People in the year of their Chiron return may be seen to be doing things differently, in their own way. At this period of time, they may behave like a 'maverick' and not be inclined to conform, which of course fuels Chiron's second most commonly used descriptive name. A maverick is an independently minded individual whose energy goes outside what convention dictates. It is likewise about building independence to sustain ourselves in case of any difficult times to come, which can in itself be a healing experience.

The symbol of Chiron appropriately resembles a key (and is also like the combined initials of Chiron's discoverer, Charles Kowell). Subject to the house and sign where it is placed, the position of the key shape can suggest a memory that may or may not be conscious, of an internal wound that is incurable, perhaps because it happened long ago, even centuries ago. This is because the wound can be cultural rather than personal, something we carry that is still affecting us for one reason or another. For example, such a wound can indicate those of us who have been forced to leave our home country because of war, dictatorship or some other intolerant regime. Yet some of us will strive to find solutions to very difficult situations in our own ways.

The fact that we know Chiron is placed in your chart at all, even if you were born before Chiron was discovered and interpreted, illustrates that the apparent nature of life on Earth incorporates experiencing damage of some kind. So the challenge is to work on healing the pain by offering healing in your own way to others, to your culture, to the planet, or to your ancestors. Maybe it is the case that without hard times and the pain that these may bring, people would not fully be able to appreciate the pleasure of the times when everything is going well!

15.
EXTRAS IN NATAL CHART INTERPRETATION

So what else is new?

Human beings like to see and name the patterns in things. In astrology, there are quite a few patterns of one kind or another, including the aspect patterns, e.g. the T-square, Grand Cross (sometimes called the Grand Square), Grand Trine, Minor Grand Trine, Kite and Stellium, the meanings of which are all explained in other astrological literature (see Further Reading list). These are probably the most commonly used aspect patterns in the toolbox of the astrologer. All these patterns bring together aspects of one sort or another between planets or between planets and angles.

But other aspect patterns are also used by some, which suggest that virtually any pattern can be formed from different combinations of types of aspect. Consider, for example, the following patterns that have been identified by various astrologers:

Thor's Hammer   Square Key
Rosetta   Mystic Rectangle
Hele   Finger of the World

Yod   Diamond

Hard Rectangle   Stretched Pentagram

Double Yod Key   Star of David (sometimes called

Grand Quintile   Grand Sextile)

Quintile Kite

I doubt whether there are many astrologers who look for, or use, all these patterns in a chart, but they sound interesting, don't they? There may be others you will come across. There are even compromises for those aspect arrangements that don't quite make it as patterns. You can have a Kite (almost), a Star of David (almost), and probably other 'almosts' for a pattern that simply has a 'just-out-of-orb' aspect to one of the points.

In this chapter, I am going to be looking at two aspect patterns listed above that occur frequently enough in charts to be considered of reasonable importance for natal work, but which are still not regarded as major aspect patterns. Whereas, for instance, a T-square occurs in about as many as 60 per cent of natal charts, the two aspect patterns described below occur in less than 20 per cent of birth charts overall. (If you are interested in finding out about any of the others, you might find more information about them online with a little research.)

One way to reach for the meaning of any aspect pattern is to break down each part into its component aspects, and then do your best to put it back together. (The concept of 'weighting' will be explained in more detail in Chapter 16, when we look at the interpretations and forecasting for Elaina and Leon's charts.)

Mystic rectangle

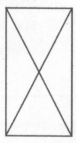

Diagram of mystic rectangle

It sounds quite exciting to say 'I have a Mystic Rectangle on my birth chart', which may be something to value! This pattern is what is known as a closed pattern, in that it neatly contains all its aspects in one 'box' made up of doubled-up aspects: two trines and two sextiles plus two oppositions.

So what is mystical about this aspect pattern? The stability of the shape and the closed nature of this pattern show its potential for self-containment, which can be a mystical kind of quality in the chaos of the world's events, or when our life threatens to become too busy and too much is going on at the same time. The difficulty represented by the two oppositions is of bringing opposing ideas, attitudes or values together even when they are diametrically opposed; these conflicting viewpoints can be between yourself and others, or even within yourself. This can be quite a challenge, requiring you to rise above the struggle or otherwise reconcile your dilemmas. The flowing aspects – two trines and sextiles – in the Mystic Rectangle are the balancing aspects, helping those with this pattern to resist going to extremes and to find a middle ground when faced with the option of reaching a compromise. It is an energised pattern which contains its own creative solution in many ways.

As an illustration of this aspect pattern, the American singer Janis Joplin's chart is given below.

As it is sometimes hard to see the shape of the Mystic Rectangle pattern amongst all the other lines on a chart, here it consists of:

Mercury trine Saturn

Pluto trine MC

Mercury sextile MC

Saturn sextile Pluto

Saturn opposition MC

Mercury opposition Pluto

Now hopefully you will see it easily. It does involve an angle (MC) rather than all planets, but it is a neat pattern with quite strong aspects. There is a school of astrological thought that would only count aspects between planets, and not between planets and angles (or Nodes), but as you see, I have not followed this. I will take you briefly through the process of breaking down each aspect in an aspect pattern, which is a way to approach any aspect pattern – in this one there are no less than six separate aspects, which can seem rather complicated.

Janis Joplin was in many ways a bundle of contradictions, and she sadly died from a heroin overdose in 1970. The oppositions in her Mystic Rectangle tell part of her story: Saturn opposition MC (♄ ☍MC) suggests that she felt different from people around her, from her school days onwards, which made her feel lonely. She migrated to the counter-culture of the early sixties, where she felt more at home, although she still found it difficult to make friends. Also Mercury opposition Pluto (☿ ☍♇) – the other opposition – illustrated her intensely passionate and powerful personal style, which came out especially in her formidable

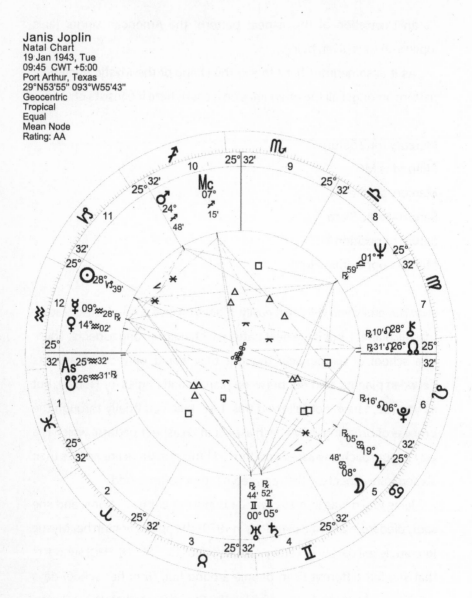

Janis Joplin's chart

singing voice, although she sometimes could be curt or brusque in her personal interactions. Her trines and sextiles helped her periodically to stop her drug and alcohol abuse and 'go straight' for a while, even to become more settled and enjoy her creative talent and increasing fame. Yet Joplin was a person who lived intensely and experimented with life, so sometimes she pushed the boundaries too far.

Nevertheless, every aspect and aspect pattern, no matter how apparently difficult to live with, has its own solution or positive manifestation. Of the 'flowing aspects' in Joplin's Mystic Rectangle, Mercury sextile MC is about communication with the world through writing or self-expression (she wrote some of her own material); Saturn sextile Pluto adds determination and persistence to make a difference; Pluto trine MC lays the groundwork for pioneering changes in the ways she presents herself in the world; and Mercury trine Saturn shows precision and depth of thought that focused her mind, and which causes others to take her and her work seriously. Altogether the balancing effect of this aspect pattern counteracts alienation and self-doubt.

One always has to remember, though, that a person's whole natal chart is a picture of a living, growing human being, and the rest of the chart needs to be taken into consideration as well when considering an overall interpretation, modified by whatever forecasting techniques are being used.

Yod – the Finger of God

Two quincunxes (sometimes also called inconjuncts), linked together by a sextile and forming an elongated triangle, together make up a Yod. This is not such a common aspect pattern, and it is always intriguing when it appears on a chart. This is because of the contrary

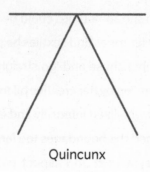

Quincunx

Yod

nature of a quincunx, which connects two planets of different elements in a rather awkward relationship. The two planets are linked by 150 degrees (with an orb of 2 degrees). It is not so much an inner contradiction, like a square, but rather an awkwardness of things not quite coming together in the way you would wish, such as an irritation, or a missed connection. It is also ironically known as the Finger of God, because it often feels as if the Almighty has set things up this way; something about it can feel like a 'fated' niggle that needs to be dealt with, but which is not simple or very easy. The solution or the outcome can often be seen in the apex planet, which will give a clue to the meaning of the Yod.

Interestingly, Janis Joplin has a Yod as well as a Mystic Rectangle in her chart, with Moon quincunx MC, Moon quincunx Mercury, and the sextile between Mercury and MC. The apex planet is the Moon in

Cancer in the 5th house. Incidentally, as two of the points in both aspect patterns are the same – Mercury and the MC – this highlights those parts of the chart. But in the Yod, the Moon stands out as a focus planet, in the apex position at the top of the triangle.

Moon quincunx Mercury (slightly out of orb) shows a relationship between these two planets, linked by about 150 degrees, which – although the aspect is rather awkward – is better than no connection. Moon in Cancer shows a part of Janis Joplin that is really sensitive and deep feeling – and in her 5th house, this is a part of her creative self, which is also connected to her career direction, Moon quincunx MC. So she puts huge energy into her performances and builds a reputation in the world when what she is doing comes naturally to her: she simply MUST express herself! Her 12th house Mercury in Aquarius reveals her desire to communicate to many, from a deep part of her soul. But in her day-to-day life, when she is not performing, the quincunx between Moon and Mercury does not make her relationships smooth and easy. She tends to over-react emotionally, and finds it hard to be rational, often feeling criticised when this is not the case.

When she was upset or angry, Joplin was often rather unfair in her comments, and later reflection probably caused her to experience anxiety and guilt. A Yod is an aspect pattern that tends towards a certain amount of inconsistency in your dealings with others at times, yet for Joplin, the powerful emotions evoked by these aspects were expressed by her uniquely passionate and wild voice in her public performances.

The value of this Yod is essentially embodied in the effort she must put in to project her eloquent passions out there to reach people, perhaps sharing her worldview with like-minded souls. Think of a 'Piece of My Heart', 'Ball and Chain', 'Me and Bobby McGee'.

WHAT ELSE HAS NOT BEEN COVERED YET?

You can go on adding more techniques, methods and systems to your astrology endlessly. You would probably need to start studying astrology at 3 years old and continue for the rest of your life, and you still wouldn't cover all there is to know! The kind of astrology I have focused on in this volume is of course natal Western astrology, which is broadly psychological and modern in its approach.

This section is included so that you will at least become aware of how much you can continue to learn and expand your knowledge if you wish to. If any of the explanations of the following methods, systems, bodies or points in space inspire you to want to know more about them, please refer to the list of Further Reading on page 326. You do not, however, need any more than what is included in this and my first book, *Astrology Decoded*, to become knowledgeable enough to read a chart, and predict the future astrologically. What you need most will be practice – so do all your friends' charts and forecasting!

Other branches of astrology

Aside from completely different systems such as Vedic astrology and Chinese astrology, you may have come across other branches of Western astrology, which require a different approach to the methods used in natal astrology.

There are some astrologers who take a 'traditional' approach to astrology, which means using many techniques from past centuries, in the belief that the 'real' astrology of the seventeenth century and earlier, back as far as the Babylonian, Greek, Roman and Medieval practitioners, was better researched and more precise than the available systems today. Some traditional astrologers do not even include the use of the 'recently' discovered outer planets Uranus (1781), Neptune (1846) and Pluto (1930), let alone the 'planetoid' or the so-called 'centaur' Chiron (discovered 1977), preferring instead to stick with the seven 'classical' planets (Sun, Moon, Mercury, Venus, Mars, Jupiter, Saturn) that have been known about, named and interpreted for thousands of years, before the invention of the telescope.

There are also branches which can act as 'extras', adding more information – as aficionados of each practice will assert. For example, in Chapter 13, page 230, we touched upon electional astrology, which focuses on choosing the best date to hold an occasion, such as a wedding or a party, open a new project, or start something new. Astro-location looks at the astrological qualities associated with different places around the world. In contrast, horary astrology is the art of drawing up a chart for the moment a question is posed, and using that chart to answer the question: this is about the idea that each moment has its own quality which contains the answer to a horary question. Horary astrology has its own rules, was very popular in the seventeenth and eighteenth centuries, and is still used a lot now.

There are several speciality subjects that can be studied using astrology. These include medical, which considers what kinds of remedies could be offered to treat an illness. Astrologers practising this skill have trained in some form of medical discipline or healing as well as astrology. There is also financial, as mentioned earlier in the book, including assessing the stock market conditions; mundane (mentioned in Chapter 13), which is the study of the countries and leaders of the world); midpoints or harmonics, both of which could be described as techniques for natal astrology; while psychological is yet another approach.

There is a unique school of astrology called Uranian Astrology, which began life in early 20th century Germany under the astrologer

Alfred Witte. Sometimes also known as the Hamburg School of Astrology, and more recently renamed Symmetrical Astrology by some astrologers in the United States, this school of thought is a quite different way of working with astrology, the most controversial part of which is that it uses eight hypothetical planets that are believed to lie beyond Pluto.

Yet another different school is Esoteric Astrology. Based on the channelled writings of Alice Bailey while receiving 'instruction' from her spirit guides, this system is about approaching astrological work from the point of view of the evolution of the soul, and your spiritual progress. In contrast, the focus in this book is on what I call 'modern astrology', and is about our personality, sense of identity, and individual development. Our soul's development may be explored as part of this, but not necessarily. In my view, if a person has issues in his or her marriage, or business problems, he or she may need a more practical focus. However, Esoteric Astrology emphasises different parts of the chart instead, and might consider an individual's situation from a karmic perspective and from the perspective of their overall life purpose. One other striking difference is that nearly all the planetary rulers are different in Bailey's esoteric system, and especially so in Esoteric Astrology. To understand why this is so, you would have to study the subject!

There are no doubt more types of astrology than those mentioned here; it is an extraordinarily wide-ranging subject and continues to expand.

Other heavenly bodies

Likewise, our knowledge of the universe carries on growing, as other bodies in space have also been discovered in recent times. Although discovered relatively recently, the aforementioned Chiron, with its irregular 50-year orbit, is now fairly well established in the work of many modern astrologers (though not all).

It seems that an increasing number of other bodies in space have been identified in the last few years, all of which are developing interpretive meanings by those astrologers who are busy studying them. For example, Eris, Sedna, Makemake and Haumea are newly designated 'dwarf planets' of our solar system, discovered in the early twenty-first century, whose meanings are being established; plus there are quite a few asteroids that are now meaningful for some astrologers. Others continue to be found in the Kuiper Belt, a region of the solar system beyond our existing eight planets. There are also various extra points on the chart or bodies in space that are considered significant by some, such as the Vertex or Black Moon Lilith; and let us not forget those astrologers who interpret other bodies in space, such as the Fixed Stars.

Asteroids

Some 400,000 asteroids and other bodies circulate in the asteroid belt between Mars and Jupiter. It is thought that these orbiting pieces of rocks and fragments were possibly once a planet that was destroyed for an unknown reason. Fortunately for the room available in a drawn birth chart, such vast numbers of space bodies have not yet made it to the scrutiny of the astrologers. The four most significant asteroids, astrologically speaking, are named Ceres, Pallas, Juno and Vesta after mythological goddesses, and were discovered at the beginning of the nineteenth century by different people within 7 years of each other. Today, they are being used by an increasing number of astrologers. In the interests of keeping the illustrations of various charts throughout this book relatively simple, I have used only the standard modern astrologer's planets in those charts, from the Sun to Pluto and Chiron.

For your interest, here follows a brief delineation of the meanings of these asteroids, as defined by the discovery charts that were drawn up using the dates on which they were discovered, and the legends of classical mythology.

Ceres ⚳

Discovered 1801

The symbol for Ceres represents a scythe with a handle. Ceres is the Roman name for Demeter, the classical Greek goddess of nature and nurture. Her daughter Persephone (also known as Kore or Proserpina in Roman mythology) was kidnapped by the god of the underworld, Pluto. During Persephone's absence from the upper world, Ceres stopped caring for the living Earth, which marked the onset of winter. The Earth was only restored to life with the return of Persephone from the underworld in the spring.

Associated with mothering, nurturing, and childbirth, as well as your relationship with the land, the crops and the cycles of nature, the position of Ceres in your chart shows your way of providing nurturing, including self-nurturing, and how you need to be loved. Also your sense of connection with the natural world, and with children. Ceres is associated with the classic 'Mother' aspect of femininity.

Pallas ⚴

Discovered 1802

The asteroid Pallas is named for the beautiful Pallas Athena, the powerful warrior queen and ancient Greek goddess of wisdom. This goddess embodies the Maiden of femininity, but also courage and skill in warfare. Her preference is to use strategic mediation if possible to avoid confrontation and violence, but if she is required to fight she will do so. Her symbol represents her spear.

In a chart, Pallas represents ways in which you plan and organise in order to arrive at solutions, and the ways you use your intellect to bring differing factors together, and create balance or unity. Intelligence is a quality that is said to be difficult to judge in planetary astrology. Mercury is the planet, of course, that describes the way your mind works and how you tend to communicate, but even its aspects and chart position do not represent how intelligent a person is. As there are so many different types of intelligence, this is not surprising.

Juno ✳

Discovered 1804

Juno was the goddess wife of Jupiter, king of the gods. In myth, she has similarities to Hera, wife of the original Greek king of Olympus, Zeus. She was staunchly loyal to her husband, although he was unfaithful many times. Juno's symbol is the sceptre of a ruler, and the star shows greatness.

The asteroid Juno is about relationships, mainly romantic ones, although any significant relationship in your life can be represented by Juno. Where this asteroid falls in your chart indicates the types of relationships you attract to yourself, or desire to have, and is said to show qualities of your marriage partner. Juno can be about soulmates, but can equally represent business connections, even political ones. For mundane astrologers, Juno is an important placement in the chart of a country or a ruler, as its position in such a chart may provide information about that country's relations with other countries.

Vesta ⚶

Discovered 1807

The symbol for Vesta represents a fire on an altar or in the hearth. Vesta is the virgin goddess of the Vestal Virgins, sister to Jupiter, and Keeper of the Sacred Flame. The fire tended by the Vestal Virgins on Olympus was never allowed to go out. Similarly, a temple was built in ancient Rome to house the earthly version of the eternal Sacred Flame and it was thought that a catastrophe would befall the city if it was allowed to go out. The flame represented Truth and Purity of the soul, burning like the flame within each person to show the way to enlightenment. As their name implies, the Vestal Virgins were completely celibate, and were trusted to tell the truth.

In your chart, Vesta represents your capacity to focus, and to be totally committed to your purpose, whatever that is, when necessary, indicating a quality of inner strength and purity that uplifts you.

To find the position of these asteroids in your chart . . .
Like all the planets, the asteroids orbit the Sun, of course. Therefore each of them has a cycle that can be followed in relation to your chart, or whoever's chart you are looking at. The transits of the asteroids can now be found on page 37 of Raphael's Ephemeris, and there are asteroid ephemerides available now too.

HOW MUCH MORE IS THERE TO KNOW?

The short answer is that it never stops. Like any subject on this Earth that has depth and meaningfulness, astrology is complex. In the field of medicine, for example, the human body seems to get even more intricate the more we discover about it. However, this does not mean that each part of astrology is complex in itself necessarily, but that there are always choices to be made about how far to go when working with various branches of astrology. I chose not to study Vedic astrology in any depth, for instance, but Western astrology instead, yet that is not to say that I will not consider learning a new astrological technique in my life. It is always possible at any time to take up a new branch.

If you are thinking about chucking the book away as too compli-cated at this stage, please don't do that yet! The next chapter is going to show you how to pull it all together – learning how to select and choose what is important and what is less so, so that you can gain a more comprehensive view – and gives suggestions about structuring what you are studying. In particular, you will discover the benefits of 'weight-ing' the information gleaned from the main forecasting methods in order to get a clear picture of what the future holds and how to make the best use of it.

16.
ELAINA AND LEON – READING THE CHARTS

What you really can't miss: the importance of weighting

You will find Leon and Elaina's natal charts on pages x to xi at the start of this book. Hopefully you have been able to print the charts out so that you have them to hand while reading. In this chapter, I am going to share my chart notes for them so that you can work with these and an ephemeris, if you wish to put the principles of forecasting into practice.

These chart notes do not form fully comprehensive chart analyses, as you will see. The notes and their identification of the main themes are simply given to provide a basis for looking at both Elaina's and Leon's forecasting for the next year or so, as this relates to their charts. In Appendix 1, the list of planetary combinations will give you a foundation for interpreting the aspects if you need a reminder. Let me encourage you to try initially to put each combination of aspects together using keywords, and then phrases, for yourself, before you consult the Appendix. It's all good practice! Take some time to make the mental connections as well as 'getting a feel' for each chart. The signs and houses where the natal planets fall, especially the luminaries and the inner and social planets, are of course also significant, as well as the house rulers. Again, use the keywords approach as above to arrive at the principles of interpretation. As a reminder, Appendix

1 contains key phrases for the aspects, but not for the planets in signs and houses. There are a number of suggested books on the Further Reading list that will help you with planets in signs and houses and with rulerships – once you have had a try for yourself at interpreting parts of the two study charts that are not included, as a basis for your own chart interpretations. Try doing an analysis of your own, or a friend's or relative's chart, using the same basic approach.

STARTING WITH THE CHART

I am starting with writing a short version of both the study charts, as I have mentioned here and there throughout this book, because this is the basis for forecasting. What you are ultimately looking to identify in gathering the information and collating it are the chart's **themes** – the main characteristics of the person, as defined by his or her astrological chart. This will then form a foundation for your predictive work.

A good place to start is by just looking at the chart in question to get an overview assessment – what stands out about the chart, what strikes you initially? Do you have a personal reaction? Is there anything on a new chart that reminds you of your own chart? There have been a number of mentions of these two charts for one reason or another in earlier sections, so you may already be reasonably familiar with them.

Just looking when approaching other charts is useful for this initial exercise in analysis. You might notice an empty, or a loaded, hemisphere or house or sign emphasis; a stellium; an aspect pattern that dominates; or any other prominent feature – even if it is a lack of any apparently unusual quality and may be simply a balanced distribution of planets. Even if the chart seems complex, remember that charts do vary a great deal in their appearance. The reality is that people are complicated beings no matter how straightforward or otherwise a person's chart may be, and approaching the chart step by step will simplify it. So don't be daunted by an unfamiliar chart! Below follows a list of suggested steps to take. If you cover these categories, and make some notes, you will have the basis of the chart:

- Assess the balance by counting *all* the planets in the hemispheres and quadrants, including Chiron, but not any other bodies than planets.
- Do the same with the elements and modes – but remember to count only the planets from Sun to Saturn, plus the Ascendant and the MC. That is, not the outer planets or Chiron, or anything that is not a planet, except the two main angles. So not the Nodes either. Because they are generational, or not planets, these bodies stay in one sign for too long to be individual.
- Moon's phase.
- Ascendant sign and the chart-ruling planet, its position on the chart.
- Sun, Moon and MC: their signs, houses and rulers' positions. Note the major aspects too.
- Mutual reception, and any stelliums.
- Moon's Nodes – signs and houses.
- Major close aspects (up to 2 to 3 degrees).
- Aspect patterns.

Once you are armed with this considerable amount of information, some of the chart's themes may already be apparent. Now you can explore any aspects or planetary placements in a bit more depth, giving deeper thought to these, or consulting what many astrologers refer to as 'cook books' – astrological interpretation books that give meanings for aspects, or houses, or whatever areas you need. It's always good to read widely when you are learning astrology, and the Further Reading list contains a number of suggestions for books to help you. The internet is always at your fingertips of course, but having the information you need in one volume that you can easily refer to instead of surfing the web clearly has its values.

Both Elaina and Leon's charts, which have been used here as illustrations for how to get going when assessing what to use, what to leave out, and why, are explored in more detail in this chapter. In putting a chart interpretation together, some of the basic points for doing this are echoed in putting the forecasting together for a coming year. (The same procedure applies if you are looking at a past year.) Have a look back at the notable points and themes for both of the case-study charts before you begin, so that you refresh your thinking and can see more easily how the coming years fit in to the natal themes. It may take a little time at the beginning, but it is worth it. Don't forget you can start just with transits if you wish, and add other methods once you become more comfortable with this.

When you feel you could have a go at looking at the chart and forecasting for someone else – your 'client' – unless he or she has some knowledge of astrology already, I suggest you try not to pepper your explanations with complicated astrological references. It is very usually the case that what your client will want to know is *what it all means* rather than specifics such as 'you have Saturn aspecting your Moon, which means you might have some problems with your mother'. This brings me to the language you use, and how you deliver it. Even if a person has what you consider to be a 'difficult' transit or solar arc starting soon, be aware of the potential effect that this news may have on the person. A person's relationship with a parent or a partner can be tricky ground to step on, for instance. So without ignoring a tough-looking transit or progression, where possible, be diplomatic or careful when broaching the subject. Perhaps ask the person if it's all right to discuss whatever it is. Imagine you are sitting in their place, listening to being told you have difficulties with whoever. Having said this, some people will tell you they prefer to hear the truth, or are not so sensitive. Let the chart be your guide.

Finding the chart themes

Essentially what you want to find are repeating or connected factors, as well as fairly obvious 'striking qualities', such as the Scorpio/Libra theme in Elaina's chart, below. As a further example, the chart of Mick Jagger, the Rolling Stones lead singer, is very obviously Leo-dominant, with no less than 5 planets in Leo, one of which is the Sun, plus the North Node (26 July 1943, 02:30, Dartford, England). This is one very clear theme – being in the limelight and on the stage are intrinsic to Jagger.

Looking for repeating factors is about seeing where signs and houses correlate, or if there are any aspects that resonate with an emerging theme, including in some cases further echoes in minor aspects. So if, for instance, a chart has a Cancer Sun that is prominently placed rising on the Ascendant, then one linked

theme would be to look at the chart ruler Moon and its position, to
see if there is back-up there for a theme of caring, nurturing,
sensitivity and a tendency to moodiness. There may be other
factors to be considered that contribute to this theme, such as
maybe the sign on the IC, and the 4th house.

NOTES FOR ELAINA'S NATAL CHART

Hemispheres and quadrants

- *Southern hemisphere dominates*: all planets above horizon
  and no planets in northern hemisphere, i.e. below the
  horizon, represented by the Ascendant–Descendant axis.
  Elaina's direction in life, her career, and her reputation are
  of great importance to her. The southern hemisphere
  influence suggests a tendency to move straight on to the
  next thing in a busy life, not always giving herself a chance
  to reflect on and absorb what she has just experienced.
- *Most planets in west*: opportunities and new possibilities
  often come to Elaina through her interaction with others,
  more than entirely through her own efforts.
- *Quadrant 3/houses 7 and 8*: emphasis on the influence of
  her relationships of all kinds. Romantic relationships and
  close friendships are where much of her learning and
  development of self-understanding comes from. Studying
  and travelling (this quadrant incorporates the 9th house
  too) will be equally important to her growth and enjoyment
  as a person.

Elements and Modes

There are different systems for choosing how to assign points for the occurrence of each planet or angle. For simplicity, it is suggested that you count one point for each one, which adds up to 9 points.

Using this system, Elaina's chart balance is:

	FIRE	EARTH	AIR	WATER
CARDINAL	Ascendant	MC	Moon Mercury	
FIXED				Sun Venus
MUTABLE	Mars Jupiter			Saturn

- *Cardinal–Mutable:* both strong modes. Both angles in cardinal (Aries and Capricorn) plus two planets makes cardinal dominant, but mutable has three planets in it (Mars, Jupiter, Saturn) – count both. Elaina can get projects going, and potentially has leadership qualities (cardinal). Can adapt her attitudes or ideas where necessary (mutable). Two planets in fixed, Sun and Venus in Scorpio, ability to see things through if that is appropriate.
- *Fire–Water:* sensitive and easily moved. Often functions on emotion and intuition. Quite often remarkably accurate if she has a 'feeling' about a situation. The air planets are noticeable too, meaning the need for mental challenge. Fire–water can be an explosive and dramatic combination

(from time to time), but Scorpio and the 8th house will mostly incline her to contain her emotions internally.

- *Earth* is a missing element, only MC in Capricorn and no earth planets. Making practical decisions may be hard (Libra and 7th). Keeping her feet firmly on the ground is not easy for Elaina. Saturn is in Pisces retrograde and 12th, so not very grounded either. She may also tend to under- or over-assess her capacity for taking on activities, or how long an activity will take.

Angles and luminaries

- *Aries Ascendant:* chart ruler is Mars in Sagittarius conjunct Pluto Scorpio 8th house.
- *Sun Scorpio, 7th house:* Ruler is also Mars Sagittarius conjunct Pluto Scorpio 8th.
- *Dissociate Sun aspect with Moon Libra 7th house:* Moon ruler Venus Scorpio 8th.
- *MC Capricorn, on the cusp 9/10th houses:* MC ruler Saturn Pisces retrograde 12th.

The fiery nature of Aries on the Ascendant, with ruler Mars, as the first impression one encounters, shows enthusiasm and keenness to rush forward and maintain a positive independence, as well as a tendency to be rather impulsive and impatient, and quite speedy.

The singleton earth MC in Capricorn, plus all planets in the top half of the chart, describes Elaina's desire to do well in life and to build in an organised way towards tangible achievements, although the shortage of earth may cause some stumbling blocks.

And Sun conjunct Moon is in a quiet Balsamic chart, each in a different sign. Sun in Scorpio, with its emotional intensity, fierce loyalty and passionate approach to life; Moon in Libra with its cooler caring, search for balance and equality, sense of justice and aesthetics; both planets in the 7th house. Relationships are key, as part of a theme that was mentioned earlier, in Elaina's life. The Sun–Moon conjunction shows a focus on the house where it falls, and a singleness of purpose, with a strong sense of self. A certain confusion as Elaina attempts to reconcile her strong emotional reactions (Scorpio) with her more rational responses (Libra) to situations, especially with people with whom she is in some kind of relationship – with friends as well as lovers.

The Sun–Moon conjunction is actually a close triple conjunction with the North Node in Libra in the 7th house – a further emphasis on learning about herself through relating to important others – Aries in 7th and Libra in 1st houses, as well as experiencing love and happiness through some of those others. The 8th house emphasis adds depth and intensity to the mix in the field of relationships.

Aspects and patterns

There are no chart patterns, as I don't count aspects between the Ascendant and MC, or where one of the pattern points is the North or South Node alone, even if the other end of the axis is conjunct a planet. But the chart is very tightly put together and most planets are in the top right-hand corner, in the 'self-expansion' section (quadrant 3), which shows a capacity to focus strongly on one thing or idea, being an intense configuration. With no planets in the lower half of the chart, she needs space and time to process her feelings (and her Balsamic Moon needs that). Her chart is more geared towards her career and learning, her direction in life, and finding the right path.

The most important aspects are usually the tightest ones, plus the ones that grab your attention. The ones in bold in this list are the aspects you really can't miss out in your assessment of the main points:

- **Sun conjunct Moon conjunct North Node, opposite South Node**
- **Sun semi-square Jupiter**
- **Mercury sextile Jupiter**
- **Venus trine Saturn**
- **Mars conjunct Pluto**
- Jupiter square Saturn
- Uranus conjunct Neptune square Sun–Moon–Nodal axis
- **Chiron square MC**
- **(Mercury on Descendant widely conjunct Chiron)**

As you see, I have not analysed each factor mentioned as we are doing this primarily as a preparation for looking at Elaina's forecasting for the near future. You just need to get to know the chart so you can see how some of her forecasting will particularly impact on her.

I have given you a brief idea of the themes of her chart, however, to help you! This is to show you ways to put the different factors together to strengthen points that are made. The core points to remember are – you are looking for repeating factors, where there are preferably at least two or three repeats of a similar theme where the various factors seem to belong together. This is not always so obvious as the 'Scorpio–Libra' theme illustrated below.

In the next section, I have listed the 'astrological significators' to show that I was looking for the astrological emphases before I put each point together with others. You'll see that I have listed more than one significator from which to draw my interpretation, which is part of **weighting** – see if you can see the connections. My intention is not to draw rounded conclusions about either Elaina's or Leon's chart, but just to give you a start.

An example: the 'Scorpio' theme and the 'Libra' theme (3 planets in each sign)

Taking two obvious areas of her chart, start with a significant factor and look for any links. If in doubt as to where to start, the Sun is always a good place. Elaina's Sun is in Scorpio plus there are two other planets in Scorpio; other connections are: the occupied 8th house; Mars conjunct Pluto; Mars and Pluto rule the Scorpio planets, so rule the Sun; and Mars is the chart ruler of the Aries Ascendant.

Her Moon is in Libra, and so are Mercury and Chiron, plus the North Node, most of which, along with her Sun, are in Libra's natural house – 7th. The ruler here is Venus, which is in Scorpio and the 8th house. Looping back to the 'Scorpio' theme.

Some themes and chart significators for Elaina

Themes need to be to the point. Try to summarise and to identify no more than six themes. If you find you have acquired more than this, go through them and try to combine them if you viably can. If you find this hard, then stay with more themes – the ability to reduce it to five or six will come with practice.

- Caring and nurturing. Sensitive to other people, awareness of another's point of view. Respectful. Wants to understand self. Greatest area of learning: through in depth relationships.

Scorpio and Pluto strong, Jupiter trine Ascendant, Venus trine Saturn,
Sun and Venus Scorpio 8th house, Moon Libra conjunct North Node 7th, opposite South Node Aries 1st.

- Deep feelings, sometimes overwhelming, intense and can be passionate. Hidden power, self-contained. Needs personal space, a bit of a loner. An independent dreamer (Uranus–Neptune). Highly imaginative inventive mind, wants to contribute to improving the world.
  Balsamic Moon, Saturn Pisces 12th, Scorpio planets/ 8th house/Plutonic theme, Sun conjunct Moon square Uranus–Neptune, Mercury sextile Jupiter, Venus trine Saturn, Aquarius cusp 11th house.

- Impatient, wants to get on with whatever the activity is, and do it well. Quietly ambitious. Few friends, but loyal and fair.
  Aries rising, MC Capricorn, Jupiter Sagittarius 9th, Balsamic Moon, Mercury conjunct Descendant and Chiron.

- Takes on too much, can be demanding, unrealistic, can be quite forceful.
  Sun semi-square Jupiter, Mars conjunct Pluto, no earth planets.

- Self-contained mind, tendency to be own harsh critic, especially re mental ability.
  Mercury conjunct Chiron on Descendant, Mercury semi-square Pluto, Balsamic Moon.

NOTES FOR LEON'S NATAL CHART

Hemispheres and quadrants

- *Southern hemisphere:* most planets above horizon but Moon and South node below add more reflectiveness. Shows that Leon's direction in life, what he is studying and learning are a major concern to him. Much of this gaining of knowledge involves deep inner exploration as well as travelling. (Very occupied 8th house.) The planets below the horizon in the northern hemisphere suggest a capacity for self-reflection in the midst of busy times.

- *Most planets west, 3rd quadrant:* support from friends. Others bring him opportunities. Wants to develop self, expand knowledge; growth through this.

- *Quadrant 3: 8th house Capricorn stellium, strong.* Prefers structure to vagueness, wants success. Practical and grounded. Willing to work to achieve an end. Few close friends, usually of long duration. Self-sufficient and self-contained. Intense and private. Fascinated from an early age with mysteries and hidden truths.

Elements and Modes

- *Cardinal–Fixed:* initiator, loyal, dependable, can be stubborn and determined.

- *Mars Scorpio (fixed) on Descendant:* steadfast in friendship or commitment. Strong opinions, fights for rights and justice. Has a temper, not good if he loses control, but does not often happen. Lacks mutable, not always adaptable

- *Capricorn* strongest (3 planets) + *Taurus Ascendant:* Serious, dedicated, pursues path with intent, conventional in some ways, values money mostly for the freedom it gives him, generally organised. Grounded, practical and forward planner.

FIRE	FIRE	EARTH	AIR	WATER
CARDINAL	Jupiter	Sun Mercury	MC	Moon
FIXED		Ascendant	Venus	Mars
MUTABLE	Saturn			

Angles and luminaries

- *Taurus Ascendant:* see above. Chart ruler is Venus in Aquarius 9th house, conjunct MC Aquarius. Very fair-minded, a believer in equality. Friendly and easy to get along with. Strong sense of aesthetic appreciation. Independent, does 'his own thing.' Politically aware and concerned about environmental and social issues, values humanity in general, cares about others and the state of the world.
- *Sun Capricorn* in the centre of conjunct Neptune and conjunct Mercury, all in Capricorn 8th house. Ruler Saturn conjunct Uranus Sagittarius 8th. Deep thinker, wants to explore depths of self and his personal growth. Leadership potential for changing others' attitudes. Reliable, wants to explore below surface.

- *Moon Cancer 2nd house opposition Sun. Full Moon phase. T-square with Jupiter apex Aries 11th house.* Exploration of ideas, philosophies, attitudes, spirituality, religions. "Split', two different sides to personality, can be indecisive yet sensitive to others. Deep feelings contained, but easily moved. Most important purpose while young – searching for meaning in his life, a traveller. Caring communicator, background and family influential.

Strongest aspects (3° or less) plus aspect patterns

- **Sun opposite Moon** (full Moon!)
- **Sun sextile Pluto**
- Moon quincunx Venus
- **Mercury square Jupiter**
- Mercury trine Ascendant
- Mars trine North Node
- Jupiter sextile MC
- **Saturn conjunct Uranus square Nodes**
- Chiron square Nodes
- Neptune sesquiquadrate Ascendant (exact)

Aspect pattern:

Cardinal T-square: Jupiter (apex) square Moon and Sun – Mercury

You will find an interpretation for the Full Moon phase earlier in this book and help with the other aspects in Appendix 1. To give you a couple of hints:

- **Sun sextile Pluto** suggests always seeking to deepen his understanding, to look below the surface and uncover what is hidden.

- **Mercury square Jupiter** suggests wide interests, curious, reaching for more knowledge, enthusiastic explorer.

Other important factors

- Generational *Uranus opposite Chiron involves Saturn – 2nd–8th square Nodes Pisces–Virgo + Sun opposition Moon:* reformer, feels the pull of both respecting tradition, and forging new ways. Sometimes embraces change, perceiving a better way, other times experiences the wisdom of past systems. Painful struggle at times.
- *Nodes: Pisces–Virgo, North–South, 11th–5th.* Needs to express own creative talent, and not get lost in ideals or collective contributions. Drawn to develop musical interest and abilities.

Some themes and chart significators for Leon

- Spiritual seeker, traveller. Wide-ranging mind, world traveller, has big plans and confidence, mental philosopher, broad interests, enthusiastic and inspiring for some.
  Practical and grounded. Willing to work to achieve an end. Sees both sides, at times torn between them. Intuitive. Business-minded, prefers order to chaos or disorganisation. Investigator, psychologist in approach, ferrets out secrets intuitively, and can put insights to practical use.
  Capricorn/8th Mercury, Neptune opposition Moon Cancer 2nd, Capricorn 8th Sagittarius cusp 8th, Full

Moon. Cardinal Jupiter 11th apex T-square Neptune Sun Mercury.

- Strong opinions, fights for rights and justice. Very fair-minded, a believer in equality and humanity. Functions well in group settings.
  Mars, Venus angular. Venus chart ruler Aquarius conjunct MC, Mars conjunct Descendant. North Node Pisces 11th/South Node Virgo 5th.

- Caring, compassionate, sensitive, family has been influential. Sensitive to others but very self-contained, can be a loner.
  Moon strong in own sign Cancer. 8th house full. Mars Scorpio. Sun conjunct Neptune opposition Moon.

- Looks at life in depth, always interested in what is below the surface. Deep thinker, questions a lot.
  Pluto strong – sextile Sun, trine Moon, square Venus–MC, closely aspected to Nodes (exact).

- Is sometimes emotionally needy, torn between needs and desires, or feels illogically guilty, even about his intelligence, yet rejoices in his mental ability.
  There may be an issue from his earlier life to do with his relationship with his mother or another female relative that could be repeated.
  Jupiter emphasis, strongest aspect is square Mercury (exact).
  Moon quincunx Venus–MC, Full Moon.

TIPS AND HINTS FOR PUTTING FORECASTING TOGETHER

I have designed a simple 1-year Forecasting Table on which to enter all three systems' activities per month: transits, progressions, solar arc directions. You will find a copy of this in Appendix 2. If you fill it in, you may find that there will probably be some months when nothing is exact, in which case you could just leave it blank. (I have not included the solar return chart in the Table, so you will need to make a separate, short list of what strikes you about the SR chart.)

I complete the Table by hand myself, but it can be completed on screen if you have astrological symbols on your computer. However, you need to be comfortable with astrological symbols in order to make writing out the planetary and sign glyphs easier in longhand! A suggested way to approach assessing transits etc. is to list these first before you write them in, marking what you consider the most important ones to interpret, and setting less important ones aside. (But keep a note of them, as questions pertaining to some of them may arise if you are doing a 'live' chart for a person.)

Knowing that you have potentially four methods of forecasting to combine, the 'normal' advice remains – keep it simple! If in doubt about whether or not to include some listing and there is already masses of material, put those uncertainties to one side and revisit them later. The fact that you doubted whether to include something or not, may help, or may be important. Think about whether the interpretation overall may seem incomplete or not if you decide not to include something. Are there any other factors in one system or another that basically echo what you have included, and could be left out? (Or you may feel that such an 'echo' acts as a back up.)

What lies ahead for Leon and Elaina – and what you really can't miss out!

These brief descriptions and main meanings overall for both of my 'case study' birth charts will now be followed by an assessment of both Elaina's and Leon's forecasting, picking out the main points for 2019–2020. I will begin by simply listing the techniques, and looking at what kind of period each is experiencing, picking out the most important. I will also prioritise and show you on what basis I do this, to help you to do the same. Obviously, the amount of different parts to this can seem quite complicated, so below are your criteria. When you are more familiar with doing this, please feel free to change priorities if that feels better. I am giving you the 'natural order' of transits. I suggest you list them in short abbreviations, and then prioritise; otherwise you may miss something of importance. There may only be one or two major – and noticeable – transits in a year. Look first for those that repeat two or three times. It is easier to put your forecasting together if you keep it simple – just notes on the essence of the meaning of each one are usually enough. Short 'one-offs' of T planets, such as Saturn or Jupiter, especially those that zip past your chart in a couple of weeks or so, are mostly not major. T Jupiter usually has a number of these short transits in most years. When the outer planets are active with longer-term transiting aspects to natal planets, then the shorter Jupiter transits mostly do not need to be taken into account, but do make a note of which part of the chart is being activated by Jupiter – which house(s) it is in.

Look for, I suggest, in this order:

Transits – Pluto, Neptune, Uranus, Saturn, Jupiter, Chiron and the Nodal axis. Any returns or half returns of these planets, e.g. Uranus, Saturn,

Jupiter. There will not be significant transits from all of these planets every year, so pick out the longest, and the most prominent. It's worth bearing in mind that an individual may resonate more sensitively to a transit of a planet that is prominent on their chart.

Secondary progressions – Sun, Moon, Mercury, Venus, Mars and angles. P Moon – just pick out the months when a progression seems relevant with a feature of the chart, or perhaps if you perceive a related transit. Changes of sign or house are important, especially for the p Moon, so do look at those. Don't try to discuss every passing Moon progression! You will need to decide whether you use only major aspects, or include the minors (which ones?) In this study I have used only major aspects for progressions and solar arcs, as you can see below, but that is mostly for the sake of brevity here.

Solar arc directions – major aspects only. Do any SAs resonate with a part of the natal chart? Any change of sign or house.

Solar Return – don't forget to shorten the orbs you are using for this chart if you are generating it yourself rather than copying it from an astrological website – but check that out too by looking carefully at what orbs have been used and discount wide orbs. Look at:

- the house position and aspects of Sun
- Ascendant sign and chart ruler
- hemisphere/quadrant or house emphasis
- Moon sign, house, ruler
- MC house, sign, ruler, if using Equal Houses
- element/mode listing and differences from natal chart

- any other things that strike you, e.g. aspect patterns
- Just make brief notes on what you consider important, otherwise you'll have too much information

Where to start in forecasting

This is a very individual decision. If you go back in your memory over the four main methods for astrological forecasting as described in the preceding chapters, you now have the basics of all of them. Knowing how to combine them, how to assess their relevant importance, indeed which ones to focus on, and which ones you can safely leave out, or even abandon altogether, is a skill that can be learnt with practice and the gaining of experience. It is at this stage that you may experience overload, and feel like giving up on this seemingly daunting task of not missing something really important, yet without focusing too much on those transits, progressions or directions that are of minor consequence. I would tend to start with the major transits (which you have previously listed) as the person is likely to recognise what you are saying. How to get the balance right and 'weight' the forecasting for a person is the true heart of this chapter.

FORECASTING FOR ELAINA 2019–2020

Transits

I have highlighted the most important transits. There are quite a few in 2019, so discrimination is needed. There are even more transits in 2020. (The forecasting for the following year will be updated on my website, for a little while: www.suemerlyn.com.) I have listed them simply as astrological significators so that you can easily see which ones I consider most important.

Elaina's main transits for 2019, with some continuing until 2020, are below, with the ones that should not be missed in bold type. These were obtained from my astrology software program, Solar Fire. (See Useful Addresses for information on astrology software etc.) I have given a brief interpretation for some of them to start you off. Try using keywords to build understanding in the same kind of process you went through with natal aspects, before you turn to interpretation books or online services. If you can arrive at a base idea as to the meaning you will be building your astrological intelligence.

Note the 'generational' type of transit which many born in the mid-1990s will experience – **Pluto conjunct Neptune**; and the long-running **Neptune conjunct Saturn** as well as more personal transits. It's worth mentioning these, as they describe background changes that are often best seen in retrospect. The repeating months of exactness, which are the months given, are of course due to retrogradation, when the transiting planet aspects the same natal point once, then for a second time usually when retrograde, and then goes direct and crosses back again. Remember that not all events occur like clockwork in the months of exactness, but the background influence is there throughout the transit/progression/solar arc. When looking up transiting months, I always count 1 degree before and after the exact degree. Computer programs are literal. If an aspect between a transiting planet and a natal planet is not pedantically absolutely exact, the computer will not iden-tify it. So sometimes perfectly valid transits are missed in software programs, which is why I quickly check my ephemeris manually, just in case.

Pluto conjunct Neptune – March, June, December 2019, January, August, November 2020

Neptune trine Venus – March/April, September/October 2019, January 2020

Neptune conjunct Saturn – June/July 2019, March, October 2020, January 2021

Uranus trine MC – June, October, March/April 2020

Saturn sextile Venus – February, June, November/December 2019

Saturn sextile Saturn – as above (because natal Venus and natal Saturn are a trine apart, T Saturn picks up her natal Saturn trine Venus)

Jupiter conjunct Jupiter – January 2019, July to early September 2019

Jupiter square Saturn – February, June, September 2019

Jupiter conjunct MC – December 2019

Interpretations

Pluto conjunct Neptune

Pluto = profound change, researching below the surface, pushing for depth understanding.

Neptune = spiritual insight, imagination or fantasy, sense of oneness with the world, universal connection, confusion.

A period where she is gaining a broader perspective on life, deepening her perspectives. Stimulated imagination opens up her thinking, and she may experience a profound sense of connection with others or with one other. She is likely to question previous beliefs about life/the world/what truth is for her. This seems to be happening also to many in her generation.

Neptune conjunct Saturn

Neptune = as above, plus creative inspiration that 'thinks outside the box'.

Saturn = grounded in practicality, the need for security, fear of loss of control, attachment to structure.

Where Saturn tests reality, and looks for the safety of clear boundaries, Neptune embraces the freedom of allowing all possibilities, and trusts life to bring what is needed.

This transit is about the effort to reconcile these opposing points of view, but can be experienced at least initially as feeling lost, or uncertain about what 'reality' means. During this period, Elaina may put an ideal into practice, or find a practical way to turn her imaginative ideas into actuality, which may help her with any sense of disorientation that Neptune may bring.

Neptune trine Venus and Saturn sextile Venus

Venus = love, affection and relationships, values and self-value, creative and aesthetic appreciation.

The combination of Neptune and Saturn with Venus in flowing aspect in a similar time period provokes feelings of love and affection towards close others or the building of this, perhaps with new people; appreciating that which is perceived as beautiful; an increased inclination to deal practically with financial affairs; and possibly developing her creative self. It is possible that a new romantic affair may begin, or an existing relationship may be treated with more compassion.

Uranus trine MC

Uranus = awakening a different vision, rebelling against the status quo, having radical futuristic ideas.

MC = future career path, public reputation, life direction, parental influence.

This is not a complicated transit to put together . . . it suggests that one of the above areas given under MC will be stimulated, and because the transit is to a chart where career options are of importance, the likelihood is that unusual or radical ways to approach career direction or maybe some breakthrough ideas will bring positive changes (changing job or similar). The transit occurs first during the period of Elaina's final exams at university, and with her hopes for employment at the museum she is working at part time, pre-exam period, it suggests a positive change of direction. This transit recurred later in 2019 and into 2020.

See what you can make of the other transits, in bold type One more transit worth mentioning in passing: Elaina's second **Jupiter return 2019**, when she is in her 24th year (before her birthday). I suggest you refer back to Chapter 7 to check out the meaning of this, and adapt it to her natal Jupiter sign and house.

Progressions and Solar Arc directions: Elaina 2019

The secrets to guarding against overload are: be discriminating, use only major aspects and, if necessary, use only the conjunction and the hard aspects if there are many, and use only progressed to natal.

As a matter of course I would tend to normally include any major aspect p Sun progressions in a year, as they don't occur that often, plus anything that strikes you as important amongst any other inner planets or a progressed angle this year. As with transits, the lists are simply for your information, and are not totally comprehensive. They are just to show you how much is going on in an average year – and to give an idea of which ones seems important and are likely to be experienced. They are shown in **bold type**.

A shortlist:

P Sun sextile p Neptune – January
P Mars conjunct p Jupiter – January

Lasting in effect from late autumn 2018 until approximately spring 2019. These two progressions coincided with a particularly busy period for Elaina, not only studying hard but also setting up an exhibition at a museum with her new boyfriend. This was the museum where she was part-time employed. Very enjoyable time with scope for creative ideas and expansion of her skills, although very tiring, perhaps not surprising because of her natal tendency to over-do things at times. Also coincided with her second Jupiter return – although inspiring probably made her feel encouraged to push herself to work too hard (Jupiter can exaggerate enthusiasm).

SA Chiron conjunct Sun – May 2019

As the influence of p Sun sextile p Neptune wanes, this direction involving the Sun manifests in more than one way – it may have acted as a healing energy, as a couple of months before it became exact, Elaina experienced a painful break-up with her boyfriend. So it could also represent that loss and the wound to her self-esteem. Chiron on her Sun was possibly reflecting the upset more in the final exam period, though there is always the possibility that Chiron may bring some inner peace and personal healing, as it moves towards exactness. Conjunct Sun may bring her to a stronger sense of herself and who she is.

SA Saturn opposition Mercury – June – July 2019

This one will have focused her thinking, and she may have experienced a time of putting in a lot of effort in order to achieve her goals. Anxiety about failing these goals suggests a determined effort to communicate in the way she wanted to. She may have had differences of opinion with someone else at some point during the period of validity, which was roughly from early summer to autumn.

MC change from Capricorn to Aquarius – August 2019

This will obviously re-orient Elaina's life path. It will probably be a process rather than a sudden shift, over a few months, as new ideas formulate in her mind. Her choices of career, at least for now, will need to give her the opportunity to make a tangible contribution to society, or to the world, in some way.

P lunation phase – Last Quarter, May 2018–March 2022

Suggests a background period of consolidating and potentially gaining recognition for her hard work, of pushing against the odds at times but achieving something lasting.

P Moon, being so fast-moving, always has a number of other progressed aspects to take into account. These can be of great rele-vance when you are looking through 1 year month by month, and should be taken into account. For the sake of brevity, I have focused only on changes to the signs or houses, but p Moon progressions that seem significant can be considered if the planets being progressed by the Moon are important on the birth chart. They need to be limited because there are too many to be properly considered – and some-times, Elaina will not particularly experience **every** p Moon aspect, as they are quite fleeting.

I have listed major progressed Moon aspects for 2019, although I have only written about one of them. I have noted the house change, plus one Moon progression. I could have chosen any of the p Moon progres-sions, but I picked out the one in bold below, for the reasons stated.

Shortlist p Moon progressions

P Moon 2019:

Square Mars – March 2019

Trine MC – May – June 2019
Change house 5 to 6 – August 2019

P Moon 2020:
Square Jupiter – February
Sextile Venus – May
Opposition Saturn – June
Trine Neptune – October

A useful progression to have at final exam time! Suggests, assuming background revision thorough, a feeling of confidence in herself and what she knows and can achieve.

P Moon enters 6th in Virgo – August 2019
The Moon will not change house again for another 2.5 years, in 2021, and will change from Virgo to Libra in 2021.
Meaning of this house change: whereas her focus during the Moon's sojourn in the 5th house has been on her social life, or on her various love affairs, amongst other experiences pertaining to the 5th house, the focus now becomes much more grounded and practical. Regular routines and habitual activities become more a part of how she chooses to organise her life, and instil a greater sense of security, which helps her to feel more settled. This may be to do with moving into the world of work more than study. Structuring her finances too gains more relevance for her. This placement is helpful for someone with no earth planets.

Her Moon makes no less than 12 progressed major aspects in 2020, so in order to distinguish a few, although they are all valid, I listed only progressed to natal.

Other major progressions and directions can usually be rounded up quite quickly, but you do need to be a little flexible with your choices:

SA Chiron conjunct Sun – May 2019

SA Saturn opposition Mercury – June – July 2019

P Mars sextile Moon – October 2019

SA MC sextile Pluto – December 2019

SA MC change signs Capricorn to Aquarius – August 2020

SA MC square Sun – August 2020

P Venus square p Saturn – October 2020

Elaina's Solar Return 2019 – valid October 2019– October 2020

Major points

- **Sun Scorpio 11** – sextile Moon, plus opposition Uranus – 'captured' from her recent transit, so remains with her throughout the 'lifetime' of the 2019 SR chart.
- **Ascendant Sagittarius, ruler Jupiter** Sagittarius 1st house.
- **Moon Leo 9, ruler Sun** Scorpio, SR Moon square Mercury plus Ascendant.
- **MC Virgo, ruler Mercury**. Many aspects to MC – sextile Venus (exact), square Jupiter, trine Saturn and Pluto, opposition Neptune. There is an emphasis on career/ direction.
- **Most planets east** (unlike natal), all inner personal planets above horizon in southern hemisphere (Sun, Moon, Mercury, Venus, Mars), six planets below horizon, four on western half of SR chart.

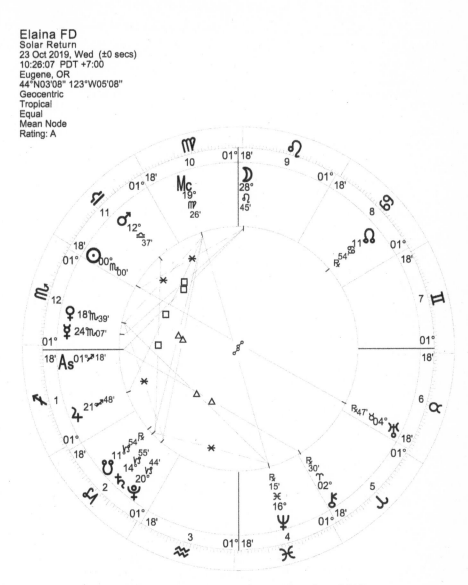

Elaina FD
Solar Return
23 Oct 2019, Wed (±0 secs)
10:26:07 PDT +7:00
Eugene, OR
44°N03'08" 123°W05'08"
Geocentric
Tropical
Equal
Mean Node
Rating: A

Elaina's Solar Return chart – October 2019

Inner Wheel
Elaina FD
Natal Chart
23 Oct 1995, Mon
17:38 EDT +4:00
Rockledge, Florida
28°N21'02" 080°W43'32"
Geocentric
Tropical
Equal
Mean Node

Outer Wheel
Elaina FD
Solar Return
23 Oct 2019, Wed (±0 secs)
10:26:07 PDT +7:00
Eugene, OR
44°N03'08" 123°W05'08"
Geocentric
Tropical
Equal
Mean Node

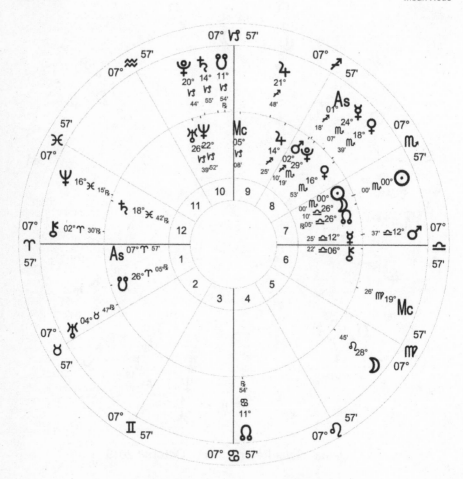

Bi-wheel for Elaina's natal and SR 2019

- **Emphasis 1st quadrant.** Self-development, finding her own way in the world (and eastern chart). Jupiter 1st house in own sign; Saturn, Pluto and South Node 2nd Capricorn. Personal values, and also financial concerns, of importance this year.

- **Emphasis 4th quadrant.** Self-transcendence, concerned with the wider world, with organisations and bodies, and environmental/humanitarian issues.

- **Fixed fire and water chart. Lacks air** (only Mars Libra). **Saturn MC in earth** (unlike natal which has virtually no earth).

- **Neptune angular, on IC in Pisces.** Inclined to need quiet space to gather her thoughts as she probably feels particularly sensitive to others or to the environment. Enhanced imagination or dream life.

- **No aspect patterns or entirely unaspected planets.**

- **Strongest aspects** – it is hard to pick these out as there are so many tight aspects on this SR chart. Possibly give emphasis to:

- **Sun sextile Moon**
  Sun opposition Uranus (because it is a repeated transit) – continuing strong need to express herself and communicate her opinions – and to act in independent ways.
  Minor Grand Trine – Venus Scorpio 12, Pluto, MC
  Mars square Saturn and square Nodal axis (exact)
  Neptune opposition MC (conjunct IC)

I suggest you try to use keywords for the remaining planets/angles, referring to the Planetary Combinations in Appendix 1 to help you!

Major connections between natal and SR October 2019 charts

- **Element/mode balance** across the two charts: SR 2019 has much more emphasis on Fixed than the natal chart, with four personal fixed planetary placements (Sun, Moon, Mercury, Venus). Enhances Elaina's staying power when she needs it.

- The SR 2019 Sun is virtually in the same place in the 7th house as on the natal chart when you put the two charts into a bi-wheel. A further focus on relationships and one-to-one friendships in Elaina's life.

- **SR Mars at 12 Libra conjuncts natal Mercury** exactly in house 7 on the Descendant. It seems as if the universe is putting a great emphasis on Elaina's ways of connecting with important others. But the planet that pushes this is Mars, which is triggered by the natal Ascendant.

- **SR Ascendant in Sagittarius conjuncts natal Mars–Pluto in the 8th house.** This connects some of the people in Elaina's life with powerful feelings. It is possible that she may know or meet someone who has strong feelings towards her, or for a particular issue, maybe leading to disagreements or needing to agree to differ.

- Other connections have already been mentioned or can be found, but those are the main ones. As I've said before, in the interests of not overloading yourself, just try not to miss the key connections or points, but keep it simple!!

Overall summary of interpretations for 2019–2020

The latter part of 2019 is a period when Elaina ceases to be a student (at least for now) and seeks work in the world. She graduates in the summer of 2019, and her avowed intent is to seek to stay in Eugene, Oregon for a while. She hopes to find employment at the museum where she has been working part-time, or a similar institution in the area. At the time of writing the results of her exams are not yet known, nor the type of employment she may find.

Overall, the year from birthday 2019 to birthday 2020 has several elements that could be said to indicate a good chance of finding suitable work. She has the repeat (because of retrogradation) of her 24th year second Jupiter return in Sagittarius in September, which usually brings good fortune – an optimum time for finding employment after a summer break perhaps. Also she has T Uranus trine her MC, which suggests her original approach to work may stand her in good stead in the coming period. A positive change of direction seems to be indicated.

Some of the pointers on her SR chart from late autumn 2019, plus her solar arc MC change from Capricorn to Aquarius, imply the kinds of opportunities that could come her way in terms of the type of work she wants – contributing to the betterment of society in some way.

With regard to the SR chart for the autumn of 2019, or a little before, the suggestion is clearly that although she will retain her need for independence she is likely to meet a new partner.

Elaina's biography

You may find it interesting to know a little more about Elaina, and see if you can tell how her chart indicates anything she has written about herself. The following brief biography is written in her own words.

'I was born in a small city on the eastern coast of Central Florida. My area was dominated by a surf/skate culture and it was a quintessential beach town. I was an only child raised by a single mother who was a teacher. My father remained distant throughout my childhood with my parents divorcing when I was 2 years old.

'I was a quiet child but I laughed a lot. I was incredibly well behaved because my mom was a hard disciplinarian. I was a little doll who did what I was told. I was introverted but able to socialise like an extrovert, but I didn't ever hang out with anyone outside of school because social situations exhausted me. I was always smiling but I think that was always just my default.

'I danced ballet from the age of four to seventeen. I also participated in figure skating and horseback riding, along with trying a long list of musical instruments. My mother was very active in the church, primarily the choir, which is where I spent much of my childhood. I attended a Lutheran elementary school, with an excellent art and music program, and a middle school focused on the arts and sciences. I quickly fell in love with botany and environmental science and achieved many accolades for my research until I switched my focus to the arts, in that my log books and the ways in which I documented my scientific research were more interesting than the research itself.

'I quickly adapted my focus to honing my artistic skills while also focusing on ways to combine art and science. This led me to study environmental science, sustainable architecture, interior design, and studio art before deciding upon the undergraduate major of art history. Still throughout my studies, my focus became art and nature.

'Now as a graduate student I have combined my interests into exhibition and museum work that acts as artistic commentary on current environmental conditions.'

FORECASTING FOR LEON 2019–2020

Transits

Once you have identified the basic themes of the birth chart and found a number of prominent planetary factors, these will help you to ascertain what is most important to consider when forecasting. For example, transits of any of Leon's natal planets are going to have an effect in his life, but he is likely to experience particularly powerful effects if the natal planets in question are prominent on his chart. In this respect, any T planets orbiting through the sign of Capricorn will conjunct each of his three natal planets in Capricorn in turn. Transits will also pick up close natal aspects to the other cardinal signs, Aries, Cancer or Libra (or other planets in degrees of other compatible signs), such as T Pluto squaring Jupiter at Aries 20° around the same time as it also conjuncts Mercury at Capricorn 20°. This highlights the exact natal square between Mercury and Jupiter, bringing out its qualities, which are about learning through exploring ideas and widening his experiences – which is what he is doing as the transit moves through 2019.

Other major themes in Leon's chart include a natural ability to perceive what lies beneath the surface of situations, and to seek for spiritual understanding and personal growth.

Leon's 2019 transit list

- Pluto enters house 9 – February and June
- **Pluto trine Ascendant** – February, June – July, December 2019 – January 2020
- **Pluto conjunct Mercury** – January – August 2018, November 2018 – February 2019, July – December 2019

- **Saturn opposition Moon** – February, July – August, October – November
- **Saturn conjunct Mercury** – April – June, December
- Saturn square Jupiter – April – May, December
- **Jupiter sextile Venus** – January, July, September
- **Jupiter sextile MC** – January – February, June – July, September
- Jupiter trine Jupiter – February, June, October
- Jupiter enters house 8 – March and October
- Jupiter conjunct Saturn – November
- Jupiter enters Capricorn – December. February – March 2020, August 2020

There are few outer planet transits in 2019 for Leon, so T Saturn and Jupiter assume more prominence. In bold are the most important transits. These are relatively straightforward, so I will just comment on two or three, for example: **Saturn opposition Moon.** The combination of planets for the others will hopefully not be too difficult to put together with keywords.

T Saturn opposition Moon
This transit can be quite hard work. If you think about the separate parts of this one, perhaps you can see that the sensitive Moon does not sit well with the maker of structure and boundaries. Essentially, Saturn is blocking free emotional expression and can make you feel frustrated and limited. Feelings of depression or loneliness may drag you down unless you can pay good attention to your emotional needs. There may be issues with women, or with family. This transit may have played a part in the change of relationship with the woman Leon met in India – they have become

'friends' rather than being in a more intimate relationship. It can make you feel alienated not only from others, but from yourself. The suggestion is to be honest with yourself about what you need, and be kind to yourself – you have sometimes pushed too hard and too seriously.

Pluto conjunct Mercury, followed and overlapped by *Saturn conjunct Mercury*. These are the last of the long passage of transiting planets in Capricorn across Leon's stellium in the 8th house. The T Pluto conjunction has of course been around since the beginning of 2018 and picks up on one of Leon's chart themes – sensing hidden agendas or buried secrets. It inclines towards deep thoughts, much pondering of the mysteries in life, and probably brings insights and new understanding. Learning and teaching are likely to figure largely during this two-year period, which is in fact the case for Leon. He has developed his skills in yoga, and teaches others, and is continuing to study Buddhism and related subjects.

During the Northern hemisphere spring of 2019, as T Saturn conjoins with natal Mercury, Leon is back home in Singapore, working and teaching, and is planning his next year or two. This transit suggests planning ahead (a Capricorn trait anyway), working out where to progress to from wherever you are now, and Leon was in the process of considering his next steps and his overall aims, especially to do with which country to move on to. It does make for much serious thought, but also a strong sense of irony about life in general.

When T Saturn joins T Pluto at the end of 2019 to the beginning of 2020, he is likely to act on his decisions and make his next moves – Saturn conjunct Pluto gives a determination to complete what you start (for everyone – the transit is affecting the world in a general sense, not only Leon). It is particularly key for those who have planets in the early 20 degrees of all of the cardinal signs – Aries, Cancer, Libra or Capricorn. Triggering Leon's Mercury in his Capricorn 8th house, T Saturn can bring feelings of depression but a dry sense of humour can temper this from going too far. T Jupiter crossing Sun and Mercury in Capricorn in 2020 brings a more philosophical view.

Progressions and directions – Leon 2019

Rather unusually, p Moon has only one major aspect throughout the year: p Moon trine natal Neptune in August and trine p Neptune in October. Likewise, there are virtually no progressions in 2019. This does happen sometimes, depending on the arrangement of the natal planets. Other years can be very busy with progressions and directions. It is interesting that this occurs during a period of relative quietness, as if Leon is gearing himself up for his next period of travel and study. He remains in Singapore in 2019, working in a customer service role for a large art gallery and museum, earning and saving enough money for future travels.

P Moon trine Neptune, from August–October 2019
Idealising about what kind of domestic set-up he would like and maybe what kind of relationship he would like (while maintaining his independence), enjoying his own company but yearning for love at the same time.

Otherwise the notable SAs are:

- **SA Jupiter conjunct Ascendant** – May
- SA Mercury square Ascendant – July
- SA Chiron trine Mars – August

SA Jupiter conjunct Ascendant and Mercury square Ascendant

Keywords: Ascendant – connection with the world 'out there', first impressions and how others perceive you, the nature of your relationships. Aspects to the Ascendant are also automatically aspects to the other end of the axis, the Descendant.

Both solar arc directions to the Ascendant are about contact with others, possibly expanding Leon's circle of friends and acquaintances. Jupiter crossing this sensitive point may have brought 'fortunate' meetings or connections that may prove significant. Mercury square to the Ascendant, as a challenging aspect, could perhaps indicate some communication difficulty with one or more people, even arguments, or simply differences of opinion. Or he may begin the task of learning a new skill, such as a language, something he has expressed an interest in trying to do.

SA Chiron trine Mars

Keywords: Chiron – healing a past hurt, doing things in your own way, helping others.

Mars – a fighter, rising to a challenge, self-assertion, courage.

Leon may encounter a challenging situation that requires him to stand up for himself, which takes some courage. An experience of a previously damaging situation may have an echo this month, which brings a chance to let go and move on.

Leon: Solar Return chart for 2020

The chart I shall look at for 2020 will be valid until early January 2021.

Major points for Leon SR chart 2020

- **Sun 11 conjunct Mercury, stellium Capricorn 11**

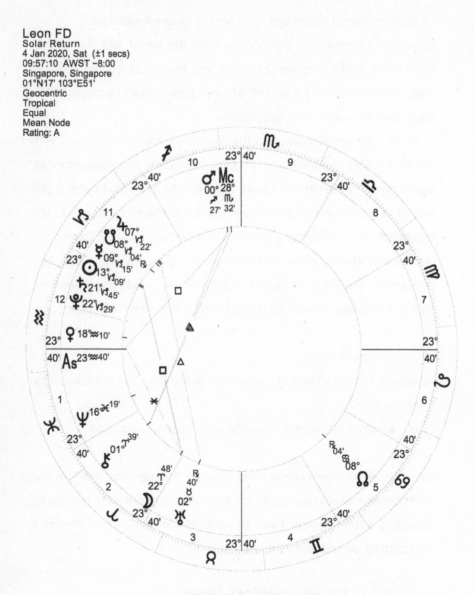

Leon FD
Solar Return
4 Jan 2020, Sat (±1 secs)
09:57:10 AWST −8:00
Singapore, Singapore
01°N17' 103°E51'
Geocentric
Tropical
Equal
Mean Node
Rating: A

Leon's Solar Return chart 2020

- **No planets in water, only MC**
- **Moon square Saturn conjunct Pluto**
- **Mercury on Nodal axis, conjunct Jupiter**

  First Quarter Moon, Eastern chart

  Lunation phase First Quarter – February 2019–February 2023

  Venus and Uranus Mutual Reception (in each other's sign)
- **Venus unaspected to a planet, widely rising**
- **Moon sextile Ascendant**

  Mars conjunct MC trine Chiron

Major comparison points with natal chart

If we superimpose the SR 2020 chart onto the natal (which of course is the essence of a bi-wheel), some interesting points emerge:

SR Saturn and SR Pluto sit tight on natal Mercury, also in a Capricorn stellium and the 8th house, thus prolonging the transit throughout 2020 (see above).

SR Mercury conjunct natal Neptune – enhances natural imagination, and maybe heights attained in meditation, but may shift at times into pure escapism, which is not necessarily spiritually enlightening. But Leon's musical interests may be stimulated and perhaps bring inspiration for new songs or the release of a new album.

The **element and mode balance** is roughly similar to the natal, except that the SR chart is shorter of water than the natal, and mutable is also not a mode that is strongly represented. This suggests that the emphasis for the year 2020 is on practicality, organisation and initiating a new direction (earth and Cardinal very strong, shortage of Mutable).

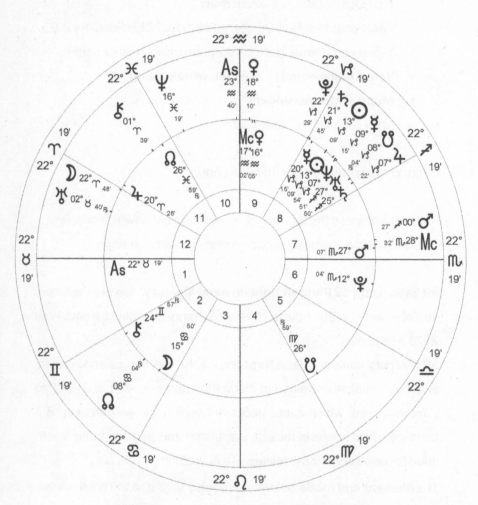

Leon's bi-wheel for natal chart and SR 2020

Circumstances are likely to emphasise groupwork or activities, community or humanitarian concerns, and spending time with like-minded friends or other individuals (emphasis 11th house on bi-wheel).

SR Moon 12 conjunct Jupiter – expanding ideas of what 'home' means, travelling as a familiar activity, questioning what emotional security and needs are and where, or if, to find them.

SR MC conjunct SR Mars and natal Mars on Descendant, 7 – echoes above remarks about home in a way, but also strongly suggests lively engagement with another person, or other friends, which may enhance Leon's ideas of building up his future direction (MC).

SR Venus – testing independence, enjoying freedom, and possibly feeling somewhat isolated at times.

Overall summary of interpretations for 2019–2020

Having experienced a relatively quiet year, mostly spent in Singapore in 2019, Leon planned to leave Singapore after a year or so of working and accumulating funds, and to go travelling again, although his plans ahead of time were not necessarily about returning, at least not initially, to Asian countries, but to visit Europe and maybe renew old acquaintances. His plans also include other Asian countries such as Laos, Cambodia and Vietnam.

As he is naturally disciplined with his strongly featured Capricorn planets, he is likely to achieve what he plans, and be able to fund himself. The spring of 2019 was a good time to tap into his thoughts about learning a language, but whether he was able to fit this into a full life of work, practice and study as well as a certain amount of social life, I am not sure. He says he is finalising his travel plans towards the end of 2019. Leon's life is likely to continue to shift and change (T Pluto), and learning and study will remain very important activities for him. He may have to use his philosophical self to put things into perspective as he experiences the T Saturn square Moon on and off throughout 2019, so that he does not fall too much into feeling down or sorry for himself. Saturn is a tough taskmaster and it always seems that challenging Saturn transits need to be seen as necessary in some way for our greater learning . . . !

Overall, however, these 2 years in his life seem to offer opportunities that he is likely to feel able to take, to continue to expand on the path he has so far chosen, and increase his knowledge of the world, physically and psychologically. Being in the second year of his First Quarter lunation phase, with an SR chart that strongly suggests finding his own way even when it is challenging (Eastern chart) is almost like picking up on past life experience that supports him (South Node in the stellium in Capricorn). He may develop and expand his abilities for teaching and educating others, which would enrich his life.

Leon's biography

The following brief biography is written by Leon, in his own words:
'Ever since a young age, I had always been fascinated by the mysterious and supernatural Universe we all live in. I grew up under a strict father and a protective (sheltering/caring) mother, along with my older sister (whom I, coincidentally, share the same birthday with 3 years apart). My parents divorced when I was 10 years old, and I was brought up by my mother. I was already reading books on UFOs by the age of 6. In addition, I was also able to recollect several mystical experiences which occurred during the first 6 years of childhood. Some were symbolic dreams while others were fragmented glimpses of past memories from before this lifetime (or perhaps, a future birth?).

'With books on UFOs, ancient mysteries and the paranormal on my bookshelves since youth, I grew up exploring those topics and subject matter in greater depths as I got older. I also read literary classics written by the great authors such as Mark Twain and H.G. Wells amongst several others. My favourite read was the World Atlas and I felt deep connections with several countries on the planet (namely, the Himalayan Regions of India and Tibet, Fiji etc.). Besides the influence from Western sources, there were also Eastern inspirations. I read the story of Ganesha (the Elephant-headed Hindu God of Wisdom/'Remover of Obstacles') and this resonated with me profoundly.

'Coming from a broken family, I was an average student at school who picked up the electric guitar at 16 years old. Being a fan of football, too, this sport alongside music and reading were my favourite passions during my teenage years. My inclinations towards picking up a musical instrument and delving into spirituality around this time is consciously unknown but it flew through me naturally; intuitively and smoothly. I formed my band Sanity Obscure (SG) while I was at polytechnic finishing up my Diploma in Information Technology (IT) and went on to release three CDs under this band's moniker in my twenties.

'I also completed mandatory National Service (conscription) at 25 years old before moving to England a week later to undertake my BA and MA degrees in Religious Studies at the University of Kent. It was during this time at university that I attended my first yoga class and later went on to take up teacher training courses in India to develop my practice. My time in England also culminated with joining several Western Mystery/Magickal schools which satisfied my appetite for the occult and I also took initiation into Tibetan Buddhism. Just a week after my 30th birthday, I returned to Singapore where I focus on my spiritual practice while alternating between working and travelling.'

17.
WHERE TO GO FROM HERE

It gets easier!

Like most new subjects in life, the more you practise astrology, the better you will become at it. However, if you don't look at any more natal charts after reading this book, or if you don't carry on reading about astrology, or attending astrology lectures or workshops, the benefits of your dedicated work in reading your way through this book will slowly fade.

So you could say that your future understanding of astrology depends on how you choose to keep going beyond this point. If your interest remains or is piqued, you will find recommendations in the Further Reading list or online recommendations to help you keep your hand in.

By now, you will have gathered that this is a very broad subject with many different branches. You may have specific ideas about what else you would like to learn: perhaps the astrology of relationships (synastry), a deeper study of the meaning of the asteroids and similar bodies, mundane astrology (the astrology of countries and organisations) or locational astrology (like astro-cartography) or the astrology of geographical place. You have plenty of choice as to the astrological direction you want to follow.

Astrology has inspired many illuminati from the past, such as pioneering scientists Isaac Newton, Galileo and Kepler, as well as twentieth- and twenty-first-century astrologers including Alan Leo, Liz Greene, Howard Sasportas and Charles Harvey. You don't necessarily need to continue with natal astrology as your focus, but could take it in a direction that suits your other interests. For example, those with a more technical or scientific approach might like to research ways in which the various astrological techniques can be written into computer software programs, or explore existing areas of controversy, such as the different house systems. There is no shortage of subjects within astrology that need more serious investigation. Others who have perhaps a more artistic bent might like to create images or paintings that illustrate the beauty of the heavens or the awesome images portrayed in the myths. Astrology is a visual subject, after all, not only based on mathematical astronomy.

Whichever way you take your studies forward and however you become involved with the wider astrological community, you will be in good company. Astrology is continuing to increase in scope. There are dedicated astrology schools in many countries who can advise you about activities in the astrological world and who might be able to recommend authentic websites if you need pointers. There are of course a plethora of websites on the subject. A word of caution here: as I'm sure you know, the internet is an excellent resource, but there is also quite a lot of false or badly written information on astrology on it, so use your discrimination.

If you are interested in continuing to expand and improve your natal work, and your ability to combine your forecasting skills with other systems for predictive work, perhaps, then do look for talks, workshops and seminars in your local area and online. If you have enjoyed the process of learning astrology, then perhaps you could consider setting up a local astrology group or class, and spread the knowledge further in this age of cynicism. If you live in a country where there are limited options for joining groups or even meeting people with a similar interest in astrology at whatever level, why not place an advert in a magazine or on the internet to see if there is anyone else that shares your passion?

When I was an astrology student, I used to enjoy getting together with fellow students over lunch once a fortnight, or once a month, simply to 'talk astrology'. We talked about our own charts, or brought a copy of a famous person's chart and learnt from each other's opinions about that chart. If there was anything particularly notable happening in the news at the time, this also made for fertile ground for discussion, if we could get the data, especially the timings, by looking them up in recent newspapers. We learnt a lot from doing this.

I likewise hope that your own astrological knowledge will continue to go from strength to strength, and that I have given you all the information you need to take you forward. Enjoy your next steps, wherever they take you! And maybe meet you one day. Who knows? The astrological world is not that large, and conferences are happening all over the world.

APPENDIX 1:

List of Planetary Combination Keywords

Please note: the following list looks at the combination of two planetary energies, but the interpretations are not specific to any particular aspect, the main point here being the principle of the two planets in combination. The combination could occur on the natal chart, or in any form of forecasting. Therefore, you will need to adapt each combination to its aspect: some will be challenging, with hard aspects (e.g. square, opposition), while some will be flowing, with soft aspects (e.g. trine, sextile). Conjunctions are neutral and could apply to any of the interpretations. You will need to use your discretion.

Each planet is represented by the first two letters of its name, e.g. SU = Sun, UR = Uranus, and so on. Each listing names one or more well-known people with that planetary combination.

☉ SUN in combination with:

MO – wants (SU) vs needs (MO); strong in its sign, intense focus (New Moon) or feels split (Full Moon); life direction influenced by past history (mother, family, childhood memories); very sensitive to others; struggles with inner security. **Susan Boyle** (opposition)

ME – mental capacity, development of the intellect, desire for knowledge, curiosity. Talkative, strong ideas, challenge is to listen. **Woody Allen, Barbara Cartland**

VE – peacekeeper, seeks harmony, charming. Sees both sides of things. Seeks to be loved and approved of; likes women. **Boris Johnson**

MA – funky energy; direct in speech/action; impatient/competitive; can be forceful; courageous; fighter, soldier. **Susan Boyle** (square), **Shirley MacLaine**

JU – reaches high; expansive nature; philosophical; explorer, adventurer; generous, open-minded; can over-reach self; spiritual seeker. **Bob Dylan**

SA – focused, structured; hard worker, grounded, ambitious; can be depressive, pessimistic, fearful, or simply serious; realistic, organised, self-disciplined; ironic; father's influence important. **Whoopi Goldberg, Al Pacino**

UR – rebellious, independent, radical attitude; freedom crucial; breaks rules or makes their own; not diplomatic, can be direct; own perception of truth important, tells it as it is, hates false news. **Donald Trump**

NE – creative, imaginative; escapist, dreamer, visionary; intuitive, empathic, can be psychic; confusion, self-doubt, avoidance; compassionate, easily moved, gullible, sensitive; drawn to glamour, beauty. **Bill Gates, Princess Margaret**

PL – insightful, perceptive, intense, self-aware; secretive, hidden, deep; drawn to power, obsessive, self-protective, can be paranoid; hard to let go, to move on, long memory. **Myra Hindley, Mark Knopfler**

CH – pain from the past colours the life until accepted, wounded sense of self; maverick, seen to be different, stands out from crowd. **Prince Charles, Tom Waits**

☽ MOON in combination with:

ME – communicates feelings in words or writing, analyses, wants to be
understood; easy to like, adaptable; loquacious, does not always
contain their conversation, story teller; changeable opinions. **Sean
Connery**

VE – adapts and co-operates; soft-hearted, sometimes overly
sensitive, easily offended; lover of peace, beauty, nature; loving,
caring, sentimental; mother's influence/love important; passive,
indirect, dislikes confrontations; can be needy, feels guilt easily,
torn between needs (MO) and desires (VE). **Woody Allen**

MA – fighting to protect others, looks after people; need to balance
self-assertion with feeling safe; hard to express anger, can be
irritable or touchy, avoids conflict; or overly fast to anger, baby
rage; fast responses, defensive (for self or others), angry with
mother. **Billy Graham** (conjunct in Sagittarius)

JU – nurtured by travelling, exploring, learning in general; big-hearted,
generous emotional reactions; carried away by feelings; needy
mother; over-promises; preacher, teacher; wants to 'grow', hates
to be tied down or classified; can be self-indulgent, may have
eating issue, indulgent parent; grandness, can patronise. **Jimi
Hendrix, Venus Williams**

SA – tight emotions, self-worth issues; defensiveness, early emotional
responsibilities; need to nurture self as early nurture is lacking;
need to please and feel secure; controlling women. **Elvis Presley,
Princess Anne**

UR – need to have emotional freedom, independence; shifting and
changeable emotions, sudden changes of heart; restless, hard to

settle, needs to find some unconventionality in personal life; can be abrupt and seem unfeeling, may break with the past more than once. **Jodie Foster, Germaine Greer**

NE – very sensitive, imaginative, impressionable, compassionate; 'missing' or vulnerable mother; actor, chameleon; yearning for love and nurture, escape or merging, readily empathises; idealises the past or rejects it; can get lost in own or others' feelings, loss of perspective, self-pity or self-indulgence. **Jennifer and June Gibbons, Shirley MacLaine**

PL – penetrating emotional insight, intense feelings; keeper of secrets, self-protective, buried emotions, controlled inner life; private person, drama king/queen, capable of emotional blackmail; transformative, instinctive, powerful experiences; hard to let go of feelings. **Leonardo DiCaprio, Kenneth Williams**

CH – emotional vulnerability, easily feels guilt; pain around mother in early life, painful experiences with women; strives for emotional independence through creative/intuitive outlet; empathy, compassion for others. **Paul McCartney, Roy Orbison**

☿ MERCURY in combination with:

VE – feelings and thinking blend well, creative combination; ease with languages, love of words, reader, writer; natural fairness and sense of balance. **John Cleese, Buddy Holly**

MA – speedy, impulsive, forceful speech and fast thinking, incisiveness; quick decision-making, the hard truth, getting on with the job; can be argumentative, competitive, impatient. **Elton John, John F. Kennedy**

JU – wide-ranging mind, an intrepid explorer of the world; big plans, futuristic approach to life, mental philosopher; self-trust, confidence; knows several subjects in depth, broad interests; inspiring, enthusiastic speaker/writer. **Harrison Ford**

SA – disciplined focused mind, sharp precise thinker; dedicated student of life, persistent researcher, serious scholar, authoritative, academic achievement; prone to negative thinking, cautiously expressive, fear of failure. **Albert Einstein, James Lovelock**

UR – brilliant thinker, inventor, thinks outside the box; originality, breaking patterns, radicality; freedom of speech, lacks diplomacy, shocks; unacceptable truths, liberating ideas, sudden insight; strong opinions, hard to change these. **Johannes Kepler, Ronald Reagan**

NE – creative imagination, thinks inspirationally, easily visualises; distorts reality or embroiders facts, glamorises information, romantic thinker; uplifted by music, art, dance; struggles with directions, maps, scientific factual thought, could be dyslexic. **Martin Luther, Gene Roddenberry, Peter Sellers**

PL – deep thinker, looks below the surface, secrets hold power; obsessive search for knowledge, researcher/scientist; dark thoughts, hidden manipulation, sabotage; getting to the roots; transforming communication with others/of others. **Bill Clinton, Galileo, Richard Nixon**

CH – communication difficulties, possible debility in speech/mentality; lack of mental self-worth; compassionate teacher/educator; inspirational voice. **David Attenborough, Marlene Dietrich**

♀ VENUS in combination with:

MA – magnetism, fascination, warmth; competitiveness, fighting for peace/what is believed to be right; seeing the other's view yet asserting self; romantic desires, sexual adventures; creative ability or artistic appreciation; financial ability, money through creative expression, discord over money; relationships very important, open relationships. **Jeffrey Archer**

JU – wanting to grow, enjoy life, expand; friendly, easy to get on with, generous; philosophical, affectionate, freely gives to others, supports the needy; easy with money, can become wealthy; can be vain, over-indulgent; spiritual quality to relationships. **Robbie Coltrane**

SA – love subject to restrictions, fear of relationships, loneliness, controlled affections, can seem cold, partners may be older; financial hardship or limitations, uncomfortable with money; hard on self, lacks self-worth; loyal and serious in commitments and committed relationships; father strict or unaffectionate; appearance neglected or over-emphasised; time-aware. **Charlton Heston, Annie Lennox**

UR – relationships need space, freedom, independence, openness; unusual tastes/appearance, unusual relationship set-ups, may behave in shocking ways, almost nothing fazes them; can be selfish, self-centred, harsh honesty in the name of truth. **Elizabeth Taylor**

NE – romantic dreamer, willingness to overlook less desirable traits; disillusion in love, unattainable partners, covert relationships; artistic talent/enjoyment; heroes and gurus; perfectionism, idealism. **Prince Charles, Vincent Price**

PL – brooding sensuality, sultry attractions, deep dark desires; hidden emotional life, money's place in relationships; obsessions, compulsions, revenge, jealousy; emotional manipulation, undying loyalty; perception, healing ability. **Antonio Banderas, Liberace**

CH – past hurts in love/friendships make them cautious; very loving but self-protective; potential counsellor, healer; artistic qualities; sensitively stylish. **Bill Clinton, Marilyn Monroe**

♂ MARS in combination with:

JU – campaigner, crusader, strong beliefs and principles; energetic, resourceful; sexual games; risk taker, sense of fun, over-extension, almost blind belief in own immortality; warmonger, large enterprises, courageous. **Winston Churchill, Walt Disney**

SA – disciplined actions, structured working and staying power; controlled sexuality, traditional attitudes; fear of loss of control, fear of failure or of violence; self-doubt (often hidden under strictly imposed rules); serious dedication and endurance, meets commitments. **Matt Dillon, Mussolini, Justin Welby**

UR – acts independently on own ideas; restless, likes to be occupied and keep moving; courage to step outside convention; decisive actions, fights for freedom; unusual sexuality, provocative excitement. **Christine Keeler, Mata Hari**

NE – ideals of fighting for peace, following a 'higher' vision, looking after the larger group; may be a victim of unscrupulous people, gullible; undermined drive, lack of direction, hard to express anger or assert self; experiences betrayal or being taken advantage of until learns to assert self; poet, 'glamorous' occupations. **Percy Bysshe Shelley, Alan Whicker**

PL – forceful reactions and actions, can push hard, sometimes too hard, ruthlessness; fighting dirty, to the kill, for survival; buried rage, taking by force, compulsively seeking power; exploration of the darker side of life, of death, mental illness, addictions. **Princess Diana, Alexander Fleming**.

CH – hard to assert self, feels guilty. Competition and conflict tend to be avoided if possible, problems from childhood relationship with family. Capacity to heal others in different ways. **Joan Baez, Tracey Emin**

♃ JUPITER in combination with:

SA – measured growth, grounded beliefs, acting on enthusiastic plans; zealous or morally upright ideas; father influential – strict or strongly opinionated; the building of wealth, materialism; acquiring assets or a philosophy, the search for meaning; fear of success or fear of failure, ambitions realised in later years; balancing doubts with self-belief; valuing education. **Susan Boyle, Pauline Collins, Isaac Newton**

UR – revolutionary ideas/plans, strong belief in freedom and truth, willingness to upset the order of things by revealing the truth; original differentness, stubborn rebellion, independent ideas; unconventional approach to life; loves to travel, physically and mentally. **Fidel Castro, Edward Snowden**

NE – mysticism, spirituality, fantasies, following a guru; disillusionment, loss of faith/a dream; drawn to magical mysteries, perceiving oneself as a saviour and sometimes being a victim; compassionate humanitarian, wants to make a difference; needs to ground grand visions. **Julian Assange, Madonna**

PL – willingness to delve deep, get hands dirty, believes anything is possible; desire to transform, to reform, to renew on a large scale; perceives hidden rot and decay and drawn to exposing it; associated with enormous power, financial, governmental, or religious. **Nelson Mandela, Justin Welby**

CH – issues of loss of faith, cynicism; accepts nothing at face value, questions a lot; can be obsessed with this, like Saint Augustine; can be a great inspirational figure later in life. **Princess Margaret, Edith Piaf**

♄ SATURN in combination with:

UR – controlled reform over time, or sudden breaks with the past; looking at old issues in a new light; struggle between tried-and-tested traditions, and the pull of the new and different; the dictator, the tyrant, or the wise authority; measured progressiveness or fierce resistance to change depends on which planet is stronger – the individual can do both in their life; strength and persistence. **Amelia Earhart, George Harrison**

NE – the weakening of authority, dissolution of structures, idealising tradition; escaping from taking control or taking responsibility; flooding awareness with visions or dreams of higher consciousness in the world; pollution and poison; subject to feelings of guilt; sacrifice, practising self-discipline. **Indira Gandhi, John F. Kennedy**

PL – stamina, endurance, keeping going in the face of obstacles;
wielding power and sabotaging control; feels being a carrier of
collective profound changes in society as a burden until
demolitions begin to happen. **Uri Geller, Stephen King, Edward
Snowden**

CH – strong personality, has the capacity to manipulate others (in hard
aspect). Can also be too self-critical. One parent (probably father)
may have been overly strict. Can be a stable influence in
supporting others if can overcome own pain from childhood.
May have unusual perceptive abilities (flowing aspects). **Jane
Fonda**

NB: Aspects between outer planets are generational rather than
personal unless a personal planet is also involved.

⛢ URANUS in combination with:

NE – holding high ideals; compassionate giving to others;
artistic revolution, force for creative change; inspired by
enhanced creativity, which may trigger spiritual insights.
  Barbara Castle

PL – transformation of goals and aims in life; may bring opportunities
to become more aware of earlier traumas (maybe from childhood)
and the effect on the current life, a chance to find ways to absorb
this. **Noël Coward.**

CH – loner with healing ability; seeker of the unusual; highly
individualistic attitude can disturb some – but can create valuable
breakthroughs though going to extremes can be a problem; wants
to make the world a better place but can alienate others. **Billy
Connolly**

Ψ NEPTUNE in combination with:

PL – attuned to the larger changes in society; potentially, depending on the rest of the chart, deep transformations of maybe long-held ideals – can be disruptive while going through the process; potential to transform personal wounds and become a mentor who can accept yet influence others. **M.C. Escher**

CH – hypersensitivity, over-imaginative; anxiety about not being liked; sensitivity can be overwhelming – needs to find an outlet to channel compassion. **Brigitte Bardot**

♇ PLUTO in combination with:

CH – potentially destructive aspect; intense feelings, emotionally reticent; powerful ability to transform self or society in some way; virtually unshockable; potential to develop a strong belief in self, and may hold equally strong opinions. **Sean Connery**

APPENDIX 2:

Forecasting Table

How to complete this table: list the transits per month, starting with the most important longer-term ones first, e.g. which of the outer planets you consider important, followed by Saturn and Jupiter's repeating transits in their various months.

List solar arcs under SA in month order, using only major aspects. Progressed Moon aspects are also listed in month order, as are 'progs' (other significant progressions over the year). Then you can see at a glance what is happening when. (I usually write the p. lunation phase in the blank space at the top of the Table.)

Name:	Jan	Feb	Mar	Apr	May	Jun	Jul	Aug	Sep	Oct	Nov	Dec	Notes
T													
SA													
P MO													
progs													

GLOSSARY

Abbreviations commonly used:

T + a planet = transiting + the planet

p + a planet = progressed + the planet

d + a planet = solar arc direction + the planet

SR = solar return

Angular: positioned within 8 degrees either side of one of the four angles – Ascendant, Descendant, MC, IC.

Aphelion: the Sun's furthest distance from Earth.

Apogee: the Moon's furthest distance from Earth.

Arc: movement in space.

Aspect patterns: see individual patterns.

Aspects: connections by degree between planets or angles.

Major aspects: conjunction, opposition, square, trine, sextile

Minor aspects: semi-square, sesquiquadrate, quincunx, semi-sextile

Asteroids: a belt of rocky orbiting bodies in space situated between the orbits of Mars and Jupiter.

Balsamic: a Moon phase. (See Chapter 9 for Moon phase definitions.)

Benefic: a traditional astrological term meaning positive energy; the planets Venus and Jupiter are both benefics.

Bi-wheel (Tri-wheel etc.): two or more charts drawn in one chart wheel shape, normally with the natal chart in the middle and the directed/progressed/transiting planets placed round the outside.

Crescent: a Moon phase. (See Chapter 9 for Moon phase definitions.)

Derived Ascendant: name given to the calculation of the progressed Ascendant.

Disseminating: – a Moon phase. (See Chapter 9 for Moon phase definitions.)

Dissociate aspect: two planets in standard orb aspect with each other yet out of modal or elemental link, e.g. a planet at 29° Aries conjunct another planet at 1° Taurus.

Dwarf planet: minor planet of a certain size found in the Kuiper Belt or the Oort Cloud. Pluto is the best known. It was downgraded to this definition by astronomers in 2006.

Ephemeris: a table of dates with their corresponding planetary positions.

Ecliptic: the apparent annual path of the Sun orbiting the Earth, as seen from Earth. Astronomically the ecliptic is the path of the Earth and all the Solar System planets that are orbiting the Sun, within a certain number of degrees of declination on either side.

Geocentric: as seen from Earth; placing the Earth at the centre of the Solar System, as if the other heavenly bodies orbited around it.

Gibbous: a Moon phase. (See Chapter 9 for Moon phase definitions.)

Heliocentric: the Sun at the centre of the Solar System.

Hemisphere: one half of the chart – N or S, E or W.

House system: mathematical system for calculating astrological houses on the chart.

Ingress: entry of a planet or sign into a new sign or house.

Karma: an Eastern concept. The belief that people die and are reborn in new bodies many times in order to learn lessons, and to rebalance current-life issues.

Kuiper Belt: a large area of our Solar System outside the orbit of Neptune and stretching for about 7 billion miles, containing many thousands of smallish planetary bodies that are orbiting the Sun. Short-term comets have their origins here.

Luminaries: refers to both the Sun and the Moon.

Lunar eclipse: occurs at Full Moon, when the Earth is between the Sun and the Moon; the Earth's shadow falls on the Moon, which often makes it appear red, and the Moon's Nodes are also aligned.

Lunation cycle: the cycle of the Moon.

Malefic: a traditional astrological term denoting hardship and suffering; the planets Mars and Saturn are both considered malefics.

Mean Node: the average position of the orbiting Moon's Node, which always moves 'backwards' or retrograde. Used in this book as it gives consistency of movement.

Midlife crisis: in astrological terms, the period between the ages of 37 and 42.

Nodes of the Moon: the two crossing points (north and south) between the ecliptic and the Moon's orbit round the Earth.

Oort Cloud: a huge icy cloud of billions of space objects that forms the extreme edges of the Solar System, far beyond the Kuiper Belt. Long-orbit comets are also generated here, or pass through here.

Orb: allowable degrees of distance away from exactitude, applied to aspects between planets and/or angles; or between Transits, progressions, and solar arc-directed planets and natal points.

Perigee: the Moon's closest approach to the Earth.

Perihelion: the Sun's closest approach to the Earth.

Placidus house system: formerly known as the Ptolemaic Method, this is the most commonly used house system in Western astrology today.

Quadrant: one quarter of the chart. Q1 = houses 1–3; Q2 = houses 4–6; Q3 = houses 7–9; Q4 = houses 10–12

Repeater: a word I have coined, meaning a chart or forecasting factor that repeats in similar terms elsewhere.

Retrograde: as viewed from Earth, the apparent temporary backwards movement of a planet in its orbit. This is actually an optical illusion, but has a significant astrological meaning. Written as a capital R or ℞.

Retrograde natal personal planets: Mercury, Venus, Mars apparently 'orbiting backwards' as seen from Earth.

Return (planetary return): the return of a transiting planet to the exact place where it appears on the natal chart.

Sidereal time: star time, which is used in astrology to calculate a birth chart, amongst other things. See Mean Node and True Node entries.

Signature sign: the strongest or keynote sign.

Stellium: three or more planets in one sign or house.

Solar eclipse: occurs at New Moon, when the Moon is aligned between the Sun and the Earth, and with the Moon's Node; the Moon's shadow falls across the Sun as seen from Earth.

True Node: the actual position of the Moon's Nodes. Can be forward-travelling, apparently stationary, or retrograding – like a planet. Recent research has shown that the True Node is no more accurate than the Mean Node. It is a matter of personal preference which one to use.

Transits: the moving orbits of the planets, aspecting a degree of a sign (usually on a birth chart, so of a natal planet or angle).

Umbra: an area of complete shadow cast by the Earth, or by the Moon, whereby the light of the Sun is prevented from illuminating another body in space.

FURTHER READING

This is not a comprehensive list, but all the books included here are of a high standard in their subject area.

Stephen Arroyo, *Astrology, Karma & Transformation* (CRCS Publications, 1984)

Bernadette Brady, *Predictive Astrology* (Samuel Weiser, 1992)

Frank Clifford, *Getting to the Heart of your Chart* (Flare Publications, 2012)

Cal Garrison, *The Lunar Gospel: The Complete Guide to Your Astrological Moon* (Red Wheel/Weiser, 2018)

Liz Greene, *Relating* (Red Wheel/Weiser, 1977)

Liz Greene, *Saturn: A New Look at an Old Devil* (Weiser Books, 2011)

Robert Hand, *Horoscope Symbols* (Schiffer Publishing, 1997)

Barbara Hand Clow, *Chiron* (Llewellyn Publications, 1987)

Robin Heath, *Sun, Moon & Earth* (Wooden Books, 2006)

Ralph William Holden, *The Elements of House Division* (L. N. Fowler, 1978)

Deborah Houlding, *The Houses: Temples of the Sky* (The Wessex Astrologer, 2006)

Richard Idemon, *The Magic Thread* (The Wessex Astrologer, 2010)

Clare Martin, *Mapping the Psyche* (The Wessex Astrologer, 2016)

Sue Merlyn Farebrother, *Astrology Decoded* (Rider Books, 2013)

Howard Sasportas, *The Gods of Change* (The Wessex Astrologer, 2007)

Howard Sasportas *The Twelve Houses* (Aquarian Press, 1985)

Percy Seymour, *Astrology: The Evidence of Science* (Penguin, 1990)

Janey Stubbs and Babs Kirby, *Interpreting Solar and Lunar Returns* (Capall Bann Publishing, 2001)

Komilla Sutton, *The Lunar Nodes* (The Wessex Astrologer, 2001)

Sue Tompkins, *Aspects in Astrology* (Rider Books, 2001)

Sue Tompkins, *The Contemporary Astrologer's Handbook* (LSA/Flare, 2009)

USEFUL ADDRESSES

Websites where you can get a birth chart

You can obtain your natal chart from my website: www.suemerlyn.com

For other websites, and sites for information about transits and progressions, see:

Astro.com
www.astro.com and www.astrodienst.com
One of the largest astrology portals, with many free features.

Astro Gold
https://www.astrogold.io/
Mobile and Mac software with high-precision calculations and astrological interpretations. Information on Natal, Transit, Progression and Synastry interpretations.

Astrolabe
www.alabe.com
Offering astrology software programs, reports, calculations and other services since 1979.

Celeste
https://alabe.com/Celeste/Android.html
Astrolabe's free mobile app for calculating charts, available for both iPhones and Androids.

Astrology shops that offer mail order to anywhere in the world

(All are based in Britain.)

The Astrology Shop: www.londonastrology.com

Watkins Bookshop: https://watkinsbooks.com/

The Wessex Astrologer: www.wessexastrologer.com

Astrology software programs

All offer to calculate birth charts for you, supplying transits, progressions, solar arc directions and solar return charts, amongst other options. You do need to spend a bit of time experimenting and learning how best to use them. All vary in price, with Solar Fire probably the most expensive, and the most comprehensive – but very good. Time Passages will supply all the above as well, and costs less, but is overall not so comprehensive.

In addition, there are the mobile apps listed above which calculate birth charts etc. All this software including the mobile apps will offer you reports on your charts – interesting perhaps, but you are in the process of learning how to look at your own interpretations for your forecasting! Use theirs, if you like, as a guide.

- https://alabe.com/solargold.html (Solar Fire)
- www.astrograph.com or search for Time Passages (Astrograph)
- http://www.astrosoftware.com/KEPLER.HTM (Kepler)
- https://www.soulhealing.com/astrosof.htm (a guide site to astrological software)

ACKNOWLEDGEMENTS

Thank you to Sue Lascelles (whose knowledge of astrology was very useful), Olivia Morris, Bianca Bexton and Helen Pisano for your invaluable help with the writing and editing of this book. I have been encouraged and supported by your input, comments, and suggestions over the months.

And thank you to Roy Gillett for your kind advice and support in sourcing the perfect astrological font (Solar Fire, www.astrolable.com) for this book.

INDEX

Page references in *italics* indicate images.